THE Tomato BOOK

Other books by Yvonne Young Tarr

THE TEN MINUTE GOURMET COOKBOOK

THE TEN MINUTE GOURMET DIET COOKBOOK

101 DESSERTS TO MAKE YOU FAMOUS

LOVE PORTIONS

THE NEW YORK TIMES NATURAL FOODS DIETING BOOK

THE NEW YORK TIMES BREAD AND SOUP COOKBOOK

THE COMPLETE OUTDOOR COOKBOOK

THE FARMHOUSE COOKBOOK

SUPER-EASY STEP-BY-STEP CHEESEMAKING

SUPER-EASY STEP-BY-STEP WINEMAKING

SUPER-EASY STEP-BY-STEP SAUSAGEMAKING

SUPER-EASY STEP-BY-STEP BOOK OF SPECIAL BREADS

THE UP-WITH-WHOLESOME, DOWN-WITH-STORE-BOUGHT BOOK
OF RECIPES AND HOUSEHOLD FORMULAS

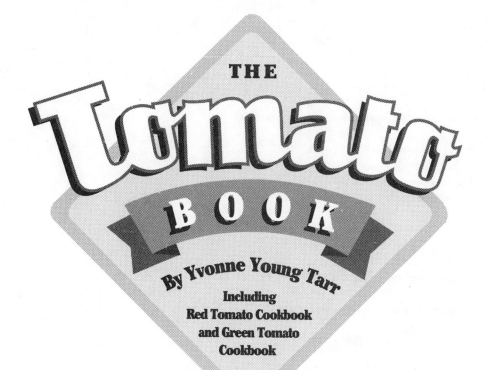

THE Tomato BOOK

By Yvonne Young Tarr

**Including
Red Tomato Cookbook
and Green Tomato
Cookbook**

WINGS BOOKS
New York • Avenel, New Jersey

A very special thank you to my friends and neighbors
George S. and Mildred Miller

Copyright © 1976 by Yvonne Young Tarr

All rights reserved under International and Pan-American Copyright Conventions.

Art from the Yvonne Young Tarr Turn of the Century Archives

This 1995 edition is published by Wings Books,
distributed by Random House Value Publishing, Inc.,
40 Engelhard Avenue, Avenel, New Jersey 07001,
by arrangement with the author.

Random House
New York · Toronto · London · Sydney · Auckland

Printed and bound in the United States of America

Library of Congress Cataloging-in-Publication Data
Tarr, Yvonne Young.
        The tomato book / Yvonne Young Tarr.
            p.   cm.
        Originally published: New York : Vintage Books, c1976.
        Includes index.
        ISBN 0-517-12267-7
        1. Cookery (Tomatoes)   2. Tomatoes—Preservation.   3. Tomatoes.
    I. Title.
TX803.T6T37   1995
641.6'5642—dc20   94-38790
                                                                     CIP

    8 7 6 5 4 3 2 1

INTRODUCTION

Tending garden was my chore back in Pennsylvania, where I was a child. Older than my two brothers (and much more amenable to promises and cajoling), every summer afternoon before my swim in a nearby creek I would kneel, cool earth beneath my knees, grasshoppers staring eye-to-eye from the tops of the plants—and weed, prune and in general coax our country garden into being. Much of that time I would rather have been somewhere else, doing something else, but looking back I realize how much I enjoyed my participation in the mysterious process that transformed a thimbleful of dormant seeds into bushels of magnificently designed, delicious and nourishing foods.

When August simmered into view with its steamy afternoons, nature took over and little was left for me to do but harvest. Daily I would invade the garden, basket in arm and saltshaker in back pocket of jeans. My reward was waiting beneath the unstaked tomato plants where I would discover, under heavy, twisted stalks as thick through as my mother's thumb and leaves as dense as in any jungle garden, hidden jewels of ripened fruit. I have cooked and consumed, since then, exotic dishes from nearly every nation, but never has any food tasted better to me than those just-picked, vine-ripened, freshly salted fruits, heated almost to the cooking point by the summer sun.

For the vast cult of tomato aficionados there are four periods of sublime pleasure . . 1. digging, planting and nurturing . . 2. harvesting . . 3. preparing and 4. consuming the fruits of our labors. This book is concerned with all four processes, but while as much in-depth planting information as you could possibly need is included, the emphasis of the book is most certainly on that ultimate pleasure . . . eating. For even the most inveterate and enthusiastic tomato farmer, the greatest pleasure is found "at table" rather than "in garden." Who has ever heard of a gardener planting and growing and then plowing the harvest under and starting over?

The recipes given here are not ordinary dishes with tomatoes arbitrarily plunked into ingredient lists, but are rather a collection of TESTED special recipes where tomatoes in some way change and/or enhance the ultimate finished product. In Green Tomato Mulligatawny, for example, the final result IS a superb rendition of the dish, but the substitution of sweet-tart green tomatoes for the sweet-tart apple adds a slightly different dimension while maintaining all the properties of the original. Green tomatoes also adapt beautifully to dessert recipes . . . the tomato is, after all, a fruit. Recipes that feature mostly tomatoes (Pennsylvania Dutch Tomatoes

In Cream Sauce, Madras Tomato-Egg Curry, Tomato-Pear Relish) have been culled from turn-of-the-century and medieval books, farmwives, foreign cooks and my own files to give the most interesting variations possible. This book is meant to show you the way to use your long-awaited crop to its fullest potential while the harvest is inundating your garden, kitchen counters, window sills and refrigerator, and to help you preserve most efficiently some of that surplus for winter feasting.

CONTENTS

TOMATO MANIA

The tomato is the superstar of the vegetable world—the most popular and widely grown plant in the home garden. Every year at least half the entire U.S. population raises tomato plants here, there or somewhere else. And little wonder—for instant eating pleasure there is nothing more delectable, and in a dazzling variety of cooked dishes the versatile tomato goes forth from soup to dessert with consummate good grace. Given the tomato's inordinately fine taste, it's hard to believe that this familiar and beloved fruit came upon the culinary scene only about five generations ago. First cultivated as a food crop by the Indians of South America, it was brought to Europe by way of Mexico, probably by the conquistadors, and found its way to Italy, where the Italians named their early yellow variety *pomi d'oro*, or "apple of gold." It was regarded by the rest of Europe as an ornamental plant and, perhaps in a distortion of its Italian name, was dubbed *pomme d'amour*, or "love apple." Whether the reputation followed the name or the name the reputation is hard to say, but the fruit was believed to be an aphrodisiac through much of its history. Not until the eighteenth century did it begin to achieve a place in European cuisine.

Early colonists brought tomato seeds to Virginia, but no record of its culture exists before 1781, when Thomas Jefferson made bold mention of planting a crop. His example, however, seems to have made little impression, since it wasn't until the beginning of the nineteenth century that the tomato made its way to market to become a fairly common ingredient in the Creole cooking of Louisiana. Most Americans shunned tomatoes until after the Civil War, believing, among other things, that they were poisonous (as a matter of fact, tomato leaves and stems *are* toxic), and long after tomatoes had achieved some esteem in American cookery, homemakers were still being enjoined to boil their stewed tomatoes and purées at least 3 hours before serving.

Tomatoes were not eaten fresh until around the turn of the century. Since then breeders have done much to improve their taste and increase their usefulness. There are varieties to suit every purpose and every area of the country. There are tomatoes for problem soils and for canning; there are early, midseason and late varieties; yellow, pink, orange and red, small and medium and pear-shaped; even some specifically created for container gardening.

Today we see the tomato as something more than just another plant with a pretty fruit. Though tomato pie may not be quite as American as apple pie, the tomato is surely as all-American a favorite as the adored apple.

GROWING

BEGIN WITH SOIL

Tomatoes are willing to grow almost anywhere, but, as in any growing process, the surest guarantee of peak flavor and top quality lies in the proper preparation of the soil. Soil is much more than a gritty handful of brown dust. Think of it as a gigantic, properly prepared dough composed of a flour of inorganic rocks, sand and silt mixed through with dead organic matter, vitalized by living organisms (earthworms and insects, hordes of bacteria, yeasts, algae, fungi and one-celled protozoans) that live in it. This lively interaction of living organisms with both decomposing organic debris and mineral particles, abetted by water and air, breaks down and converts nutritive ingredients, speeding the release of the essential soil elements on which plants thrive. The ultimate result of this dynamic and incessant activity is humus, the dark, rich, loamy substance that improves and enriches soil and helps it maintain its vigor. Humus acts as an anchor to hold soil particles together. Its spongy, porous texture increases water-holding capacity and enables both moisture and air to penetrate the soil more deeply and efficiently.

A rich, workable, fertile soil, then, depends not only on its mineral makeup and the twin effects of water and air but also on the presence of organic debris and the myriad soil inhabitants that do the vital work of relaying nourishment to green plants.

The ideal soil for raising tomatoes is friable (crumbly), loamy earth, a rich repository of organic matter. Chances are fairly good that whatever corner of the garden you select for your seedlings will be loamy to some degree, but you can usually upgrade or restore the structure and fertility of unpromising soil by working enough organic matter into it. The compact structure of clay soil forms a bond that is practically impervious to air or moisture. Integrated organic matter loosens and lightens this soil, permitting air and water to penetrate more easily so that plant roots have room to stretch and grow. In overly sandy soil, air moves freely but so does water, which rushes down and away from the roots, leaching out valuable nutrients in the process. When organic matter is added, water and nutrients are held and concentrated in upper soil levels where roots have access to them.

CONDITIONING THE SOIL

COMPOSTING: The easiest and cheapest way to enrich your soil and/or help it stay that way is to nourish it with liberal lacings of compost at regular intervals. If soil is the heart of the garden, compost is the bloodline that supports and sustains vital growth with transfusions of decayed twigs and grasses, nuts and seeds, leaves, feathers, manure and all kinds of healthy natural

12

wastes. To build a compost heap is to repeat and accelerate what nature does in converting organic debris into new and revitalized growing materials. Almost any waste material can be used, but there are some important elements you should incorporate right from the start. Primary among these is some form of nitrogen, which plants need in abundance not only because it builds plant proteins and stimulates leaf and stem growth and strong green color, but especially because this valuable nutrient also encourages the proliferation of the soil bacteria that hasten decomposition. Fresh manure is a fine source of nitrogen, but if this is unavailable, you may substitute one of the dried packaged manures or a commercially prepared compost starter. In addition, you might want to include in your compost heap other nitrogen-producing materials like cottonseed meal, blood meal, soybean meal, animal hair, feathers or even activated sludge.

Healthy green plants—weeds, grass clippings, spent flowers, fruits, vegetables, leaves and tree prunings—are a good source of extra minerals. Your compost heap makes a perfect recycling agent for these otherwise hard to dispose of wastes. Straw and waste hays are good compost materials, too, if you have access to them, and bone meal, rock powders and wood ashes are especially valuable because they are high in phosphorus and potassium, two other very important soil nutrients.

You may build your compost heap without benefit of structural support directly on the ground or below ground level, but probably the most satisfactory method is to drive 3 or 4 six-foot stakes firmly into the earth and wrap wire mesh around them. Any location—preferably one convenient to your garden and watering hose—will do. Start the heap off by spreading a fairly deep layer of plant and kitchen wastes on the ground. Follow with a 3-inch layer of manure topped off with a thin blanket of soil. Break up large waste ingredients (twigs, weeds and so on) by hand, or shred them with a power mower or shredder, before adding them to the heap. Be sure to stack the heap at least 5 to 6 feet high to encourage the heat build-up that bacteria thrive on. Too shallow—or too high—a heap creates a poor environment for bacteria, and may even mean loss of bacterial life.

Throw some rock powder, wood ashes or limestone over each layer of wastes if you wish, to give your compost an added boost. Keep light materials like leaves and hay in place with a thin covering of soil. As you add new layers, wet each enough to moisten it, but *do not* saturate—a waterlogged heap will be heavy and sodden and will severely limit the air supply that bacteria need to flourish. If properly layered and prepared, the clean-up materials you assemble in your out-of-the-way corner will begin to heat up almost overnight as bacteria set to work oxidizing them. Given the correct proportions of materials, the heap should register a temperature of around 150 degrees F. by the second day, as nature goes about her miraculous transformation. A heap that doesn't warm up sufficiently indicates a lack of nitrogen-producing elements. This is your cue to correct the balance and begin again. Tend the pile by watering fairly frequently during dry spells and, in seasons of heavy rainfall, by shielding the compost with a tarpaulin or piece of heavy plastic.

A compost heap begun one spring can usually be counted on for use the following spring. Fork over your compost from time to time during the year. Turning loosens and redistributes materials so they can decay evenly, and also introduces into the pile the air that is so necessary to hurry decomposition along.

QUICK COMPOSTING: Composting does take time but the wait is surely worthwhile. If you're in a hurry, however, you might give quick composting a try. This is an accelerated process that reduces wastes to compost in a matter of weeks. The trick here is that all the raw materials must be ground or shredded to less than one inch. Decomposition in this case is more rapid because the bacteria have a greater working surface. Quick composting also demands extra attention to details. Adequate moisture is important. The heap must be kept continuously damp but not soggy, and since more air is required, forking over every couple of days or so is a must.

Air is always vitally important even in conventional composting because the bacteria that reduce the waste materials to nutrient-rich fertilizer flourish and multiply on oxygen. An airless atmosphere fosters the growth of the usually objectionable, odoriferous anaerobic bacteria, which thrive without oxygen. While these bacteria are discouraged from growing in conventional composting, there is a somewhat unconventional method which encourages and employs their services. This system involves gathering materials like grass, leaves or other wastes that mat together easily and covering them tightly with black plastic or sealing them in dark clean-up bags. At this point your chores are completed. Just leave the materials strictly alone until decomposition is finished and the end product is completely free from odor, then use in the usual way.

SHEET COMPOSTING: If you haven't the space or inclination to establish a compost heap, traditional or otherwise (although you really should), you can resort to other quite effective means of improving the physical characteristics of your soil and/or correcting its deficiencies.

Sheet composting is a process in which leaves, grass clippings or manure are recycled into the soil simply by spreading the material over the garden bed and spading it in. During the process of decomposition any one of these materials performs the same basic function as compost. Although you may apply these up to two months prior to planting, the best time to sheet compost is in the fall, particularly when fresh manure is used, since this will burn seedlings if it hasn't sufficient time to rot.

GREEN MANURES: A soil that is low in organic content can be improved by the use of the so-called green manures. These are grass or legume cover crops that are planted, allowed to mature and then dug into the soil. Green manures have strong root systems which very effectively loosen heavy soils or bind sandy soils. They have a higher nitrogen content than their dried counterparts and decompose more rapidly, so you can plan on setting out your seedlings within a month of turning the crop under. Check with your agricultural agent or extension service for the cover crops most suitable for your climate and soil.

MAULE'S NEW IMPERIAL

SOIL NUTRITION

Soil properly conditioned with organic matter is much more receptive to any nutrients you may wish to add to increase fertility or correct a particular deficiency. Sixteen chemical elements supplied by the combination of air, water and soil are crucial to the healthy life of green plants, but three—nitrogen, phosphorus and potassium—are utilized in greater quantities than any of the others. A deficiency in any one of these will seriously affect both the growth and yield of your crop. For example, nitrogen promotes leaf and stem growth. Phosphorus stimulates early and strong root growth, helps to produce plant sugars (photosynthesis) and is also responsible for relaying the energy produced by the sugars to all parts of the plant. Potassium is essential to all the growth processes and contributes to general plant health.

Like all green-leaved plants, tomatoes thrive on a well-balanced diet of nitrogen, phosphorus and potassium. Once you have restored your soil to top condition by restructuring and enriching it with organic matter, you can probably count on a good balance of these essential nutrients and look forward to healthy, vigorous, productive plants right from the start. Despite your best efforts, however, it is still possible for your plants to display some signs of deficiency in one or another of the major nutrients.

NITROGEN DEFICIENCY: Yellowing leaves usually signal that your plants need additional nitrogen. This condition is particularly evident in the older leaves, which may drop off as a result. Often general plant growth is stunted. It is always best to take care of this problem before it starts by incorporating compost, well-rotted or dried manure, blood meal or cottonseed meal into the soil at planting time. Unfortunately, by the time you notice the yellowing leaves, it is too late for preplanting remedies.

The best advice at this point is to water with a *very light* manure tea (½ cup of dried manure steeped in one gallon water). Whatever you do, don't overreact. Knowing how much extra nitrogen to add when you suspect a deficiency can prove somewhat tricky. Too much nitrogen in the early stages of growth may promote luxuriant foliage at the expense of further fruit setting.

PHOSPHORUS DEFICIENCY: Plants deficient in phosphorus display many symptoms identical to nitrogen deficiency: slow stem and flower growth and poor root development but the leaves of a phosphorus-poor plant tend to be dullish, with purple tints. Either bone meal or phosphate rock, both of which are rich in phosphorus, are recommended for increasing your soil's supply of this nutrient.

POTASSIUM DEFICIENCY: A potassium deficiency also leads to stunted growth with tips and edges of leaves exhibiting yellow patches. The best way to restore the potassium balance is to apply a thin layer of wood ashes, especially those left over from the burning of hardwoods. Keep wood ashes stored in a dry place until needed, then spread over and work in your garden. Other organic sources of potassium include granite rock or a green manure used as a mulch prior to planting. If you suspect a potassium deficiency this year it is wise to take steps to prevent it from occurring again next year.

ACIDITY OR ALKALINITY

Plants have a hard time utilizing the nutrients present in soil that is too acid or too alkaline. Acidity and alkalinity refer respectively to the degree to which a soil is either sour or sweet as measured on a pH scale. The scale ranges from 0 to 14, with 7.0 regarded as neutral. Your soil will most likely be on the acid or lower side of neutral if you live in an area with plentiful rainfall. Alkaline soils tend to predominate in drier climates.

Tomatoes, like other vegetables, prefer to grow in soil that is on the acid side. Acids help to unlock the soil's minerals and make them available to soil bacteria. Since humus-rich soils produce some of their own acids, your garden, unless it is compacted with hard and poorly aerated clay, will undoubtedly fall within the slightly acid range of pH 6.0 to pH 6.8.

A soil analysis is suggested when preparing a new garden bed or if growth problems arise in an old one. You can determine the degree to which your soil is acid or alkaline with a soil-testing kit available at most garden supply centers. As an alternative, ship a sample of your problem soil to your state university agricultural station or state agricultural extension service, where (sometimes for a small fee) its shortcomings will be analyzed and suggestions for improving it will be recommended.

You can reduce acidity in a soil that is below the accepted pH level by applying lime, preferably finely ground dolomitic limestone, once every three years. Moderately alkaline soils can be restored to a more neutral pH by digging in substantial amounts of compost. Shredded oak leaves, acid peat, leafmold, wood shavings or sawdust are also very effective in reducing alkalinity. Whether you are raising or lowering your soil's pH, be sure to do it well in advance of planting time. Ideally, this operation should take place in the fall to assure that your garden will be in great shape for spring planting.

SELECTING A SITE

Tomatoes will adjust to just about any kind of well-prepared soil that has been nourished in advance with organic materials and nutrients, but they also require those two vital ingredients without which few vegetables will prosper—sufficient light and warmth.

Choose a sunny site with a southern or southeastern exposure and some protection from the wind where seedlings can receive 6 or more hours of sun. Light stimulates stocky growth, and warmth prods the growing plants into performing their best. Setting your plants along a wall or fence, or shielding them with some sort of plastic windscreen will boost soil temperatures and add weeks to the growing season. A sunny spot close to or up against the house offers both wind protection and convenience, with a source of water right at hand.

The tomato bed should be reasonably well drained. Avoid sites where water collects. Poor drainage weakens your plants and makes them much more susceptible to disease. Try to locate the garden away from trees and good-size shrubs. Their shade blocks the sun and their roots have the furtive habit of draining the soil of most of the moisture and nutrients you've expended time and energy adding.

STARTING RIGHT

As good-natured as the tomato plant is in general, it is, in particular, rather fussy about its outdoor growing climate. Most varieties are temperature-sensitive and will balk at setting fruit unless days, and particularly nights, are sufficiently warm. Since most varieties need an extended time to mature, tomato enthusiasts in areas where winter lingers into spring can get a jump on the season by starting seeds indoors and transplanting well-established seedlings to the garden when the weather and soil warm up.

Although it is easier to buy nursery seedlings, you can grow your own successfully if you keep a few basic rules in mind.

First—seeds need a disease-free starting medium. Unsterilized soil harbors a fungus known as "damping off," which rots tender stems at the soil line.

Second—good germination depends upon warmth, moisture and light. A moist, warm growing environment speeds sprouting, and ample light, either natural or artificial, assures compact, stocky growth.

Third—own-grown tomato seedlings require an adjustment period in order to withstand the shock of being moved outdoors when spring arrives. A gradual "hardening off" will acclimatize them to temperature changes and exposure to wind and sun (see page 22).

"SOIL" FOR SEEDS

Prepare your own planting mixture from commercial starting mediums or select one from the varied assortment of synthetic premixed soils, peat pellets, cubes or blocks, minigreenhouse arrangements or seed-starting kits available in most garden supply centers. Whatever planting method you elect, be sure you choose disease-free, lightweight materials that hold moisture well.

Many starting mediums meet these qualifications, and most are sold in small quantities as well as in bulk.

Vermiculite, an expanded mica that is sterile, clean and simple to handle, makes transplanting easy.

Perlite, of volcanic origin, has similar qualities, although it is usually combined with other materials.

Equally good soil substitutes that will satisfy both the novice and experienced gardener include milled *sphagnum moss* or equal parts of *peat moss* and *builder's sand*.

19

Some commercial starting mediums work well with organically enriched soil from your own garden, provided you sterilize the latter beforehand. A mixture I've had great luck with is one of equal parts of sterilized garden soil, vermiculite and peat moss. To sterilize garden soil, sift it through a fine mesh screen to give it an even texture, then spread the soil over the bottom of a shallow pan, dampen it a bit and set it in an oven preheated to 160 to 170 degrees F. A 30-minute period of baking on each of two successive days should render the soil disease- and weed-free.

CONTAINERS FOR SEEDLINGS

Your starting soil can go into just about any kind of container, from the large wooden or plastic flats that commercial growers use to conventional flower pots. One of the easiest and most successful ways to start seeds off is in individual peat pots filled with starting mix or in solid peat growing blocks or expandable peat pellets. These reduce the shock of transplanting since the pot, block or pellet can be set directly and neatly into the garden. Recycled juice or milk cartons, plastic bleach bottles, egg cartons, coffee cans and plastic ice cream containers also make fine receptacles for your starting mix when drainage holes are punched in the bottoms before filling.

SEEDS FOR SEEDLINGS

Tomatoes do best in the garden when days and nights are warm, so check the average date of the last frost in your area and begin 6 to 8 weeks prior to that. Plants set into the garden too early may succumb to a late frost. On the other hand, seedlings held indoors too long waiting for warm weather tend to turn lanky and do not take well to transplanting.

Most tomato gardeners like to plant a combination of early, midseason and late varieties to insure a steady harvest. If you end up with an excess of seeds, and you probably will, store them in a cool, dry place and they'll remain usable for up to 5 years past the "packed for" date stamped on the packet.

Before sowing, dampen your soil to the consistency of a well-squeezed sponge and prepare furrows or make holes about ¼ inch deep. To sow, fold a piece of paper in half, drop some seeds along the crease and tap the paper lightly with your finger as you move your hand along the rows. This method makes it easier to distribute seeds evenly and avoids overcrowding which results in spindly plants. Sow 3 or 4 seeds per inch in rows 2 inches apart when using flats or other large containers, or 3 or 4 seeds per pot in smaller containers. Sift soil lightly over the seeds, slip the container into a clear plastic bag and twist closed.

If you've chosen to start your seeds off in peat pellets or blocks, follow the instructions provided, cover with clear plastic and seal tightly. Sheet plastic is a great convenience in indoor gardening. It helps maintain the constantly moist soil that seeds need for good germination. Water condenses and gathers on the plastic and drops back on the soil in this improvised terrarium. If your daily check reveals the soil is soggy from excess condensation, simply roll back the plastic or open the bag to permit a little drying out.

In addition to moisture, your germinating seeds need a soil temperature of 70 to 80 degrees F., so find them a corner in the warmest spot in the house. A cozy place in a sunny room or on a radiator set at low heat will do nicely. Electric heating cables available through garden supply centers work well, too. Some elaborate types come equipped with plastic trays to accommodate the cable and hold your seed containers as well, or if you really feel like pampering your plants you can buy them anything from automatic heat timers to thermostatically controlled miniature greenhouses.

After the first set of leaves appears, remove your seedlings from their plastic incubator. They will require at least 12 hours of light per day and daily spraying of the soil to keep it spongy. Avoid spraying the leaves if you can. Set your containers where they will receive full sun through a window with southern exposure and turn the containers every day to keep seedlings from bending toward sunlight. The fluorescent lighting arrangements or growing lights designed for plants are worth investigating, since they provide abundant overhead light and therefore encourage hardy, compact seedlings. Keep the bulbs dust-free and the seedlings well aired.

The second set of leaves to appear are the true leaves of the mature tomato plant. As soon as these form, begin a weekly feeding program of ¼ strength water-soluble fertilizer. If you are using a synthetic soil, this is also the time to transplant to flats or containers with equal parts of sterilized garden soil, sand and peat moss. Space your seedlings 2 inches apart, or set in individual peat pots. Seedlings that reach this stage in deep containers filled with a mixture of sterile garden soil may be left where they are, but give them space to grow by keeping the hardiest and snipping off the rest.

Handle seedlings carefully and try not to disturb roots too much. Clean hands are a must also, especially if you are a smoker (see page 45). Lift the seedlings with a large, clean spoon and replant so that the seed leaves sit about ½ inch above the soil.

HARDENING OFF

Even sturdy young tomato plants should not go directly from their protected indoor environment to their home in the garden. They must adjust gradually to cold, sun and drying winds. If you have one, a coldframe makes a perfect temporary shelter for your plants. Keep the cover open on warm days but shut at night or when rain or cold is expected and don't forget to keep plants well watered. As soon as they have successfully weathered 24 hours of complete outdoor exposure they are ready for the garden.

If you have no coldframe, any fairly sheltered, partially shaded outdoor spot will do. About 2 weeks before planting date, begin a program of gradual exposure by setting out your seedlings for 15 minutes the first day and gradually lengthening the time on each successive day. As soon as they can be left outdoors for 24 hours, they are ready for transplanting to the garden.

Regardless of the hardening-off method you choose, cut back on moisture and warmth a week before transplanting to accustom your plants to outdoor conditions. And remember that even after hardening, young plants are tender, so don't set them into the garden until all danger of frost is past.

STARTING SEEDS IN A HOTBED

A coldframe works on the greenhouse principle. Sunlight streams through the glass or plastic cover and heat is trapped within the box, creating a tropical miniclimate which is controlled by opening or closing the cover.

If you happen to have a working coldframe, you can make it double as a hotbed by adding a second source of heat—either by underlaying the soil with a thick blanket of fresh, heat-producing manure or with a soil-heating cable—to maintain steady warmth. Set your pots or trays of seeds directly in the bed or spread a 4- to 6-inch layer of starting mixture over the heat source and sow your seeds in this. A thermometer will tell you at a glance when—or if—the cable needs unplugging or the cover must be raised to decrease heat or whether additional insulating materials (blankets and the like) are needed to increase heat. Once your seedlings are well established and transplanting time approaches, allow the hotbed to return to its original function and use it to harden off seedlings.

BUYING TRANSPLANTS

If you lack time, space or a sunny southern exposure, you are probably better off buying your seedlings. These are generally inexpensive and save a great deal of effort, but of course you are limited to the varieties that suit your nurseryman's (and not your own) fancy.

If you do buy, look for stocky, succulent young plants with at least 4 to 6 sets of true leaves. Do not buy plants that are in flower or fruit (especially if they are growing in small containers) or any that appear pale or off-color or seem overly leggy. These characteristics usually result from overcrowding or nutritional deficiencies. Make a concerted effort to purchase plants labeled disease-resistant. Nursery transplants need no hardening off.

SAVING SEEDS FROM YOUR OWN TOMATOES

Saving seeds from tomatoes you grow this year for next year's planting is easy but not entirely practical. Many tomato varieties are hybrids, which means each seed is a controlled cross between two distinct parent lines carefully bred to reproduce the best characteristics of both. Seeds carried over from hybrids frequently revert back to one or another remote ancestor and produce inferior fruits.

If you have had luck growing a particularly delicious and/or vigorous variety and want to experiment, select very ripe, perfect fruits from strong, healthy vines. Cut each tomato into eighths and shake or scoop the seeds into a very fine sieve. Rinse away bits of pulp under running water, spread the seeds on paper towels and set them in a warm spot to dry. Label and store in a cool, dry place. A few weeks before actual indoor planting time, sow in sterile potting soil as you ordinarily would, but keep track of the number you plant. If most of these test seeds sprout, it's safe to go ahead with indoor sowing at the proper time, but you won't know until your first bite of ripe fruit whether or not your experiment was a success.

PREPARING GARDEN SOIL

Tomatoes are single-season plants. All their growth takes place in one year, so the best time to prepare outdoor soil is the season before the actual planting takes place—in fall for spring planting or in spring for fall planting.

This advance preparation has several important benefits. Digging aerates the soil; spading in organic matter greatly improves fertility and texture; and the nutrients supplied by compost, well-rotted manure, bone meal, wood ashes, blood meal, peanut shells or activated sludge, aided by snow and rain, are gradually released into the soil. Lime is slow to permeate, so if a pH test reveals excess acidity, it, too, should be added well in advance. In established gardens, prior-season preparation in the form of cleanup and mulching is good housekeeping practice. Cleanup gets rid of weeds and dead plants which may harbor insects and disease, and mulch materials decay right down into the soil, adding beneficial nutrients to its structure.

If you are planting your first garden, select a well-drained site with maximum sunlight (see page 18). Sample shovelfuls of soil from the various areas available to you. If one seems to have richer, more loosely packed earth than another, plant there unless poor drainage is a problem. If the area is rich with earthworms, so much the better.

Mark off garden boundaries and strip the area of grass or weeds, or incorporate these into the soil. Tomatoes are deep-rooted plants, so dig to a depth of at least 10 inches, and deeper if it is possible to do so without disturbing the subsoil. Remove stones and debris, break up heavy clods of earth and spread about 2 inches of organic material over the top of the soil. Spade this in deeply and distribute it well.

Add a second organic layer in about a week, but try to keep the materials from matting together. Aim for a good mix of half organic matter and half soil in the top 10 inches. The idea is to create a crumbly, nicely textured medium to which your tomatoes will respond enthusiastically. Just prior to planting, or as soon as the soil can be worked, enrich it with another application of organic materials.

Avoid planting tomatoes near ornamentals like dahlias, petunias or close relatives like peppers, eggplants, okra, potatoes, nightshade and other members of the Solanum family. Keep them away from cucumbers, celery and muskmelons, too. Seasoned gardeners, accomplished in the art of tomato raising, report increased harvests when they practice crop rotation. Insects and diseases that establish themselves in one particular location seem reluctant to join the tomatoes in their move from place to place.

Lay out your rows parallel to the short side of the plot, with more room between rows than between plants. This makes for easier access and more comfortable harvesting. If your ground slopes, set out your plants in rows that traverse the slope to minimize erosion during heavy rain. Leave about 2 to 2½ feet between plants you plan to stake, 4 feet between unstaked plants.

Your seedlings should go into the ground as soon as days are pleasantly warm and night temperatures reach and remain above 55 degrees F. Handle seedlings tenderly and try not to disturb the roots when transplanting. Plants in clay or plastic pots slip out easily if you soak them beforehand just enough to loosen the outer edges of the soil. When separating seedlings growing together in large containers or flats, use a clean, sharp knife and lift each plant singly, along with whatever soil clings to it. Seedlings grown in peat pots, blocks or pellets suffer little root disturbance when transplanted, but be sure to set the containers well below ground level or the root ball will dry out too rapidly.

Tomatoes are deep-rooted vegetables and appreciate lots of underground living space. Make their holes wide and deep so the roots can sprawl and get a firm hold beneath the soil. Lighten the earth you take from each hole with some compost to simulate the light-textured growing mixture your plants are accustomed to and to minimize transplant shock. Loose soil also encourages deep root growth, so put some of this mixture at the bottom of the hole and use the rest to fill in around the settled-in plant.

If you plan to stake your tomatoes (and to stake or not to stake is really just a matter of personal preference since all the evidence pretty much indicates they grow just as well either way), the time to do so is just before setting in the plants to eliminate the possibility of root injury. Staking and ways of training plants so that fruits are up off the ground are discussed on pages 28 to 31.

Like most aficionados, I have my own favorite planting technique which may sound like witchcraft but is merely a tried method utilizing available materials (with sensational results). Begin with a hole about 10 to 12 inches deep (provided this doesn't disturb the subsoil, the depth of which varies with the location), layer in an inch or so of crushed corncobs, cover with about 4 inches of soil, set in a fish or eel head (use a bit of well-rotted manure if fish heads are not available), and you are ready to plant. The corncobs soak up and hold moisture and the heads decompose slowly, causing roots to reach deep for water and nourishment. The result is a particularly well developed root system and bushels of perfect fruit.

I have my pet method of setting out seedlings, too, which I am convinced produces stronger plants and therefore more abundant fruit. Instead of planting upright with just the roots below ground, set the plant into its hole at an angle, so that the first two sets of true leaves lie almost parallel to the ground. New roots form along the stem and the plant soon straightens up to become a hardy and vigorous bearer practically immune to disease, dry spells, high winds and other natural phenomena.

Soak each hole well before setting in the plants, leave each root ball intact and never spread out the roots. Fill in the hole with organic matter and soil mixture, tamp down firmly to eliminate air pockets and follow up with another good soaking. In 8 to 10 days give your plants a boost with a mild compost-water solution or some other very diluted water-soluble fertilizer.

Your newly planted tomatoes may be a bit droopy during their first few days in their permanent home. Although recovery is generally rapid, you can usually avoid this setback by doing your transplanting on a cloudy day or by providing a little light shade for each plant if the clouds don't cooperate. I find that baskets with open-slatted sides turned upside down shelter the seedlings from the hot sun very effectively, and also help to keep the soil moist during this recovery period. As an alternative, when baskets are scarce, shield your plants with pieces of cardboard box, anchored with heaped-up soil.

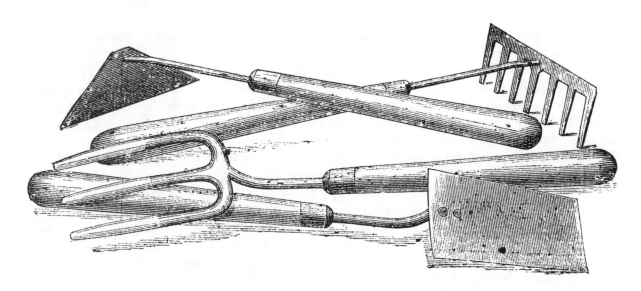

WATERING

Normal spring rainfall should furnish most of the moisture your tomatoes need during their early stages of growth. If you feel the urge to get out the hose during an excessively hot, dry spell, water in the morning so wet foliage can dry by evening. Better still, use the flat, soaker-type hose with holes on one side. This kind of watering allows moisture to penetrate to the level where it will do the most good. Shallow watering has an adverse effect, encouraging roots to surface in a quest for moisture, weakening a plant's structure and making it more vulnerable to high winds or heavy rain.

MULCHING

Once fruit is set, it is important to maintain even moisture. Soil that fluctuates between dry and wet encourages stunting and blossom-end rot. The best way to keep your soil evenly moist and cool is by mulching ... an age-old garden technique that retards evaporation and makes water necessary only during the driest and hottest weather. Mulch is helpful in many ways. Spread between rows, it keeps fruit off the ground, discourages pests and even seems to retard disease. Heaped up around the stems, it protects the leaves from soil splash and the danger of soil-borne disease, particularly if you have decided to forego staking and are allowing your plants to sprawl. For lazy gardeners or those with a minimum of time to spare, mulching holds down weeds and makes your garden practically maintenance-free.

Organic mulches, and there are many of these, decompose and enrich the soil with valuable nutrients and improve soil structure at the same time. Grass clippings can go directly from mower bag to garden, but should be spread out rather thinly to avoid matting. Old straw or hay that is free from weed seed works superbly well, and ground bark, peat moss, cocoa shells, fine wood chips or sawdust do an effective job. All of these may be allowed to reach the final humus stage right on the soil they will ultimately enrich.

Where we live in eastern Long Island, the salt hay that grows so abundantly near the bay is widely, and successfully, used as a mulch, and because it doesn't decompose, it can be reused year after year. Seaweed is also popular in this area. It, like all mulches, modifies the environment in which plants grow, protects the roots from cold, heat or drought, reduces the possibility of erosion and helps the soil to retain beneficial amounts of water.

The best time to apply a mulch is when your plants first set their blossoms after the sun has warmed the soil during the initial growth period. Light, bulky materials should blanket the soil to a depth of 6 inches, and denser mulches should be layered less thickly—2 to 3 inches are quite sufficient. Mulch immediately after a good soaking rain (or a thorough hosing) to give your garden a head start and keep your soil moist all summer long. Incidentally, since organic mulches tend to decompose, you may have to replenish or supplement them from time to time with additional layers of the original material. This is not really a drawback, since the greater the degree of rotting, the richer your soil becomes.

The use of black plastic as a mulch has risen dramatically right along with the current boom in vegetable gardening. Perhaps the most complimentary thing you can say about its appearance is that it is neat; nevertheless, its popularity is outdistancing many organic mulches because of its particular advantages to tomato growers. Once the soil has warmed in the spring, black plastic permits earlier planting because it absorbs the sun's rays and keeps the soil warm and moist. In addition to retarding evaporation, it diverts the greater part of a heavy rainfall away from your garden and prevents nutrients from leaching away. Weeds won't grow under it, and it effectively keeps fruit off the ground.

Mulching with black plastic does, however, have some drawbacks. It is lightweight and can easily be whipped away by high winds unless you anchor it securely. And while it is helpful in raising soil temperature during the spring, on hot summer days it makes root-damaging heat soar high. Devotees of black plastic argue that as the plants mature they shade the plastic, and thus less heat is absorbed into the ground, but to be on the safe side it's probably wise to remove the plastic when spring yields to summer and replace it with a more conventional mulch. The prime reason to avoid it, in my opinion, is that it is not organic, does not decompose and enrich the soil and is totally unnecessary, since natural mulches work as well.

TRAINING FRUIT OFF THE GROUND

To stake or not to stake . . . that issue has created more controversy than any other among tomato gardeners. Staking proponents argue that this practice results in cleaner produce and also makes cultivating and harvesting lots easier. Fruit that stays off the ground, they say, is less subject to soil-borne insects and disease. But since the natural inclination of tomatoes is to sprawl as they grow, antistake gardeners are just as staunchly convinced that thick lower branches give the plants all the support they need and that mulching keeps fruit sufficiently clean and disease-free.

Actually, to stake or not really depends to a great extent on the growth pattern of the varieties you choose to grow. Most early varieties fall into the *determinate* category, which is characterized by plants with fewer than three leaves between each flowering cluster. Determinate or bush tomatoes, as they are commonly called, set fruit low on bushy plants and seldom, if ever, need staking.

Indeterminate varieties, on the other hand, just keep growing until the first frost. This growth is characterized by the pattern of flower cluster, three leaves, and then another flower cluster. Most late, straight-growing varieties are indeterminate and do very well when staked and trained.

Semideterminate tomatoes have some characteristics of both determinate and indeterminate varieties and may be staked or not as you prefer.

Whether or not to stake also depends on garden size. The sprawling habits of determinate varieties call for more distance between plants. Indeterminate tomatoes may be pruned to one, two or even three stems, trained to stakes or trellises and set closer together. If you garden exclusively in containers, any variety you plant will need some kind of support (see page 33).

My own inclination is to heavily mulch determinate or bush varieties and let them grow free but to stake later or indeterminate plants. Actually, though, it can never harm tomatoes to stake them (unless you handle plants roughly), and even determinate varieties seem to benefit when they are fastened loosely to small stakes or are allowed to sprawl over a low platform of slats or a ladder-like frame, where freer air circulation around lower branches may result in a higher degree of pollination and fruit set.

There are literally hundreds of ways to hold fruit vertically off the ground—almost as many ways as there are tomato gardeners. One of the simplest and easiest to use is a strong stake or pole embedded deeply into the soil at transplanting time, about 6 inches away from the seedling. Stakes should be thick and tall—at least 8 feet high for indeterminate varieties to allow plenty of room for the plant to grow on even after you bury one end of the stake 10 to 12 inches deep in the soil.

Use finished or unfinished wood, bamboo poles or healthy, trimmed tree branches. Forget about the pencil-thin, green-dyed stakes that are a familiar staple at garden centers. These are too light to support plants and usually yield to the first stiff breeze of summer.

Secure the plant to the stake, or fence, or trellis, by looping some strong, soft material—rag strips, discarded nylon stockings or soft thick yarn—several times around the stake, then crossing it loosely over the plant not far below a leaf stem. Finish up with a square knot. This arrangement keeps the ties from damaging the stalk, while giving the stalk some freedom of movement. As the plants grow taller and branches show the first signs of developing fruit, tie them in similar fashion at strategic points.

Don't hesitate to devise other methods of using stakes or poles. You can set them out in rows with horizontal wooden or wire cross supports in between, or stack and tie them teepee fashion with one well-pruned tomato plant set at the base of each pole. You can also use the teepee arrangement when setting out one heavy-bearing vine; or for any heavy-bearing variety, you can try a two-pole stake with rigid cross supports. Fasten your plants to any of these supports with soft materials in the manner described above.

Another increasingly popular way to train tomatoes is to cage them in wire cylinders. Growth is upright and confined, yet cages provide lots of space for the plants to develop naturally. The wire cylinder not only supports the plant but the leaves grow in such a way that they protect the ripening fruit from sunscald and cracking. There are other advantages to cages, too. They are very durable and may be used from year to year, even if they are left outside all winter. You can easily slip a clear plastic cover right over the outside where it will protect the plant, both as young seedling and, at season's end, from cold weather. Unless your cage is very small, no tying or pruning is necessary. The plant simply grows up through the cage.

Ready-to-use cages are available at many garden centers, but you can also fashion your own out of 6-inch concrete reinforcing wire, 4 to 5 feet in height. Bend the wire into a cylinder 24 to 30 inches in diameter and secure the edges where they meet by crimping them with a pair of pliers. Cut out enough cross wires at the bottom so that the cage can be pushed into the ground at transplanting time. Some leaves and stems will poke through the 6-inch holes as they grow, but try to keep them inside until the plant reaches its full growth.

The Japanese ring is a variation on the wire cylinder. It's also a great space saver if you have limited garden area. You'll need a spot that's about 4 by 4 feet in all. To make the ring, bend 6-foot high reinforcing wire into a cylinder 24 to 30 inches in diameter and line the sides of one end with 2-foot high fine mesh screen. Set the screened end into the ground, and starting with a 6-inch layer of peat moss, fill the screened part of the cylinder with alternate 3-inch layers of compost-enriched soil and peat, ending with a layer of peat or other mulch (and a sprinkle of fertilizer if you desire).

Set four young seedlings outside the ring at equal distance from each other. As growth proceeds, attach the vines to the wires with soft materials. Water the seedlings while they're getting started, and water the layers of nutrients from the beginning and keep them moist. Once established, the ring's interior materials should give your plants nourishment for the entire season.

PRUNING

At the point where a leaf stem joins the main stem, there is always a shoot or sucker that will eventually blossom into a full-fledged, fruit-bearing branch. Each of these will, of course, add to the number of tomatoes you will eventually harvest. In this case, however, the plant may direct its energy toward vine growth, and fruit production will be delayed. I've found also that these late-developing branches rarely bear top-quality fruit.

If your tomatoes are the staked, indeterminate varieties, and you want to confine growth to a limited space, pruning has advantages. You have fewer vines to tie and there is less rambling.

Pruning demands a weekly regimen, but you don't need to adopt the severe single-stem method. Instead, try the more manageable double-stem method. Here the first sucker near the base of the stalk and below the first flower cluster is allowed to grow and form a two-stemmed plant. The stems may be tied and trained to one or two stakes or a trellis, and the rest of the suckers are removed. Double-stem pruning assures denser foliage to protect against sunscald and cracking as well as more fruit over a longer period. If you have lots of time to devote to your tomatoes, you might want to try the multiple-stem method, which involves training 3 or more stems. You'll have more fruit and more foliage protection—and lots more work.

Pruning your staked plants does not necessarily mean that the fruit will be better than those you harvest from varieties allowed to sprawl. Both pruned and unpruned plants yield good crops. But there are times when pinching off some foliage helps sprawling plants immeasurably. If your plants have huge stalks with lots of leaves and green fruit, or summer weather proves exceptionally humid or rainy, try removing some of the heavy foliage. Instant pruning speeds up ripening as the sun reaches the fruit, and both fruit and soil dry more rapidly.

Pruning by hand is best. Simply grasp each shoot between thumb and forefinger at its growing point and bend it to one side until it snaps, then pull it off in the opposite direction. This reverse maneuver prevents injury to both leaf axil and stalk. Make your snap flush with the stem, taking care not to disturb any fruit buds in the immediate vicinity.

PLANTING SUCKERS

One advantage pruning gives is that with no extra expense and very little effort you can increase your stock of tomato plants and boost your total yield. The only requirement is space. As long as there's a vacant spot or two in your garden, it's a relatively simple matter to cut off some of the suckers at pruning time and plant them immediately.

Suckers from 8 to 10 inches in length are a good size for transplanting. Take them from healthy, heavy-bearing plants. Prepare holes in advance in the same organically rich earth you have provided for the rest of your tomato crop, then bury the cut-off ends at least 4 inches deep, tamp down the soil and water thoroughly.

Give these cuttings a little light shade following surgery. A bushel basket turned upside down over each transplanted sucker for a few days will not only keep the ground cool and moist but will also prevent transplant shock. Some of the transplanted suckers may not survive, but most should form roots quickly and take hold quite well.

TOMATO GROWING IN CONTAINERS

Gardenless city dwellers and would-be tomato gardeners whose real estate is not conducive to tomato production need not be deprived of a home-grown harvest. The adaptable tomato makes an ideal container plant. As long as the sun shines six or more hours a day on patio, porch, fire escape, rooftop, doorstep—or even window sill—the tomato lover can sow and reap to his or her heart's content. All it really takes is a desire to nurture, plus a little extra attention.

There are both small-fruited and standard varieties perfect for container gardening. Tom Thumb, Red Cherry, Red Pear, Small Fry and the nonacid Yellow Pear are all small varieties that provide a nonstop harvest, excellent flavor and a decorative focal point when trained to grow from hanging baskets. Standard varieties will grow in containers anywhere there is sun, provided you aren't stingy with water. For full-season production, you might try planting early, midseason and late varieties, or devote your containers exclusively to hybrids which give heavy yield in a limited space. There are even tomatoes especially bred for growing in containers, varieties like Patio, Pixie, Stakeless and the low-acid Dwarf Champion. These tend, however, to be not quite as tasty as are standard varieties.

The nice part about container gardening is that you can shift your plants about to follow the sun or, when frost threatens, push them to a protected place. For containers, use whatever you have at hand—your choice can be as far out as your imagination.

Small-fruited tomatoes thrive in containers as small as 8 inches across but deep enough to hold 2 quarts of soil. Try cut-off plastic bleach bottles and plastic buckets or baskets, as well as the more conventional planter boxes or clay or plastic pots. Hanging any of these consists simply of slipping them into heavy cord or hemp bags, the kind available in dime stores, or of outfitting them with wire holders. Or try lining wire baskets or wire cylinders (see page 31) with sphagnum moss, fill with soil mix and hang in a sunny place.

Bigger tomato varieties will take easily to any large container provided it can hold at least 2 gallons, and preferably more, of soil mix. Even with 2-gallon containers you'll probably have to plan on more frequent watering and feeding to compensate for the limited root space. With the really large-growing varieties you'll need 5-gallon tubs.

Readymade oversized planters or tubs of wood, clay, metal or plastic make ideal receptacles, but don't limit yourself to these. Try barrels, wooden crates or plastic laundry or garbage pails,

33

all eminently suitable. Wood and clay containers do "breathe" and give freer circulation to air, so be prepared to water them more often. Safeguard any wooden container from wear and tear by finishing it first with wood preservative inside and out.

Wood, clay and some readymade plastic containers usually come equipped with built-in drainage, but you will have to provide some kind of drainage facilities for your improvised plastic containers. Proper drainage calls for lots of small holes (depending on the container's size) drilled in a random pattern around, and at least 1 to 2 inches above, the container's bottom. A deep laundry or bushel basket whose open sides will not confine the soil properly may be lined with heavy plastic punched in a dozen or so places for drainage. Gravel, pebbles, broken clay shards or even a recycled collection of bottle caps should fill the container's bottom right up the drainage holes. Another way to assure good drainage is to line the bottom of your container with an inch or so of peat moss. This works especially well in small containers because soil loss is cut to a minimum.

Fill your containers with a suitable planting medium of commercial potting soil, peat moss and builder's sand combined in equal parts to make a well-blended mixture. City dwellers may beg some ordinary garden soil and/or compost from suburban friends. Both of these will have to be sterilized, of course, before using (see page 20), but you can substitute them for the potting soil and peat moss respectively. Soil in containers also profits from occasional additions of organic material worked deeply in.

You also might want to consider using one of the lightweight soil substitutes sold at garden supply centers. These hold moisture and nutrients very well, and are very utilitarian if you have large containers to fill and lug around to keep up with the sun. There's even a lightweight soil substitute you can prepare yourself by combining 1 bushel of vermiculite with 1 bushel of shredded peat. Add 1½ cups of crushed limestone (the dolomitic kind, which contains magnesium), 1 cup of 5-10-5 fertilizer and ½ cup of 20 percent superphosphate. Sprinkle with a bit of water to minimize dust reaction while you're elbow deep, and mix all ingredients thoroughly.

Start your plants off as described on pages 19 to 22, or if you don't want to fuss with indoor planting, you can buy transplants that have been started at your local nursery (for tips on buying, see page 22). Nursery transplants won't need hardening off, but your well-established seedlings grown indoors should be gradually conditioned to life outdoors.

Follow the same general instructions for hardening off plants destined for the garden outlined on page 22. Tomato plants are tender and should not be set outside until all danger of frost is past, but because city temperatures generally grow warmer and settled far sooner than those in suburban areas, it's a fairly safe bet to say that if you are a city dweller, you'll be able to harden off and transplant a week or two earlier than your country cousins.

Ready your containers shortly before transplanting. Cover the bottom of each container right up to its drainage holes with 2 to 3 inches of drainage materials. Prepare your soil mixture, moisten to the consistency of a damp sponge and fill your containers to within 1 inch of the rim.

Unless they're quartered in hanging baskets, containerized tomatoes will need some kind of support. The time to install this is before the seedlings go into their new homes. You can use stakes or trellises, tying the vines as they grow with strips of cloth or strong, soft twine, or even improvise a cage arrangement (see page 31). Some gardeners like to train vines up with strong string attached to a cross brace at the top of two stakes. If you're not hanging your small varieties in baskets, a soft string or piece of yarn looped loosely around will keep branches from breaking with the weight of the fruit.

Pick a cloudy day for transplanting, or move your plants into partial shade for a day or two so they'll recover more quickly. Plants started in peat pots, blocks or pellets can be set into their containers without further ado, but be sure that each is placed well below soil level to prevent its drying out. Loosen seedlings in individual starting containers by moistening the soil a bit, then run a sharp knife around the inside of the pot, turn the pot over and sharply tap its bottom. The plant and soil should slide out quite easily. If your seedlings started life in flats, separate them from one another with a clean, sharp knife and lift out each seedling separately, together with whatever soil clings to it. Keep the roots as close together as possible.

Scoop out a hole in the waiting soil deep and wide enough for roots to sprawl effortlessly once they take hold. Set in each plant so that its first leaves are just above soil level, or try the productive technique of burying part of the stem (see page 26). Water well after planting and tamp the soil down with the heel of your hand.

Follow a regular routine of watering, fertilizing and cultivating once your tomatoes are settled in. Knowing how often to water your plants can be a bit tricky. Soil should be kept moist but not soggy, so if necessary get out the watering can as often as twice daily—plants exposed to warm winds and sun will dry out very rapidly.

A good rule is to water when the soil feels dry to your touch about ½ inch down. It's a bit harder to regulate the water supply for tomatoes growing in plastic containers because air cannot circulate as well as in wood or clay. To guard against soggy soil, make sure your containers have plenty of drainage holes and are well lined with drainage materials. You'll appreciate this help when summer rains come. Mixing peat into the soil also alleviates the drainage problem. If frequent watering tests your patience, or you just want to keep the soil cool, carefully dig a layer of finely textured mulch material (see page 27) into the top inch of soil.

Containerized tomatoes are heavy feeders, yet cannot send roots sprawling to seek nutrients. It helps to start with a good, nourishing soil mixture supplemented with bone meal, but it's also a good idea to begin a regular fertilizing routine about three weeks after transplanting. Use a diluted liquid fertilizer so you won't burn the roots, and continue to fertilize at 3-week intervals throughout the season for rapid growth and good production.

Airborne weeds turn up in most unlikely places. Pull them up by hand, taking care not to damage tomato plant roots. Turn surface soil over occasionally by loosening gently with an old tablespoon or fork, or put down a mulch and let it serve double duty as a moisture conserver and soil conditioner by keeping the soil loose and porous.

Tomatoes in containers sometimes suffer from the same diseases and pests that their garden brethren do. For diseases and pest control for your plants, see pages 42 to 50.

Scratch a tomato enthusiast, and chances are you'll uncover a home gardener who not only wants a huge crop of ripe, juicy tomatoes but also wants them *soon*. In frost-free regions, of course, and often in areas where the last hard frost occurs in the middle of March, there is usually time for two harvests each year. In most parts of the country, however, tomatoes cannot be put outdoors much before midspring, and only one crop is possible every year.

Originally a tropical plant, the tomato is fussy about temperatures, especially at night. A light frost can cause considerable damage, and even in early spring when days may be blissfully warm, night temperatures can, and often do, fall below 55 degrees F. Most of the early-maturing varieties set fruit at lower temperatures than this, but main-season varieties do not. Pollen germination and tube growth slow down in cool weather, and blossoms drop off before they have a chance to be fertilized.

GETTING A JUMP ON THE SEASON

The tomato's sensitivity to cold, plus the long growing season needed for most varieties, makes some kind of extra help necessary to increase soil temperatures and provide the plants with protection when early planting is planned. The idea is to get the tomato seedlings into the ground soon enough to assure early and continuous fruit production, but not so early that the seedlings succumb to spring cold.

Those few gardeners who happen to have a greenhouse handy can easily get a good jump on the growing season, but for most of us the easiest way to get early fruit is to buy early-maturing varieties and to get them into the ground as soon as is feasible.

Some experienced tomato gardeners believe in acclimating their seedlings to cool conditions right from the start. They raise seedlings at an indoor temperature that hovers around 60 degrees F., then harden them off and put them out early.

If you plan to ignore the calendar you will have to exercise a bit of ingenuity. Your own backyard, for example, has many different climates. Choose a planting area with a southern exposure well protected from the wind and your tomatoes will be degrees warmer. Or provide your young plants with some kind of protective covering, and expose them gradually until they are sufficiently hardened to make it on their own.

Good protective covering is any kind of sheltering device you design or resort to. A surprising number of temperature modifications can be effected with inexpensive or recycled plastics. You can rig up a minigreenhouse right over your planting bed using a cover of polyethylene film stretched over a square or A-shaped wooden frame. (When daytime temperature is mild, the plastic can be laid back.) If temperatures threaten to zoom downwards, fill plastic jugs with water and lay them on the soil. These will warm up during the day and throw back heat on a chilly night. Water-filled plastic bags also serve this purpose, but these tend to be a bit fragile. Bushel baskets outfitted with plastic covers work well over single plants. Just remove the covers when the weather warms up.

The hotcaps available in garden centers give very good protection during cool weather. The trick is to remember to widen the slits in the caps as the days warm up. Your own-made hot-caps of plastic hardware cloth wrapped around and supported by a long pointed stick afford as good, if not better protection. These circumvent the danger of excessive heat build-up which sometimes occurs under the commercial variety.

A collection of glass gallon wine or cider jugs will give similar greenhouse service. These allow air to enter from the top and furnish a clear view of your plants' progress. Remove the bottom of each jug with tools from one of the currently popular glass-cutting kits, or crack the bottoms by boiling the jugs and plunging them into 1-inch deep ice water. You may not achieve a smooth break, but it will be a break you can easily tap out. Set a jug over each of your transplants as soon as you've planted and watered it. Remove the jugs whenever you notice any heat build-up through the glass.

Gallon jugs made of plastic have an advantage over their glass counterparts—it's much easier to cut off their bottoms. Their opaque composition makes it impossible for sunlight to penetrate, but don't hesitate to use them on cold nights or blustery days. Screw the tops on if you like and anchor them well or they'll take off in a strong wind.

Really frigid climates call for even more protection. One way to keep young transplants warm outdoors is to shelter them in a snug buffer zone. Dig out your holes and layer them with rich, well-fertilized soil, then set in your plants. Build a circular wall of thickly stacked salt hay around each plant, heaping it above the soil. A piece of glass or clear, rigid plastic laid on top of each circle of hay affords a warm greenhouse atmosphere for the plant underneath. Remove the glass on sunny days as you gradually acclimate the plants to cooler weather.

Another countermeasure to take when spring temperatures plunge is to bury a bottomless glass jug right along with the roots. As the plant grows, lift the jug and raise the soil level, then replace the jug. Substitute gallon-size plastic ice cream containers for the glass jugs if you wish. When extra protection is needed, simply attach the plastic covers.

Many of these techniques designed to shelter your young tomatoes in early spring work equally well at the other end of the growing season. If you can get your plants through early fall frosts, ripening should continue through Indian summer and even after. Even a light frost clinging to vines and fruit can be damaging because the early morning sun burns right through, rotting the fruit and drying the leaves. By repositioning the large plastic structure so helpful in spring, or by lightly blanketing the plants at night with polyethylene film or other lightweight covering (including ordinary blankets), you can keep production going. Remove protection during the day, however, or the consequent heat build-up will do in your tomatoes as surely as any frost.

Sooner or later the calendar runs down and tomatoes, though they try their best, are unable to ripen out-of-doors. Then it's time to bring them in. Gnarly, small dark green tomatoes will probably never ripen. Use the *best* of these for green tomato recipes (see pages 145 to 181), pickles or relishes (see page 171). Green tomatoes paling to white at the bottom will usually ripen gradually indoors in cool storage (see page 204), or if you prefer, dig up the plants and shake the soil loose from the roots, then hang upside down in any cool, sheltered place while fruits ripen and color. Green tomatoes tinged with pink may be brought directly to a cool kitchen or pantry counter to ripen at their own pace out of the sunlight. It's best not to ripen tomatoes on a sunny window sill because direct sun rays deteriorate quality—warmth, not light, ripens tomatoes.

GROWING TOMATO PLANTS IN WINTER

If during the winter months you are unwilling to settle for those woolly textured, tasteless red golf balls that grocery chains sell as tomatoes, you may want to try one of the various ways of growing tomatoes indoors. There's no guarantee you'll be successful, and your extra efforts probably won't yield a really abundant harvest, but if you do decide to try your hand, you may be able to garner enough of a crop to give your family a once- or twice-weekly winter treat of home-grown fruits.

Indoor tomatoes can be raised from seed or from branches cut from mature plants growing in the garden. Don't bother to dig up and pot the mature plants that have been busy supplying your summer and early fall tomato needs. Their well-developed root systems will never survive transplanting. But if you've been doing part or all of your gardening in containers, there's no harm in shifting these indoors come fall.

To start your indoor crop from seed, simply follow in autumn the same procedure for sowing seeds in spring (see page 20), then transplant into larger containers. When taking cuttings, you may either cut vines from summer-bearing tomatoes, housing them afterwards in water until roots appear, or layer some branches until they form roots by cutting each stem half through or girdling it around with your clean knife. Hold each cut open with moist compost. A plastic bag may be wrapped around the layered area to help keep the compost in place.

Pot the cuttings taken by either method in appropriately sized individual containers (see page 33) filled with an organically rich mixture of garden soil and compost or peat, plus a sprinkling of bone meal. You may get them off to a head start outdoors while the weather is still warm, but it's a good idea to treat them like house plants that summer outside and bring them in a bit before it turns cold enough for you to heat your house, so the change won't be too drastic.

Tomatoes are long-day plants and require lots of sun. A southern sun porch or sunny window sill will do nicely. It's best if your plants can receive a day-long dose of full sun. Supplement this if necessary with fluorescent lights. If your only source of light is a fluorescent setup, you'll have to keep them glowing for at least 16 hours a day to provide the equivalent of outdoor sunlight. You can, however, transfer your maturing plants to a sunny window if you do it in gradual stages. Keep them a bit on the sheltered side before exposing them to the bright winter sun.

Aim for indoor daytime temperatures that range between 70 and 75 degrees F. A thermometer reading of around 60 degrees F. is fine for night. Windows that frost up during frigid nights may be insulated with cardboard, or you can move your plants out of danger until morning sun warms the windows.

Frequent mistings will provide the kind of humidity your plants need most. The dry conditions that prevail in most homes can also be offset by setting bowls of water in between the pots or simply by arranging your plants on trays of pebbles filled with water. Give plants a thorough watering when necessary with tap water which has been allowed to stand at room temperature overnight, but don't water so often that the plants get wet feet. The soil should be moist but not soggy. At regular intervals, add some water-soluble fertilizer at half-strength to your watering can, or mix the water with a little compost.

One of the difficulties with growing tomatoes indoors is that the same environment that spurs indoor growth also inhibits pollination. Outdoors, breezes and insects move pollen grains from one blossom to another. Indoors, you'll have to help nature along. Try shaking each plant a bit to scatter the pollen, or tap each wide-open blossom with a soft camel's-hair artist's brush. Garden centers can also supply you with a fruit-setting hormone spray that will help any recalcitrant plant along. Once fruit has set, keep temperatures a bit on the cooler side if you can manage it, around 65 degrees F.

Varieties that are most successful indoors are generally those that are small-fruited or medium-size because they grow fast and ripen early. Keep the soil in the pots loose and porous, and bolster with applications of bone meal once blossoms appear. Stake your plants if you wish, and prune them on a regular weekly schedule so that leaf growth doesn't outbalance root growth. Your tomatoes won't go on bearing indefinitely, but they will provide you with some mighty good winter eating and, don't forget—there's always spring.

Growing tomatoes can be as simple or as complex as you decide to make it. Relaxed, almost indifferent gardeners frequently grow glorious fruit with a minimum of effort, while more ambitious gardeners achieve the same results with endless hours of pampering. The truth is that tomato plants are a hardy lot, and as long as you follow the basics of good tomato gardening, your plants will pretty much take care of themselves.

Now that your fears have been allayed, I must, in the interest of thoroughness, describe all the absolutely terrible things that can happen to your plants and/or fruits. Chances are that you won't need this advice, but just in case your plants are struck down by a Job-like sequence of unhappy happenstances it is probably better "to take arms against a sea of troubles, and by opposing, end them." Don't let the thought of potential disaster discourage you. It is most probable that once they are off to a good start your plants will thrive by themselves while you sip cool drinks on the veranda.

PREVENTING PROBLEMS

Raising tomatoes successfully involves buying named, disease-resistant varieties and then providing them with a healthy growing environment from planting to harvest. The key is good soil management.

- Begin with well-drained, organically rich soil. Soil deficiencies and excesses and nutritional imbalance impair nature's harmony.
- Turn over the soil at fall cleanup. Good garden housekeeping—disposing of weeds and diseased plants—limits the spread of disease and curbs the insect population.
- Give your tomatoes all the growing space they need and rotate their location every year or two. Pests and disease comfortably settled in one locale are usually loath to move to another.
- Provide adequate moisture and mulch to maintain it evenly. Soil that fluctuates between dry spells and soakings weakens even healthy plants and makes them much more susceptible to insects and disease.

COPING WITH PROBLEMS

Get in the habit of taking routine strolls to the tomato garden throughout the growing season, not just at feeding and watering times. A regular check on each plant's progress will permit you to spot early signs of trouble. Knowing what kind of problems to expect gives you time to remedy the situation before it gets too advanced, and may even help you avoid it altogether.

- If your carefully tended seedlings fail to germinate, or shrivel at the soil line soon after they do emerge, then a wilt called *damping off* is the reason. Occasionally seedlings will survive the attack of this fungus (also responsible for soil rot), but the subsequent stunting makes them useless as transplants. Damping off is preventable. Use only sterilized soil as a starting medium, and don't overdo either moisture or fertilizer. When all else fails, buy nursery transplants.
- Probably the most common problem among tomato gardeners is their plants' *failure to set fruit*. (Blossoms don't become fruit, or drop off prematurely.) The culprit here is temperature. Optimum temperatures for productive fruit setting range between 65 degrees F. and 75 degrees F. When night temperatures dip below 55 degrees F., germination and tube growth are so slow that plants drop their flowers. On the other hand, hot summer days above 90 degrees F. accompanied by nights when temperatures remain above 75 degrees F. contribute to the loss of later-forming blooms.

Your plants won't go on dropping blossoms indefinitely, but to relieve aggravation it helps to take action. When the weather turns cool and humid at fruit-setting time, try covering the plants at night (see pages 37 to 39), or try shaking or vibrating each plant a bit to spur pollination. The best time to do this is at midday when the air is warm and the humidity low. Where summers are hot and dry, try growing varieties best suited to the area.

- If your plants are *all bush and little fruit*, blame excessive watering or too much nitrogen. Curb your zeal for watering and fertilizing. Maintain a good, even level of moisture right from the start and fertilize with a light touch. If you must use extra nitrogen, do so only after fruit production gets going.
- On the other side of the coin, tomatoes do occasionally suffer from one or another nutritional deficiency. If you notice *foliage yellowing*, suspect a shortage of nitrogen or soil that is too acid. Feed with small doses of additional nitrogen or, if necessary, have a soil test made and compensate for irregularities. It's a good idea to apply dolomitic limestone to your soil routinely once every three years.
- Stunted growth and dull, purplish leaves signal a *lack of phosphorus*. Remedy this with bone meal worked into the soil.
- If you find black, leathery scabs at the base of your fruit, the trouble is *blossom-end rot*. Although the fruit is still edible, it is not very attractive. The cause of this trouble is a calcium deficiency in the soil, aggravated by dry conditions or too much nitrogen. A properly limed soil is the answer, but mulching around plants also helps by maintaining even moisture.
- Another common source of concern is the appearance of *cracks* in tomatoes. Some varieties crack more easily than others, either radially or in concentric rings around the stem end of the fruit. Cracking usually occurs when plants are subject to drought stress, although it can also appear during hot, rainy spells. Again, keep soil evenly moist. If cracking is unusually bothersome, next time try planting crack-resistant varieties like Glamour, Heinz 1350, Campbell 1327, Park's Extra Early Hybrid or the Roma plum tomato.
- Small, brown, irregular patches on the leaves of tomato plants, or dark, slightly concave spots around the stem ends of the maturing fruit, are signs of *early blight*. This fungus will ultimately perforate the leaves and cause fruit to drop or decay. Early blight is most prevalent in those eastern and central parts of the country where tomato leaves frequently remain wet because of rain or dew. Chances are that early blight will be minimized if you start off with disease-free seeds initially, plant in sterile soil, then stake plants and mulch with a suitable material. When watering is necessary, use a soaker-type hose to keep water off the leaves. Dig up and destroy all infected plants, and next year plant in a different, disease-free location.

- The fungus that produces dark, water-soaked patches of greenish-gray on mature leaves and fruit is *late blight*. A pale, fungus growth also spreads over the fruit surface, especially if damp, cool conditions prevail. Like early blight, this fruit rot can be controlled by destroying infected plants and moving the tomato garden yearly.

- When tomato leaves roll or curl up and nothing else seems wrong, the cause is excessive watering, especially after the soil has been allowed to go dry. *Leaf roll* won't interfere with quality or yield, but to prevent it, make sure your soil has good drainage.

  Some kinds of leaf curl are normal, however. Leaves often curl during dry, hot spells and during and after a long period of wet weather, and some varieties curl more than others.

- When tomato leaves turn yellow, then roll upward and inward as a dark brown discoloration gradually spreads through the stems, the cause is either *Fusarium wilt*, which is widespread in the South, or *Verticillium wilt*, which can be a serious problem in the northern states and Canada. Both wilt fungi enter through a plant's roots and block its food and water channels. Once established in soil, these fungi persist for many years. An easy solution is to plant disease-resistant varieties. These are clearly labeled V-, F- or VF-resistant and there are lots to choose from. Don't use home-saved seed unless you can be sure it came from plants completely free from wilt.

- Black, round water-soaked spots that show up in a random pattern on ripening tomatoes are a sure sign of *anthacnose*, caused by soil splash on leaves and fruit. Mulching is the best antidote. Take care not to brush against wet plants, and dig out and destroy any infested specimens.

- If the leaves on your tomato plants develop dark, water-soaked spots with gray centers and then begin to drop off, blame *Septoria leaf spot*. Rain splashes the fungus spores onto the leaves, or they may be spread by people and animals brushing against wet plants. Eventually all foliage drops, exposing the fruit to sunscald. Staking and mulching plants in clean, well-drained soil is a good method of control.

- Deformed or puckered tomato foliage, plus mottling of leaves and fruit, is the mark of the *tobacco mosaic virus*. This disease is spread by direct contact. To prevent it, gardeners who smoke or use tobacco in any form should wash their hands and tools well in soap and water, or dip their hands in milk, before attending to garden chores.

- Those nasty looking, slightly concave circles of dark brown that suddenly appear on your tomatoes mean that the fruit has been attacked by *soil rot*. Entry can be made through whole skin as well as wounds. Rainy weather and excessively wet soil encourage it, especially on sprawling tomatoes liable to soil splash or directly in contact with soil. Avoid in advance by mulching and/or staking.

INSECTS AND OTHER GARDEN PESTS

Tomato gardeners are fortunate where insects are concerned. Tomato plants themselves contain a built-in repellent called solanine, which many chewing and sucking bugs find distasteful. As a result, only a handful of insects are attracted to the plants, and if gardeners are on the alert, most can be easily controlled before too much damage is done.

One way to keep the bug population within manageable proportions is by encouraging natural allies.

Selective plantings of flowers and herbs not only lend color and fragrance to the tomato garden but also make effective insect repellents. Marigolds have long been traditional companion plants to tomatoes. Their striking colors make a bold contrast to green tomato foliage, their musky scent is repugnant to many insects and above all they suppress infestations of soil nematodes (see page 49).

Other ornamentals also make good companion plantings because they keep insects away. Try calendulas (pot-marigolds), coreopsis, cosmos or nasturtiums. The latter won't put forth a showy bloom in the rich, fertile soil of the garden but they do help to control aphids. So does the castor bean (ricinus), a quick-growing, tall, showy annual, which helps keep moles and deer away. However, all parts of the castor-bean plant are poisonous, so keep children well out of the way, too. The low, green foliage of scillas (wood hyacinths) is another effective mole deterrent.

Planting soybeans around or near the tomato garden sidetracks overeager rabbits, who prefer them to tomatoes. Other vegetables and herbs that not only create a relatively pest-free growing environment for your tomatoes but also complement them in almost any recipe are garlic (which contains a potent insect control called allyl), onions, chives, all kinds of parsley, basil, borage and dill.

Even some insects are valuable allies to have around. Ladybugs, praying mantises and trichogramma wasps are all natural insect predators who make short shrift of other insects, and

46

lacewing larvae, often called aphid lions, feast voraciously on aphids. If you can't find any evidence that any of these helpful insects are hard at work in your garden, you can import some (seedhouses supply them), but time your purchases to coincide with the emergence of their natural prey. There's no guarantee these good bugs will take up residence in your garden, but you can always try.

Keep in mind that a few crawling, sucking or chewing insects on your tomato plants do not an invasion make. A chewed leaf or two will do no harm. If the creatures are not numerous, you have several options; pick them off by hand and drop them in kerosene; go after them with the fine spray of your garden hose; or douse them with soapy water (at a ratio of 1 tablespoon soap flakes to 1 gallon water). Chewing insects find gritty substances most uninviting, so sprinkle the ground around your tomato plants with rock powder or wood ashes.

In emergencies, there are some very potent insect-repelling mixtures made from common kitchen ingredients that you can whip up at home without resorting to lethal pesticides. A generous amount of any hot, spicy seasoning—onions, garlic, hot peppers or cayenne—will do. Chop or whirl these in your blender, alone or in combination. Add soap flakes, if you wish—it helps the homemade brew cling to leaf surfaces. Then steep the mixture in water for a few hours or even overnight, if you have time, and strain. Dilute by a ratio of 1 tablespoon mixture to 2 cups water and pour into the sprayer. When spraying, be sure to cover the undersides of the leaves, too. For added protection, distribute the strained pulp around the base of your plants.

Unfortunately, these methods are not foolproof. Insect allies may still depart from companion plantings for the greener pastures of your tomato plants, and home-brewed sprays must be repeatedly applied on a routine basis and after heavy rains to carry any impact.

In case it comes down to a question of losing your entire crop to rapacious hordes of insects, there are some sprays and powders you can use.

The most common are pyrethrum and rotenone (used mostly in combination with pyrethrum). Each is spectacularly effective against specific pests. Regard them as a last resort, however, since these botanicals may kill off beneficial as well as harmful insects, and when purchased as commercially prepared dusts and sprays may be dangerous to the health of the gardener as well.

A good control for caterpillars and grubs is the biological insecticide *bacillus thuringiensis*, marketed in powder form under trade names like Biotrol, Thuricide and Dipel. Another specific control, the spores of milky spore disease *(bacillus popilliae)*, is highly detrimental to Japanese beetles. Use all these according to manufacturer's directions.

All these substances are properly biological controls rather than insecticides because they are naturally occurring phenomena. Pyrethrum and rotenone are derived from plants, and *bacillus thuringiensis* and *bacillus popilliae* are both bacteria.

- Those tiny, plump-bodied sucking insects that range themselves along the stems and foliage of tomato plants are *aphids* or *plant lice*. There are many different species, all exceedingly prolific. They usually shun humus-rich soils, but if large colonies show up on your plants, try flooding them with soapy water or spray with a garlic preparation. Use pyrethrum or rotenone as a last resort. Aphids' bodies produce a sweet fluid much favored by ants. The grateful ants in turn helpfully move the aphids from one garden spot to another. Covering ant holes with bone meal helps get rid of both.

- A long, greasy, semicircular brown to black grub is responsible for cutting off your newly set seedlings at soil level. You probably won't see the culprit, but you'll know a *cutworm* has been busy. Cutworms hide during the day and feed at night. To protect your plants, girdle each seedling as you set it out with a large paper cup, cut-off milk carton or tin can, sinking the enclosure 1 or 2 inches deep into the soil.

- Tiny holes in your tomato foliage? It's the work of the *flea beetle*, a minuscule, black hopping bug that scoots away at your approach. Flea beetles are most active in dry weather. The damage they do is usually minor, but if they get to be a problem, keeping the soil moist discourages them.

- Those large green or brown (larvae change color as they mature) caterpillars chomping on the foliage of young tomato plants or burrowing through the fruit are *tomato fruitworms*, also familiar to gardeners as corn earworms or cotton bollworms. They are a particular nuisance in the South and in California. Pick them off by hand, try a garlic or onion spray or, if the infestation gets out of control, try rotenone.

- That formidable, horned green caterpillar with white stripes along its sides is the *tomato hornworm*. Of prodigious appetite, these awesome 2- to 3-inch creatures will hollow out a tomato in no time at all. Even if the hornworms themselves evade your scrutiny, which is highly unlikely considering their size, you probably won't miss the green fecal droppings on the soil that announce their presence in your garden. If you're not too squeamish, go after the worms by hand. If you lose courage, sprinkle some cayenne pepper or wood ashes around. Hornworms also find dill alluring, and their enormous bodies stand out more prominently on this wispy herb than when hidden under tomato foliage. Allow any hornworms whose backs bear tiny eggs to survive. This is a sure sign that trichogramma wasps have been doing their job, and all those eggs will soon hatch more wasps to feed on more hornworms.

- Anyone who has spent more than a few hours at garden chores is familiar with the large, shiny green and bronze *Japanese beetle*. These hard-shelled insects may spend up to two years as ½-inch milky white grubs in the soil, then emerge to nibble on whatever is handiest. White geraniums, odorless marigolds and roses have great appeal, and beetle predators are easy to spot on these plants. Pick them off by hand in the morning when they're less likely to take flight, and drop into kerosene. If your local colony experiences a population explosion, you might resort to a long-lasting powder, appropriately tagged by the trade name Doom, which contains the spores of the milky spore disease and is very effective. Apply by teaspoonful directly to the soil at 3- to 4-foot intervals, or according to manufacturer's directions. It works by infecting the beetle grubs who in turn pass the disease on to their neighbors.

- Gardeners in midwestern and western states who discover the foliage of their once-lush tomato plants has suddenly become twisted, rolled up and leathery may recognize the handiwork of the *beet leafhopper*. These far-ranging creatures spread a virus called western yellow blight or curlytop. This disease is hard to eradicate because weeds on vacant, uncultivated lands are a preferred breeding spot. If you live in a section of the country where these pests are a problem, don't plant beets if you're planting tomatoes. Get some advice from your local agricultural extension service about what and when to plant. If your tomatoes are infested, dig out and destroy them.

- If your plants, despite your best efforts, seem especially susceptible to stunting, wilts or rot, the problem may very well be *soil nematodes*. Because these tiny worms feed on plant roots, they provide a convenient entry channel for destructive soil bacteria or fungi. Humus-rich soil discourages their presence, but you should also try planting marigolds nearby as a preventive measure, or set your tomato seedlings in soil previously reserved for marigolds. Another solution when nematodes are a headache is to plant resistant varieties, plainly marked on seeds and seedlings with an N.

- Some soft-bodied, light-shy creatures you may never see at all can be responsible for much tomato damage. *Snails* and *slugs* (not insects at all but properly mollusks) hide by day and creep forth to feast at night. Place inverted cabbage leaves around in strategic areas to trap these when they seek daytime shelter, then drop them in kerosene. If the thought of touching them repulses you, spray them with salty water or set out shallow pans or cans set flush with the ground and filled with beer. If you're lucky, the slugs, attracted by the smell, will crawl in, get soused and drown. Snails and slugs abhor gritty substances, so another control is to scatter wood ashes or sand over the soil around tomato plants, or to mulch with salt hay.

- The clouds of tiny *white flies* that emerge from the undersides of tomato leaves at your touch are the same "flying dandruff" so bothersome to house plants. These pesky creatures breed fast, so get out your sprayer and give them routine squirts of a garlic preparation (see page 47). Don't forget to hit the undersides of the leaves—that's where the eggs are hiding. Some good companion plants for controlling white flies are garlic, marjoram or mint.
- If all that remains of your once-sturdy tomato plants are 1-inch stubs cut off at a slant, then *rabbits* are afoot. Wire fencing sunk at least 10 to 12 inches into the ground will usually foil these and other animal pests, but for instant measures against rabbits, shrews and woodchucks, try scattering blood meal (but not too near the tomatoes, please), spraying the plants with watered-down Epsom salts or a garlic or onion brew or dusting the ground liberally with ground limestone, wood ashes or cayenne pepper. (For companion plants that curb animal pests, see page 46.)

VARIETIES

Tomatoes come in a bewildering array of varieties—early, late, big, little, round or pear-shaped, medium-size to oversize. Tiny cherries to giant beefsteaks, pink and orange, yellow and red and, just to be different, even white.

If you think of it, chances are some zealous grower has produced it and some progressive seed dealer sells it. All in all, over 100 varieties of tomatoes are being sold and grown in the United States—a variety for every need and every purpose.

Some are ideal for canning. Others shine at juicing or pickling or preserving. Some tomatoes are superpiquant and thus made-to-order for sauces, pastes and purées. Still others are suited for use in salads or sandwiches. And some expecially versatile varieties are equally competent doing all of these.

Above all, tomatoes are adaptable. Lots of space? Plant a combination of early, midseason and late tomatoes for the longest possible harvest. Limited space? Try indeterminate types which, when staked or pruned, require less room. Problem soil? There are attractive and flavorful varieties for every growing condition . . . even productive ornamental varieties especially designed to flourish in containers (see page 33) or to climb trellises, and there is even a tree tomato!

A close relative—the Husk Tomato (also called the Ground Cherry or Pohaberry)—grows just like a tomato and yields cherry-size fruit ideal for jams. New varieties boast improved flavor and appearance and are especially resistant to soil-borne disease.

To help you through the maze, I have listed a number of varieties and their general characteristics. This listing is not meant to be an unqualified endorsement . . . merely a helpful guide. Most are varieties you will find in catalogues, seed racks or in the form of seedlings found at your friendly neighborhood garden center. The list is not complete . . . nor could it ever be since new varieties are constantly being developed and introduced.

The rule of thumb in choosing varieties is to buy only named, disease-resistant seeds or seedlings that fit your soil and climatic conditions. If your growing season is short, for example, you should choose early and early-midseason types. Then you should be influenced by the space you have available and your family needs. When in doubt about any of these considerations, consult your county agricultural extension service or rely on the advice of your local nurseryman.

NOTE: The number of days shown on the list that follows refers to the time of setting out transplants to the first fruits.

TOMATO VARIETIES

VARIETY	DESCRIPTION
Burgess Early Salad (45 days)	For regions with short summers. Bears early, 1½-inch fruit throughout season.
Rocket (50 days)	Where growing season is short, dwarf-size plants bear extra early.
Pixie Hybrid (50–55 days)	Early, 1¾-inch fruit. Continuous production. Grow outdoors in containers, also especially good for winter growing indoors.
Tiny Tim (50–55 days)	Small, compact variety with ¾-inch bright scarlet fruits. Makes ideal container plant.
Swift (54 days)	Extra early. Where summer arrives late, sets medium-size fruit at lower temperatures than most other varieties do. Determinate.
Stokesalaska (55 days)	Another extra early for northern U.S. and Canada. Sprawling plants with mild-flavored, 2-ounce fruits. Can be grown in tubs or staked.
Starfire (56 days)	Produces early, medium-size fruit on compact plants. Prefers light, sandy soil.
Stokes Early Hybrid (56 days)	Early, medium-size fruits and long producing season. Stake for best results.
Burpeeana Early (58 days)	Early, continuing through long growing season. Medium-size fruits.
Earliana (58 days)	This all-purpose, extra-early tomato is a favorite. Medium-size.

VARIETY	DESCRIPTION
Hybrid Red #22 (58 days)	Indeterminate variety, large-size fruit. Bred from cross between Valiant and Earliana.
Gardener 67 (59 days)	Full-flavored round fruit. Should be staked. Crack-tolerant and verticillium-resistant.
Maritimer (59 days)	This variety is still green when ripe. Fine for pickle makers.
Fordhook Hybrid (60 days)	Especially suitable where summers are short. Early yields of bright red, uniform fruit, continuing throughout season.
Quebec #314 (60 days)	Especially for northern climes. Determinate plants bear medium-size fruit.
Burpee's Big Early (62 days)	Fruits largest of early varieties, continuous production. Somewhat susceptible to cracking.
Springset (62 days)	Sets blossoms in cool weather, gives high yield where growing season is short. VF-tolerant.
Fireball (65 days)	A favorite with home gardeners. Medium-size fruit on determinate vines. Don't stake. Verticillium-resistant.
Globemaster Hybrid (65 days)	Very popular in the home garden. Bears early and continues until frost.
Park's Extra Early Hybrid (65 days)	Early and high yielding. Resistant to cracking.

VARIETY	DESCRIPTION
Hybrid Red #23 (65 days)	Later than Hybrid Red #22 (see above) but also bears large fruit. Cross between Rutgers and Pritchard.
Small Fry (65 days)	An All-American selection. High-quality, 1-inch cherry-type fruits. VFN-resistant.
Valiant (65 days)	A home garden favorite and good, all-purpose variety. Mild flavor.
New Yorker (65–70 days)	Medium-size fruit on determinate, vigorous vines. Verticillium-tolerant.
Springset Hybrid (67 days)	Early, medium-size fruit on determinate vines. Recommended for North, Midwest and East. VF-resistant.
Spring Giant (68 days)	An All-American selection. Particularly suitable for southern Canada and northern U.S. Semideterminate and VF-resistant.
Campbell 1327 (69 days)	Semideterminate vines bear early. Especially developed for canning. VF-tolerant, also tolerant to cracking.
Beefmaster (70 days)	Giant, red beefsteak-type tomatoes—everybody's favorite. VFN-resistant.
Early Giant (70 days)	Large and early, too. Indeterminate.
Patio (70 days)	For containers or garden. Sturdy, compact plants bear continuous supply of tasty, 2-inch fruit. A favorite.

VARIETY	DESCRIPTION
Fantastic (70 days)	Medium-large fruits on indeterminate vines. An early yielder. Stake or train.
Red Pear (70 days)	Pear-shaped, 1-by-2-inch fruits grow in scarlet clusters.
Terrific (70 days)	Earliest of new VFN-resistant hybrids. Stake or allow to sprawl. Continuous production.
Yellow Pear (70 days)	Pear-shaped 1½-inch fruits borne in clusters are mild-flavored, excellent for pickling or preserving.
Yellow Plum (70 days)	Another favorite for preserves. Sweet, 2-inch yellow fruits are low in acid.
Red Cherry (72 days)	Clusters of small, scarlet tomatoes ⅞-inch in diameter all season long.
Better Boy (72 days)	Vigorous, indeterminate vines with large fruits. Grows just about everywhere. Stake or train. VFN-resistant.
Jubilee (72 days)	An All-American selection. Tops in flavor, high in vitamins, too. Bright, gold-orange fruits are medium-large. Best for Northeast, Midwest and Northwest.
Sunray (72 days)	Another yellow-orange, low-acid variety. Similar to Jubilee but best where Fusarium wilt is a problem.
Dwarf Champion (73 days)	Small, bushy 2-foot plants with mild-flavored pink fruit. Excellent for container growing.

VARIETY	DESCRIPTION
Bonus (75 days)	Strong-bearing, determinate vines with medium-size fruit. VFN-resistant.
Glamour (75 days)	Pale green outside, vivid red interiors make this a good canning variety. Crack-tolerant. Best for Midwest and Northwest.
Heinz 1439 (75 days)	For all-purpose cooking and canning. Crack- and disease-resistant.
Red Top (75 days)	Large and plum-shaped. Best for tomato paste, but also suitable for canning whole.
Rutgers (75–80 days)	Another favorite. Semideterminate. Staking optional. Especially good for southern states. Crack- and VF-resistant.
Roma (76 days)	Prolific vines bear tremendous crop of plum-shaped fruits. Eat fresh, but ideal for purée and paste. Don't stake.
Burpee's Delicious (77 days)	Extra-large fruits, excellent flavor. Low in acid.
Big Boy Hybrid (78 days)	Indeterminate vines bear extra-large fruits. Will grow almost everywhere. Stake or train.
Supersonic (79 days)	Large fruits on indeterminate vines. Best for East and Midwest. VF-resistant.
Stakeless (78 days)	Dwarf-size, with dense foliage. Good-size red fruit. Fusarium-tolerant.

VARIETY	DESCRIPTION
Marglobe (79 days)	A very popular tomato. Heavy vines and large, sweet uniform fruit. Has some resistance to Fusarium wilt.
Beefsteak (80 days)	Largest red-fruited tomato and a home garden favorite. Low in acid.
Golden Boy (80 days)	Large, smooth yellow fruits are low-acid and mild-flavored. Indeterminate. Best for Northeast, Midwest and Northwest.
San Marzano (80 days)	Tops for canning, purées and paste. Bright red, elongated fruits form in clusters.
Tropic (80 days)	Medium-size fruits with good flavor. Indeterminate, fine for staking. Highly resistant to disease. Recommended for South.
Ponderosa (83 days)	Large, solid fruits, purple-pink in color, are juicy and mild-flavored. Often weigh over 1 pound each.
White Beauty (84 days)	Silver white from skin to core. Sweet and low in acid.
Ramapo Hybrid (85 days)	Indeterminate variety for late harvesting. Stake or train. VF-resistant, also resistant to cracking and blossom-end rot.
Oxheart (86 days)	Large, pink tomatoes average 1 pound apiece. A home garden favorite.
Manalucie (87 days)	An old standby in the South because of its strong resistance to disease.

NUTRIENTS IN FRESH TOMATOES AND TOMATO PRODUCTS BY POUND

	Fresh Green Tomatoes	Fresh Ripe Tomatoes Whole	Fresh Ripe Tomatoes Peeled	Canned Tomatoes (Regular Pack)	Tomato Juice	Tomato Purée
Food Energy (calories)	99	100	88	91	86	177
Protein (grams)	5.0	5.0	4.4	4.5	3.6	7.7
Carbohydrate (grams)	21.1	21.3	18.8	19.1	19.5	40.4
Calcium (milligrams)	54	59	52	27	32	59
Phosphorus (milligrams)	111	122	108	86	82	154
Iron (milligrams)	2.1	2.3	2.0	2.3	4.1	7.7
Potassium (milligrams)	1,007	1,107	974	984	1,030	1,932
Vitamin A Value (International Units)	1,110	4,080	3,590	4,080	3,630	7,260
Thiamine (milligrams)	0.26	.29	.26	.24	.21	.39
Riboflavin (milligrams)	0.15	.18	.16	.13	.11	.24
Niacin (milligrams)	2.0	3.0	2.6	3.1	3.1	6.3
Ascorbic Acid (milligrams)	83	102	90	76	73	148

RED TOMATO COOKBOOK

TOMATO CROSTINI
YIELD: ENOUGH TO SERVE 6

1 Small onion, peeled and minced
1½ Tablespoons butter
2 Medium-size ripe tomatoes, peeled, seeded and chopped
1 Egg yolk
2 Tablespoons grated Parmesan cheese
  Thin slices from small Italian bread,
    buttered on both sides

Directions: Sauté the onion in butter until soft and transparent. Do not brown. Add the chopped tomatoes and cook over low heat, stirring occasionally, until no liquid remains. Cool and work in egg yolk and cheese.

Preheat oven to 400 degrees F.

Sauté bread slices on both sides, spread one side with tomato-cheese mixture and bake until topping is bubbling and lightly browned. Serve immediately.

PINT-SIZE NEAPOLITAN PIZZA
YIELD: ENOUGH FILLING FOR 6 6-INCH PIZZAS
OR 12 3-INCH PIZZAS

I'll wager this is the most delicious pizza you have ever sampled.

1 Recipe Pizza Dough (see page 184)
10 Medium-size ripe tomatoes, peeled, seeded and chopped
1 Clove garlic, peeled and minced
6 Tablespoons olive oil

1 Teaspoon granulated sugar
½ Teaspoon salt
¾ Pound Fontina cheese, grated
  Anchovy fillets (optional)
  Oregano

Directions: Prepare dough according to recipe directions. While it is doubling in bulk, place tomatoes, garlic, 3 tablespoons oil, sugar and salt in a saucepan. Cook over low heat, stirring occasionally, until most of liquid has evaporated, about 30 minutes.

Roll out dough as directed. Spread tomato mixture over each dough circle and sprinkle with cheese. Top each individual pizza with anchovy bits, if desired. Sprinkle with remaining 3 tablespoons oil. Season to taste with oregano and bake as directed.

PIZZA CALABRESA
YIELD: ENOUGH TO SERVE 6

When you care enough to serve something really spectacular—try this pizza in the form of an honest-to-goodness pie with tomato, olive and tuna filling.

4 Cups all-purpose flour
1 Teaspoon salt
½ Package (1½ teaspoons) dry active yeast
½ Cup lukewarm water
2 Egg yolks
6 Tablespoons vegetable shortening
1 Recipe Tomato-Olive Conditi (see page 59)
  Anchovy fillets (optional)
  Vegetable oil

Directions: Combine flour and salt and sift together into a large bowl. Mix yeast into lukewarm water, allow to dissolve and add to flour. Add as much additional lukewarm water as necessary to make a soft but not sticky dough. On a lightly floured surface, knead dough for several minutes, then place in a floured bowl, cover with a dish towel and set in a warm, draft-free place for about 1 hour until dough rises and doubles in bulk.

Punch dough down. Set aside a small portion of egg yolk and work remaining yolks and shortening into dough with your hands. When these ingredients are well incorporated, knead dough vigorously for 10 minutes.

Break off ⅓ of dough and set aside. Roll out large piece and use it to line bottom and sides of a 12-inch pie plate. Spoon tomato-olive conditi into crust. If desired, arrange anchovy fillets spoke-fashion over mixture. Roll out remaining piece of dough to a size large enough to cover pie and place over filling. Roll edges of lower crust over top crust to form a ropelike edge about ½ inch in diameter. If edging turns out thicker, trim lower crust a bit.

Preheat oven to 450 degrees F.

Glaze top of pie with a little vegetable oil and the reserved egg yolk. Let pie stand in a warm, draft-free place for 20 minutes to rise again, then bake for 25 to 30 minutes. Cut into wedges before serving hot.

TOMATO-OLIVE CONDITI
YIELD: ENOUGH TO SERVE 6

12 Medium-size ripe tomatoes, peeled, seeded and coarsely chopped
¾ Cup olive oil
2 Cloves garlic, peeled and minced
1½ Tablespoons minced fresh basil
1 13-Ounce can tuna fish, well drained
1¼ Cups pitted and halved black olives
3 Tablespoons chopped anchovy fillets
1½ Tablespoons drained capers
⅛ Teaspoon black pepper

Directions: In a heavy stainless steel skillet, simmer together tomatoes, oil, garlic and basil until mixture reaches thick consistency. Remove from heat and cool to room temperature, then stir in remaining ingredients.

Preheat oven to 350 degrees F.

Heap mixture into pie plate, cover with foil and bake for 15 minutes. Remove, cool to room temperature, then chill. Serve cold with crackers or Italian bread.

SWEET AND RED CHICKEN WINGS
YIELD: ENOUGH TO SERVE 8

Serve as an hors d'oeuvre or double and serve as a main course.

20 Chicken wings
½ Cup vegetable oil
¾ Cup tomato catsup
½ Cup honey
½ Cup soy sauce
½ Cup sherry or rum
¼ Teaspoon each anise and ground ginger
Generous pinch of cloves

Directions: Remove the skin from the chicken wings. Bring several cups of water to a boil in a large saucepan, drop in the wings all at once and cook only long enough for the water to return to a boil. Drain wings, rinse in cold water and pat dry with paper towels. Cut each wing into 3 sections, discarding the tip. Heat the oil in a large skillet and brown the wings on both sides, turning once. Remove the wings and drain briefly. Discard the oil. Combine the remaining ingredients in a large saucepan, add the browned wing pieces and boil over medium heat until the sauce thickens and sticks to the wings. Serve warm or cold.

STUFFED TOMATO HORS d'OEUVRES
YIELD: ENOUGH TO SERVE 6

BASIC RECIPE
6 Medium-size firm, ripe tomatoes
  French Dressing I (see page 189)

Directions: Cover tomatoes with boiling water, allow to stand for about 12 to 15 seconds, then dip in cold water and peel. Cut ¾-inch slice from stem end of each tomato and scoop out pulp, taking care not to damage shells. Marinate tomato shells in French dressing for at least 30 minutes before filling.

STUFFED TOMATOES WITH HERBED RICE

Ingredients listed in Basic Recipe plus:
  2 Cups cooked and cooled rice
  1 Tablespoon each minced fresh dill
      and thyme leaves
½ Cup cooked green peas
  3 Flat anchovy fillets, minced
      French Dressing I or II (see page 189)

Directions: Prepare and marinate tomatoes as directed in Basic Recipe.

Combine rice, herbs, peas and anchovies and mix with as much dressing as necessary to bind mixture. Spoon into tomato shells, chill and serve.

STUFFED TOMATOES WITH PESTO

Ingredients listed in Basic Recipe plus:
  1 Cup chopped fresh basil leaves
  1 Cup chopped fresh parsley
  2 Cloves garlic, peeled and chopped
½ Cup olive oil
½ Cup Parmesan cheese, grated
      Salt and black pepper
¼ Cup finely chopped pine nuts
  2 Cups Garlic Bread Crumbs
      (see page 185)

Directions: Place basil, parsley, garlic, oil and cheese in blender. Whirl until mixture is smooth and thick. Season to taste with salt and pepper, then stir in pine nuts and bread crumbs. Cover and refrigerate for 1 hour.

Meanwhile, prepare tomatoes as directed in Basic Recipe. Spoon filling into marinated tomato shells. Serve cold.

TOMATOES STUFFED WITH HARD-COOKED EGGS AND BACON
YIELD: ENOUGH TO SERVE 6

6 Ripe, firm tomatoes
¼ Pound country-cured bacon, minced
4 Small onions, peeled and minced
1⅔ Cups bread crumbs
3 Hard-cooked eggs, minced
1 Teaspoon granulated sugar
⅛ Teaspoon marjoram
 Salt and pepper
 Butter

Directions: Preheat oven to 450 degrees F.

Cut a slice from the top of each tomato. Scoop out as much of the inside as possible without spoiling the shape of the tomato. Mince the scooped-out insides.

Fry bacon for 2 minutes over high heat, stirring to separate the pieces. Add onion, stir for 2 minutes longer, then add minced tomato. Stir over medium heat until most of the liquid has disappeared and the bacon fat begins to spatter in the pan. Stir in 1½ cups of the bread crumbs and then add the eggs, sugar and spices.

Fill the tomato shells with the stuffing, sprinkle each with some of remaining bread crumbs and top each with a bit of butter. Arrange in a buttered baking dish and bake for 8 minutes. Serve immediately.

BAKED TOMATO-STUFFED EGGS

To serve any one of these Stuffed Egg Recipes as a hot lunch or supper dish, arrange stuffed eggs in an ovenproof serving dish, top with 2 cups hot White Sauce (see page 187) or Curry Sauce (see page 187) and bake for 20 minutes in a preheated 350 degree F. oven. Serve with hot, buttered Toast Points (see page 185).

TOMATO-STUFFED EGGS WITH ANCHOVIES
YIELD: ENOUGH TO SERVE 6

12 Hard-cooked eggs
3 Large ripe tomatoes, peeled, seeded and finely chopped
1 Large onion, peeled and finely chopped
2 Tablespoons butter
1½ Teaspoons minced fresh or ¼ teaspoon dried basil
1½ Tablespoons sour cream
 Salt
12 Flat anchovy fillets, cut in half and
 drained on paper towels

Directions: Cut eggs in half lengthwise. Separate whites from yolks, then mash yolks and set aside.

Sauté tomatoes and onions in butter until moisture evaporates. Stir in mashed egg yolks, basil, sour cream and salt to taste. Spoon the mixture into egg-white halves, crisscross with anchovy pieces, chill and serve.

BACON-AND-TOMATO-STUFFED EGGS
YIELD: ENOUGH TO SERVE 6

12 Hard-cooked eggs
6 Strips country-cured bacon
3 Large ripe tomatoes, peeled, seeded and finely chopped
6 Large mushrooms, minced
1½ Teaspoons minced fresh or ¼ teaspoon ground thyme
2½ Tablespoons sour cream
Salt

Directions: Cut eggs in half lengthwise and separate whites from yolks. Mash yolks and set aside.

Crisp-fry bacon, set the slices aside and sauté tomatoes and mushrooms in the bacon fat until moisture evaporates. Stir in mashed egg yolks, thyme, sour cream, salt to taste and finely crumbled bacon bits. Spoon the mixture into egg-white halves, chill and serve.

TOMATO-AND-ZUCCHINI-STUFFED EGGS
YIELD: ENOUGH TO SERVE 6

12 Hard-cooked eggs
3 Large ripe tomatoes, peeled, seeded and finely chopped
1 Cup finely chopped zucchini
2½ Tablespoons butter
¼ Teaspoon oregano
1½ Tablespoons sour cream
Salt

Directions: Cut eggs in half lengthwise. Separate whites from yolks. Mash yolks and set aside.

Sauté the tomatoes and zucchini in butter until moisture evaporates. Stir in mashed egg yolks, oregano, sour cream and salt to taste. Spoon the mixture into egg-white halves, chill and serve.

STUFFED TOMATOES, ITALIAN STYLE
YIELD: ENOUGH TO SERVE 6

Serve hot as a vegetable or cold as an appetizer.

6 Medium-size ripe tomatoes
3 Tablespoons olive oil
1 Large onion, peeled and chopped
6 Anchovy fillets, coarsely chopped
⅓ Cup bread crumbs
1 Tablespoon capers, drained
½ Teaspoon oregano
Pinch each nutmeg and pepper

Directions: Preheat oven to 375 degrees F. Cut ½ inch from tops of tomatoes and hollow out, taking care not to damage the shells. Reserve ½ cup tomato flesh. In olive oil, sauté onion until soft and transparent. Remove from heat and stir in remaining ingredients, including reserved tomato.

Fill tomatoes with mixture. Bake 30 minutes.

COLD ZUCCHINI AND TOMATO HORS d'OEUVRE
YIELD: ENOUGH TO SERVE 6

1½ Pounds medium-size ripe tomatoes, peeled and seeded
2½ Pounds small zucchini (about 1½ inches in diameter), peeled
3 Large cloves garlic, peeled and minced
3½ Tablespoons olive oil
2 Tablespoons lemon juice
1 Tablespoon each minced fresh tarragon and chervil
Salt and black pepper
1 Large lemon with skin and seeds removed (be certain you cut away all the bitter white underskin)
1 Tablespoon minced fresh thyme leaves

Directions: Cut tomatoes into coarse dice and zucchini into ½-inch slices. Sauté vegetables and garlic in olive oil for 1 minute. Add lemon juice, tarragon, chervil and salt and pepper to taste. Bring to boil, then lower the heat and simmer uncovered until zucchini are tender and most of the juices have evaporated. Chop lemon, stir it into the vegetable mixture and chill well. Sprinkle with thyme leaves before serving cold.

BROILED MUSHROOMS WITH CHERRY TOMATOES
YIELD: ENOUGH TO SERVE 6

The texture of broiled mushrooms and the mellow cushion of sour cream set off sweet, juicy cherry tomatoes superbly well.

18 Large mushrooms
¼ Cup melted butter
  Salt and black pepper
⅓ Cup sour cream
18 Cherry tomatoes

Directions: Remove the entire stem from each mushroom and reserve for other use. Use a damp cloth to wipe the mushroom caps or wash them if they feel gritty and pat them dry. Fresh, tender mushrooms need not be peeled. Arrange the caps stem side down on an oiled broiling pan and brush with the butter. Broil for 2 to 3 minutes or until caps are lightly browned, then turn and brush with the remaining butter, and broil 1 minute longer. Place a dab of sour cream in each mushroom cap, top each with a cherry tomato and broil for 1 minute longer. Serve hot.

THREE-CHEESE AND TOMATO COCKTAIL SPREAD
YIELD: 1 POUND

Serve this zesty spread with toast points or as a topping for grilled tomatoes.

½ Pound sharp Cheddar cheese,
    at room temperature
¼ Pound each Roquefort and cream cheese,
    at room temperature
¼ Cup soft butter
2 Tablespoons tomato paste
1 Teaspoon each Tabasco sauce and
    garlic juice
  Crackers or Toast Points (see page 185)

Directions: Cream all ingredients together thoroughly, pack into oiled mold and chill until firm. Unmold and serve with crackers or toast points. This mixture may also be stored and served in crocks.

ROSY TOMATO-CUCUMBER DIP

1 Large cucumber, peeled and seeded
1½ Teaspoons salt
2 Hard-cooked eggs
1 Recipe Rosy Tomato-Cream Sauce (see page 128)
2 Tablespoons capers

Directions: Grate the cucumber, sprinkle with the salt and drain in a colander for 15 to 20 minutes, stirring from time to time. Rinse under cold water, then squeeze dry using paper towels. Put the hard-cooked eggs through a food mill or force through a fine sieve. Stir all ingredients together.

Tomato soups are among the most popular, but when you think tomato, you probably think "cream of tomato that comes in a can." Creamed tomato soups are good, of course, but classic tomato soups run from hearty to delicate, from chunky to clear, from New England to Manhattan, from Greece to Italy, from "Deep South" to Near East.

Real homemade tomato soup may contain rich chunks of tomato, sausage slices, chicken pieces, eggplant, scallops and/or fiery chili peppers. Try turning part of your tomato crop into soups, chowders and stews and see if you don't agree that the ultimate soup is one that is tomato-based.

DILL WEED AND TOMATO SOUP
YIELD: ENOUGH TO SERVE 6

10 Large ripe tomatoes
 1 Large onion, peeled and sliced
 2 Cloves garlic, peeled and minced
 3 Tablespoons butter
 5 Tablespoons flour
1½ Tablespoons tomato paste
 5 Cups Basic Chicken Stock (see page 192)
 ¾ Cup heavy cream
 4 Tablespoons minced fresh dill
   Salt and black pepper
   Sour cream (optional)

Directions: Wash and core tomatoes. Set 2 aside and coarsely chop the rest without removing the skins.

Sauté onions and garlic in butter until onions are lightly browned. Stir in half the chopped tomatoes and cook over high heat for 3 minutes, stirring constantly. Remove the saucepan from the heat. Blend in the flour until well incorporated, then mix in the tomato paste and stock. Return the soup to the heat and bring to a boil. Lower the heat, add the remaining chopped tomatoes and simmer for 15 minutes. Strain the soup and stir in the cream.

Peel, seed and chop the 2 reserved tomatoes and add to the soup along with the dill. Reheat over low flame, taking care not to boil. Season to taste with salt and pepper. Serve hot with dollops of sour cream, if desired.

SWEET-TART VEGETARIAN VEGETABLE SOUP
YIELD: ENOUGH TO SERVE 6

 5 Large onions, peeled and chopped
 5 Carrots, scraped and chopped
 1 Bunch celery with leaves, well washed and chopped
 ¼ Cup tomato paste
10 Cups tomato juice
 ⅓ Cup granulated sugar
 3 Tablespoons lemon juice
 3 Tablespoons Worcestershire sauce
 2 Teaspoons peppercorns, coarsely crushed
 2 Teaspoons each rosemary and caraway seeds
 ½ Teaspoon ground cloves
   Salt

1 Cup grated Swiss cheese
½ Cup sour cream
2 Large ripe tomatoes, peeled, seeded and chopped
6 Scallions, with 3 inches green top, chopped
2 Green peppers, seeded and chopped
3 Tablespoons minced fresh dill

Directions: Add onions, carrots and celery, along with the tomato paste and tomato juice, to a kettle. Stir in sugar, lemon juice, Worcestershire sauce, peppercorns, rosemary, caraway seeds, cloves and salt to taste. Cover the kettle and bring liquid to a boil; then lower the heat and simmer soup one hour, adding more tomato juice or water if necessary to maintain the level of the liquid.

Stir in additional sugar and lemon juice if desired, until the soup is as sweet and tart as you like it. Pour into soup bowls and top each portion with a sprinkle of cheese and a dollop of sour cream. Pass the fresh tomatoes, scallions, green peppers and dill in small bowls on the side.

BEERY TOMATO-BEEF SOUP
YIELD: ENOUGH TO SERVE 6

8 Medium-size ripe tomatoes, peeled
1 Cup flour
2 Tablespoons butter
1 Tablespoon vegetable oil
¼ Cup tightly packed light brown sugar
⅓ Teaspoon dry mustard
2½ Cups beer
2½ Cups Basic Beef Consommé (see page 193)
　Garlic Croutons (see page 185)

Directions: Discard tops and slice tomatoes into thick slices. Dredge thoroughly in flour and fry in hot butter and oil until brown on one side. Sprinkle with sugar and dry mustard, then turn the slices and fry until brown on the other side. Pour in the beer and consommé, and stir until the soup thickens slightly. Break up any large pieces of tomato and serve hot over garlic croutons.

CREAMED TOMATO-BEEF SOUP
YIELD: ENOUGH TO SERVE 6

All ingredients listed in Beery Tomato-Beef
　Soup (see above) with the exception of
　Garlic Croutons plus:
2 Tablespoons heavy soy sauce
　(or 3 tablespoons regular)
4 Tablespoons cream cheese, pressed through a sieve
4 Scallions, with 3 inches green top

Directions: Follow directions for Beery Tomato-Beef Soup but stir above ingredients into the thickened soup. Heat again to bubbling. Serve hot.

BAKED-TOMATO SOUP WITH CREAM CHEESE AND MINT
YIELD: ENOUGH TO SERVE 6

6 Medium-size ripe tomatoes, peeled, seeded and chopped
2 Small onions, peeled and finely chopped
1 Cup chopped mushrooms
2 Tablespoons butter
1½ Tablespoons flour
2 Teaspoons granulated sugar
1 Large clove garlic, peeled and minced
¼ Teaspoon each basil, rosemary and thyme
6 Cups Basic Beef Stock (see page 191)
3 Ounces cream cheese, at room temperature
Salt and white pepper
1 Tablespoon chopped fresh mint leaves
1 Tablespoon minced fresh parsley

Directions: Preheat oven to 325 degrees F.

Place the tomatoes in a lightly buttered casserole, cover and bake for 20 minutes. Meanwhile, sauté the onions and mushrooms in the butter until the onions are soft, stirring occasionally. Blend in the flour and sugar. Add the garlic, basil, rosemary and thyme. Pour in the stock and bring to a boil, then add the tomatoes. Cover and cook over low heat for 30 minutes. Combine the cream cheese with salt and white pepper to taste. Use the back of a spoon to force the cream cheese mixture through a fine sieve into the soup. Cook only long enough to heat through. Serve hot. Garnish each portion with mint and parsley.

DILLED TOMATO-EGGPLANT SOUP
YIELD: ENOUGH TO SERVE 6

1 Medium-size eggplant, peeled and cut into 1-inch cubes
3 Tablespoons each butter and oil
6 Medium-size ripe tomatoes, peeled, seeded and chopped
2 Medium-size onions, peeled and finely chopped
1½ Cloves garlic, peeled and minced
2 Bay leaves, crumbled
Pinch marjoram
8 Cups Basic Beef Stock (see page 191)
⅓ Cup uncooked rice
Salt and black pepper
½ Pound finely ground veal
⅛ Teaspoon each nutmeg and oregano
Flour
Garlic Croutons (see page 185)
2 Tablespoons minced fresh dill

Directions: Cover eggplant pieces with salted water. Soak for 20 minutes. Drain. Sauté in butter and oil, covered, for 30 minutes or until lightly browned, stirring frequently. Add tomatoes. Reserve 2 teaspoons chopped onion and add remaining onions to the tomato-eggplant mixture, along with the garlic, bay leaves and marjoram. Cook over low heat for 15 minutes, stirring occasionally. Add stock and rice and season to taste with salt and pepper. Simmer soup covered, for 40 minutes, then bring to a boil.

Mix together the veal, reserved onions, nutmeg, oregano and salt and pepper to taste. Shape into ½-inch balls, roll in flour and cook in the boiling soup for 15 minutes. Serve hot, garnished with croutons and dill.

TOMATO-WHOLE WHEAT BREAD SOUP
YIELD: ENOUGH TO SERVE 6

2 Cups peeled, seeded and chopped tomatoes
1 Large onion, peeled and coarsely chopped
2 Tablespoons butter
¾ Teaspoon granulated sugar
1 Tablespoon flour
7 Cups Basic Chicken Stock (see page 192)
3 Tablespoons vegetable oil
1 Clove garlic, peeled and minced
8 Slices whole wheat bread, trimmed and cut in half
3 Hard-cooked eggs, sliced
  Grated Parmesan cheese

Directions: Sauté tomatoes and onions in butter until the onions are soft and transparent. Sprinkle with sugar. Combine flour and 1 cup chicken stock, stir into tomato mixture and bring to a boil, stirring constantly. Remove from heat. Purée by forcing through a fine sieve with the back of a spoon into a large soup kettle. Add the remainder of the stock and bring to a boil, then reduce heat and simmer for 15 minutes.

Meanwhile, heat the oil and garlic and sauté the bread until golden on both sides, turning once. Serve the soup hot, garnished with bread slices, sliced eggs and cheese.

CURRIED TOMATO AND EGG CHOWDER
YIELD: ENOUGH TO SERVE 6

Tomatoes, hard-cooked eggs, curry powder and dill are friendly companions whether they are served in chowder or in a classic curry.

2 Small onions, peeled and coarsely chopped
1 Small clove garlic, peeled and crushed
2 Tablespoons butter
2 Teaspoons curry powder
2 Large ripe tomatoes, peeled, seeded and coarsely chopped
½ Cup tomato purée
1 Tablespoon granulated sugar
5 Cups Basic Chicken Stock (see page 192)
1½ Tablespoons flour
⅓ Cup water
4 Hard-cooked eggs, sliced
3 Tablespoons minced fresh dill

Directions: In a deep kettle, sauté onions and garlic in the butter for 3 minutes. Add curry powder and sauté for 2 minutes more. Stir in chopped tomato, tomato purée and sugar. Cover with stock and bring to a boil. Lower heat, cover kettle and simmer for 10 minutes.

Blend flour and ⅓ cup water to a smooth paste and add to soup. Stir constantly until soup thickens slightly. Serve hot, garnished with sliced egg and dill.

FARMHOUSE TOMATO AND BRUSSELS SPROUTS CHOWDER
YIELD: ENOUGH TO SERVE 6

3 Cups ripe tomatoes, peeled, seeded and chopped
3 Tablespoons butter
3 Cups cooked Brussels sprouts, coarsely chopped
6 Cups thin Basic White Sauce (see page 187)
1 Cup dry white wine
⅛ Teaspoon grated nutmeg
  Salt and black pepper
3 Hard-cooked eggs, sliced

Directions: Sauté the tomatoes in the butter for 5 minutes. Combine with Brussels sprouts, white sauce and wine in a large saucepan. Season with nutmeg and salt and pepper to taste, then cook over low heat, stirring occasionally, until the soup heats through. Garnish each serving with egg slices. Serve hot.

MEXICAN CHILI-TOMATO SOUP
YIELD: ENOUGH TO SERVE 6

6 Medium-size ripe tomatoes, peeled, seeded and chopped
4 Green tomatoes, seeded and chopped
3 Onions, peeled and thinly sliced
4 Medium-size potatoes, peeled
8 Cups tomato juice
1 Chili Verde pepper, sliced
2 Teaspoons salt

Directions: Bring tomatoes, onions, whole potatoes and tomato juice to just under a boil, then reduce heat and simmer, covered, until the potatoes are tender but not mushy. Cut potatoes into ½-inch cubes. Return to the soup, along with the pepper slices and salt, and cook over low heat, covered, until the pepper is soft. Serve hot.

TOMATO-SAUERKRAUT SOUP WITH SAUSAGE SLICES
YIELD: ENOUGH TO SERVE 8

6 Cups tomato juice
3½ Cups Basic Beef Stock (see page 191)
1 Teaspoon granulated sugar
1¾ Pounds delicatessen-style sauerkraut
4 Medium onions, peeled and finely chopped
6 Slices country-cured slab bacon, diced
3 Medium-size potatoes, peeled and grated
1 Tablespoon tomato paste
1 Tablespoon paprika
1 Teaspoon each salt, caraway seeds and fennel seeds
2 Barenwurst, sliced
½ Cup chopped baked or boiled ham
2 Tablespoons chopped fresh chives

Directions: Combine tomato juice, stock and sugar in a large soup kettle and bring to a boil. Rinse and drain sauerkraut and add to kettle, then lower heat and simmer for 30 minutes. Meanwhile, sauté onions and bacon in a separate pan until onions are soft. Soak potatoes in cold water to cover for 5 minutes. Drain. Stir onions, bacon, potatoes, tomato paste and seasonings into tomato-sauerkraut mixture. Cover and simmer over low heat for 20 minutes. Add barenwurst slices and ham to soup and cook 10 minutes longer. Sprinkle with chives and serve hot.

VALLEY OF GOD'S PLEASURE DRIED CORN AND TOMATO CHOWDER
YIELD: ENOUGH TO SERVE 8

1½ Cups Pennsylvania Dutch dried corn
2 Teaspoons granulated sugar
  Salt
  Water
¼ Pound salt pork, sliced
2 Cups peeled, seeded and chopped tomatoes
1 Medium-size onion, peeled and finely chopped
1 Green pepper, seeded and finely chopped
1 Medium-size potato, peeled and diced
2 Cups Basic White Sauce (see page 187)
  Salt and black pepper

Directions: Cover the corn, sugar and salt to taste with 4 cups water. Soak for 3 hours. Add additional water to cover and bring to a boil, then reduce heat and simmer for 1 hour, or as directed on package. Meanwhile, render salt pork until golden brown. Discard pork pieces. Add tomatoes, onion, pepper and potato cubes to pork fat. Sauté over low heat until potato is soft, about 15 minutes. Add vegetable mixture to the corn. Stir in the white sauce and cook the soup over low heat for 10 minutes, stirring occasionally. Season to taste with salt and pepper before serving hot.

TOMATO-ZUCCHINI SOUP
YIELD: ENOUGH TO SERVE 8

2 Medium-size onions, peeled and chopped
2 Ribs celery, chopped
⅓ Pound country-cured bacon, chopped
3 Tablespoons olive oil
1½ Cups uncooked rice
5 Ripe tomatoes, peeled, seeded and finely chopped
½ Teaspoon granulated sugar
2 Quarts Basic Beef Stock
  (see page 191)
5 Small zucchini, thinly sliced
3 Tablespoons fresh minced chives
  Salt and black pepper
1½ Cups grated Parmesan cheese

Directions: Sauté onions, celery and bacon in olive oil until the onions are golden. Add rice and sauté for 3 minutes, stirring once or twice. Stir in tomatoes, sugar and stock. Cook over medium heat until the rice is barely tender. Stir in zucchini and chives. Cover and cook the soup for 5 minutes, then remove from the heat and let it stand for 5 minutes more. The zucchini should still have a bit of "crunch" left. Season to taste with salt and pepper. Ladle into soup bowls and serve with grated cheese on the side.

HEARTY TOMATO GUMBO
YIELD: ENOUGH TO SERVE 8 GENEROUSLY

1 Chicken carcass
1 Fresh lobster shell (ask your seafood
    store owner when you buy the shrimp)
½ Pound raw shrimp, peeled and shells reserved
½ Pound each lean beef and pork, cut into 1-inch cubes
1 Pound ham, cut into 1-inch cubes
4 Strips country-cured bacon, cut into 1-inch pieces
2 Large onions, peeled and finely chopped
2 Cups well-washed and chopped celery, including leaves
1 Green pepper, seeded and chopped
1 Sweet red pepper, seeded and chopped
1 Cup chopped okra
4 Cloves garlic, peeled and finely chopped
8 Medium-size tomatoes, peeled, seeded, and very
    coarsely chopped
½ Cup tomato paste
2 Tablespoons granulated sugar
1 Bay leaf, crumbled
½ Teaspoon leaf thyme
  Salt and pepper
¼ Cup minced fresh parsley
1 Tablespoon filé powder
3 Cups cooked rice

Directions: Cover chicken carcass and lobster shell with water, add shrimp shells and bring to a boil. Boil for 10 minutes, skimming off any froth that accumulates. Lower heat and simmer the broth, covered, for 1 hour. Strain the broth, return it to the kettle, add the beef, pork and ham and bring to a boil. Boil for 10 minutes, skimming off any froth, then lower the heat and simmer for 1 hour longer.

Meanwhile, in another large kettle, sauté the bacon for 3 minutes. Add onions, celery, peppers, okra, garlic and shrimp. Sauté until onions are transparent and the shrimp are pink. Remove and reserve the shrimp.

Add cubed meats, chopped tomatoes and enough of the broth to bring the liquid level at least 1 inch above the vegetables and meats. Stir in tomato paste, sugar, bay leaf, thyme and salt and pepper to taste. Simmer the gumbo, covered, for 1 hour, adding more broth if the mixture seems too thick. Adjust the seasonings to suit your taste. Remove from the heat and stir in the reserved shrimp, parsley and filé powder. Spoon some cooked rice into each soup bowl and ladle the gumbo over. Serve hot.

SOUTH-OF-THE-BORDER TOMATO-OATMEAL SOUP
YIELD: ENOUGH TO SERVE 6

1 Cup rolled oats
6 Tablespoons butter
3 Medium-size ripe tomatoes, peeled, seeded and chopped
1 Medium-size onion, peeled and finely chopped
2 Large cloves garlic, peeled and minced
¾ Teaspoon salt
5 Cups Basic Chicken Stock (see page 192)

Directions: In a heavy skillet, heat rolled oats, stirring frequently, until they are brown. Take care not to let them burn. Heat the butter in a large saucepan, add the tomatoes, onions, garlic, salt and browned oats, then cover with stock. Bring mixture to a boil and cook for 8 minutes over medium heat. Serve hot.

TOMATO BURGOO
YIELD: ENOUGH TO SERVE 6 GENEROUSLY

1 Pound lean lamb
1 Turkey carcass (or 1 stewing chicken)
2½ Quarts water
2 Cups coarsely chopped leftover turkey
    (or the chicken meat)
5 Large ripe tomatoes, peeled, seeded
    and coarsely chopped
3 Large onions, peeled and diced
3 Large potatoes, peeled and diced
4 Medium-size carrots, scraped and diced
1 Green pepper, seeded and chopped
1 Sweet red pepper, seeded and chopped
½ Small head cabbage, cored and
    coarsely shredded
1 Cup well-washed and chopped celery,
    including leaves
1 Cup chopped okra
1 Cup whole corn kernels cut from the cob
1 Cup lima beans
1½ Tablespoons granulated sugar
    Salt
    Cayenne pepper
    Worcestershire sauce
    A-1 sauce
    Tabasco sauce
¼ Cup minced fresh parsley

Directions: In a large kettle, cover lamb and turkey carcass with water and bring to just under a boil. Skim off the froth and simmer the broth, covered, over low heat until the meat is very tender (2 to 3 hours). Chop the meat and chicken and add to the hot broth along with the tomatoes, onions, potatoes, carrots, peppers, cabbage, celery, okra, corn and lima beans. Mix in the seasonings to taste, keeping in mind that their flavor increases during cooking. Cover the burgoo and cook over very low heat for 1 to 2 hours, stirring occasionally at first, then more frequently as the mixture thickens. Adjust the seasonings to taste just before serving hot, garnished with the minced parsley.

TURKISH-STYLE TOMATO-GREEN PEPPER SOUP
YIELD: ENOUGH TO SERVE 6

6 Large ripe tomatoes, peeled, seeded
    and chopped
3 Medium-size green peppers, seeded and chopped
1 Large onion, peeled and grated
¼ Cup uncooked rice
1½ Tablespoons butter
8 Cups Basic Beef Stock (see page 191)
1½ Cups light cream
1 Tablespoon each minced fresh chives
    and parsley
    Salt and black pepper
    Croutons (see page 185)

Directions: Place tomatoes, peppers, onion, rice and butter in a large soup kettle. Add the stock and simmer over low heat for 30 minutes. Stir in the cream, a little at a time, and continue to cook over low heat until the rice is just tender. Add the chives and parsley, season to taste with salt and pepper and cook 5 minutes longer. Serve hot, garnished with croutons.

GREEK TOMATO WITH CABBAGE SOUP
YIELD: ENOUGH TO SERVE 8

A thick, hearty peasant-style soup.

1 Large onion, peeled and finely chopped
⅓ Cup olive oil
8 Medium-size ripe tomatoes, peeled, seeded and chopped
1 Teaspoon granulated sugar
9 Cups Basic Chicken Stock (see page 192)
1 Medium-size head cabbage
5 Ounces vermicelli, broken into pieces
  Salt and black pepper

Directions: Sauté onion in the oil until lightly browned and transparent. Stir in tomatoes, sugar and stock. Bring to a boil, cover and simmer over very low heat for 1½ hours.

Meanwhile, pull the tough outer leaves from the cabbage, cut away and discard the core and shred the cabbage finely. Add to the soup, along with the vermicelli. Cook, stirring frequently, for 15 minutes, or until the vermicelli is tender. Season to taste with salt and pepper before serving hot.

ITALIAN TOMATO AND SAUSAGE SOUP
YIELD: ENOUGH TO SERVE 6

4 Strips country-cured bacon, minced
1 Medium-size onion, peeled and minced
6 Ripe tomatoes, peeled, seeded and diced
½ Teaspoon granulated sugar
1½ Pounds sweet Italian sausage
8 Cups Basic Beef Stock (see page 191)
1 Cup uncooked rice
1½ Cups grated Parmesan cheese
4 Tablespoons butter
2 Tablespoons fresh chopped parsley
  Salt and black pepper

Directions: Sauté the bacon and onions in a large soup kettle until lightly browned. Add tomatoes, sprinkle with sugar and cook 10 minutes more, or until the tomatoes are soft.

Meanwhile, in a separate skillet, cook the sausages in water to cover for 15 minutes over medium high heat. Drain the sausages and cut into 1-inch pieces. Add sausages and stock to the tomatoes, browned onions and bacon bits. Bring the mixture to a rolling boil and stir in the rice. Cook, covered, over medium heat until the rice is tender, adding additional stock or water if needed. Remove from the heat and stir in the cheese, butter and parsley. Season to taste with salt and pepper. Serve hot with extra Parmesan.

SCALLOP AND TOMATO STEW
YIELD: ENOUGH TO SERVE 6

   1 Quart scallops, washed and rinsed
1½ Cups Basic Chicken Stock
      (see page 192)
1½ Cups dry white wine
   4 Medium-size ripe tomatoes, peeled,
      seeded and coarsely chopped
   3 Large cloves garlic,
      peeled and crushed
   3 Tablespoons butter
   2 Tablespoons flour
   3 Tablespoons minced fresh parsley
   2 Tablespoons fresh minced basil,
      thyme or rosemary
   3 Hard-cooked eggs, chopped
   6 Large Garlic Croutons
      (see page 185)
½ Teaspoon anchovy paste

Directions: Cover the scallops with stock and wine and bring to just under a boil, then remove from the heat and let stand for 10 minutes.

Meanwhile, sauté the tomatoes and garlic in the butter until most of the liquid has evaporated. Mix in the flour and seasonings. Strain the scallops and measure the liquid. There should be 4 cups. If not, add enough chicken stock to make up the amount. Stir the liquid into the tomatoes and cook over medium heat, stirring constantly, until the mixture boils and thickens slightly.

Place the scallops, tomato mixture and chopped eggs in a hot soup tureen. Spread each of the garlic croutons with anchovy paste and float on the stew. Serve immediately.

TOMATO SOUP ANDALUSIAN STYLE
YIELD: ENOUGH TO SERVE 6

   2 Cups tomato purée
   6 Cups Beef Consommé (see page 193)
½ Teaspoon granulated sugar
¼ Teaspoon salt
½ Teaspoon freshly ground black pepper
   2 Teaspoons tapioca
18 Chicken Quenelles (see page 193)

Directions: Bring tomato purée and consommé to a light boil. Stir in the sugar, salt, pepper and tapioca and continue stirring for 15 minutes. Remove soup from the heat and ladle into soup bowls. Float 3 warm chicken quenelles in each. Serve immediately.

FISH SOUP NORMANDE
YIELD: ENOUGH TO SERVE 6

   4 Medium-size ripe tomatoes, peeled, seeded
      and cut into quarters
   1 Pound sole fillets
   2 Medium-size onions, peeled and sliced
   1 Rib celery, chopped
¾ Teaspoon salt
   1 Teaspoon whole peppercorns
   1 Bay leaf
   2 Teaspoons minced fresh thyme
   4 Cups water
   1 Cup dry white wine
½ Cup cooked, shelled shrimp
   1 Slice white bread, crumbled
   1 Cup heavy cream
      Ground nutmeg
   2 Tablespoons each minced fresh chives and parsley

Directions: Place tomatoes, sole fillets, onions, celery, salt, peppercorns, bay leaf and thyme in a large soup kettle. Cover with the water and wine, bring slowly to a boil, then lower heat and simmer for 30 minutes. Strain the broth into another large pot. Discard the peppercorns and bay leaf and purée the fish and vegetables, with ½ cup broth, in a blender or Cuisinart. Add purée to broth. Purée shrimp, bread and ½ cup broth together in blender and stir into soup. Heat to just under a boil and gradually stir in the cream. Season with nutmeg to taste and serve garnished with chives and parsley.

MANHATTAN CLAM CHOWDER
YIELD: ENOUGH TO SERVE 6

1½ Quarts fresh clams
 1 Large onion, peeled and finely chopped
¼ Pound salt pork, sliced
 3 Cups tomatoes, peeled, seeded
     and chopped
1¾ Cups chopped celery
 1 Cup chopped carrots
 2 Tablespoons minced fresh parsley
⅓ Teaspoon thyme
 1 Bay leaf
 2 Large potatoes, peeled and cut into
     ½-inch cubes
   Salt and black pepper

Directions: Scrub clams well under running water. Place in a large kettle with water to barely cover. Steam until clams open. Strain clam juice through several thicknesses of cheesecloth and reserve. Chop clams finely. Fry salt pork until lightly browned, then remove the pieces. Sauté the onions in the fat until golden. Stir in tomatoes and cook over low heat for 5 minutes, stirring constantly. Add celery, carrots, parsley, thyme and bay leaf. Combine reserved clam juice with enough water to make 2 quarts liquid and add to the vegetables. Cover and cook over low heat for 1 hour. Add potatoes and cook for 15 to 18 minutes, or until tender, then stir in the minced clams and continue to cook for 4 minutes longer. Season to taste with salt and pepper before serving hot.

SEASIDE GARDEN STEW
YIELD: ENOUGH TO SERVE 6

 4 Lobster tails
 6 Cloves garlic, peeled and minced
¼ Cup olive oil
 5 Large ripe tomatoes, peeled, seeded
     and coarsely chopped
 3 Cups tomato juice
 2 Cups white wine
 1 Teaspoon granulated sugar
 2 Cups Basic Chicken Stock (see page 192)
 2 Dozen small clams
 2 Dozen uncooked shrimp, shelled
½ Cup minced fresh dill

Directions: Separate meat from lobster tails and cut into ½-inch slices. In a soup kettle, sauté the lobster meat and garlic in hot oil for 3 or 4 minutes, turning the lobster pieces once or twice. Add the tomatoes, tomato juice, wine, sugar and stock and bring the mixture to a boil. Scrub the clams under running water, then add to the boiling soup along with the shrimp. Cook only long enough for shells to open. Serve hot, sprinkled with dill.

CIOPPINO
YIELD: ENOUGH TO SERVE 6

1 Pint fresh clams
1 Pint fresh mussels
8 Cups water
⅓ Cup chopped dried mushrooms
4 Cloves garlic, peeled and finely chopped
¾ Teaspoon salt
½ Cup olive oil
2 Medium-size onions, peeled and finely chopped
2 Green peppers, seeded and finely chopped
1 Cup fresh chopped spinach
6 Ripe tomatoes, peeled, seeded and coarsely chopped
1 Cup tomato purée
2½ Cups red wine
  Salt and black pepper
1 Medium-size sea bass
2 Small live lobsters
½ Pound large uncooked shrimp, shelled

Directions: Cover the clam and mussel shells with water and soak for 3 hours, changing the water several times. Meanwhile, soak mushrooms in water to cover for 1 hour.

Drain and scrub the clam and mussel shells. Steam in 1½ cups water only long enough for the shells to open. Remove the clams and mussels. Strain and reserve the juices. Crush garlic with the salt, using the back of a spoon.

Heat the oil and sauté onions, peppers, spinach and garlic for 5 minutes, stirring once or twice. Add the tomatoes, tomato purée, wine and reserved clam and mussel juice. Season the mixture with salt and pepper to taste and bring to a boil. Cover and simmer over low heat for 30 minutes. Cut the sea bass into 2-inch slices and the lobster into pieces and add to the soup, along with the shrimp. Cook only long enough for the lobster pieces to turn bright red, about 10 minutes. Place the clams and mussels in their shells in the soup just long enough to heat through. Serve immediately.

CREAM OF TOMATO SOUP
YIELD: ENOUGH TO SERVE 6

2 Medium-size onions, peeled and finely chopped
½ Teaspoon each dried basil and thyme leaves
  Salt and black pepper to taste
2 Tablespoons each butter and olive oil
6 Medium-size ripe tomatoes
3 Tablespoons tomato paste
5½ Cups Basic Chicken Stock (see page 192)
4 Tablespoons flour
1½ Teaspoons granulated sugar
1½ Cups heavy cream
1 to 2 Tablespoons butter (optional)

Directions: Sprinkle onions with spices and sauté in butter and oil until the onions are golden and transparent. Add tomatoes and tomato paste and simmer for 10 minutes, stirring occasionally. Blend ½ cup stock with the flour and stir into the tomato mixture. Add the remaining stock and cook for 30 minutes, stirring frequently with a wooden spoon. Force the soup mixture through a fine sieve with the back of a spoon, or purée in a food mill, blender or Cuisinart. Return to a clean kettle, add the sugar and cream and simmer over low heat, stirring frequently, until the soup is piping hot. If desired, stir 1 or 2 tablespoons butter into the soup before serving.

TOMATO BOUILLON
YIELD: ENOUGH TO SERVE 6

---

3 Tablespoons butter
4 Large ripe tomatoes, peeled, seeded
   and chopped
1 Medium-size onion, peeled and
   coarsely chopped
½ Small clove garlic, peeled and speared
   with a toothpick
  Salt
4 Cups Basic Beef Consommé (see page 193)
2 Cups tomato juice
1 Small bay leaf
  Sour Cream
  Grated orange zest (the thin outer skin of the fruit
   with none of the bitter white underskin included)
  Mint leaves, chopped (optional)

Directions: In a large skillet, heat the butter and stir in tomatoes, onion and garlic. Season with salt to taste, then cover and simmer over low heat for 30 minutes. Remove the vegetables from the heat and discard the garlic. Purée the vegetables by pressing through a fine sieve and pour the mixture into a large saucepan. Stir in consommé, tomato juice and bay leaf and simmer over low heat, covered, for 30 minutes. Discard bay leaf and serve the bouillon hot, topping each portion with a spoonful of sour cream sprinkled with orange zest and mint.

TOMATO AND ORANGE CONSOMMÉ, GOURMET
YIELD: ENOUGH TO SERVE 6

---

3 Cups tomato juice
3 Cups strained orange juice
  Lemon juice
  Celery salt
2 Tablespoons chopped fresh chives or mint
  Sour cream (optional)

Directions: Combine tomato and orange juices and season to taste with lemon juice and celery salt. Serve hot or cold, garnished with chives or mint and a dollop of sour cream, if desired.

Unlike recipes featuring green tomatoes, ripe tomato recipes abound. The trick here was to ferret out only the most interesting and/or useful dishes and then to make sure each recipe really performed perfectly. Although a tomato is absolutely marvelous when merely sliced and set forth fresh from the garden, you really owe it to yourself and your family to fry it, stew it, broil it, bake it or soufflé it while the price is right.

CANNELLONI
YIELD: ENOUGH TO SERVE 6

Cannelloni Noodles (see page 186)
1 Recipe Meat Sauce Florentine (see page 123)
2 Cups Béchamel Sauce (see page 187)
1 Egg yolk
2 Tablespoons grated Parmesan cheese
  Light cream

Directions: Prepare cannelloni as directed. Mix together half the meat sauce, 2 tablespoons béchamel sauce, egg yolk and cheese. Place spoonfuls of mixture along center of each cannelloni, roll up and arrange in shallow baking dish.

Preheat oven to 350 degrees F.

Cover cannelloni with remaining meat sauce. Mix remainder of béchamel sauce with equal amount of cream and pour over meat sauce. Sprinkle with extra cheese and bake for 15 minutes, or until bubbling and lightly browned on top. Serve hot.

LASAGNE
YIELD: ENOUGH TO SERVE 6

1½ Tablespoons each salt and vegetable oil
18 Lasagne noodles (see page 186)
 6 Sweet Italian sausages
 4 Cups ricotta cheese (small-curd
     cottage cheese may be substituted)
 2 Small eggs
⅓ Teaspoon dried tarragon leaves
⅓ Teaspoon salt
1½ Pounds ground chuck
 1 Medium-size onion, peeled and chopped
4½ Cups Spaghetti Sauce (see page 122)
¼ Teaspoon each ground cloves, ground sage and thyme
⅓ Pound mozzarella cheese, cut in
     small cubes

Directions: In a very large kettle, heat 6 quarts of water. As soon as the water boils rapidly, add 1½ tablespoons each of salt and oil, then slip in the noodles and cook until nearly tender. Meanwhile, cook the sausages according to general directions on page 195.

Drain noodles and rinse in cold water to stop any further cooking. Drain them again and spread them flat on clean dish towels or paper towels.

Beat the ricotta cheese for 5 minutes in large bowl of your electric mixer, scraping the bowl occasionally. Add the eggs, tarragon and ⅓ teaspoon salt, beat the mixture for 30 seconds longer, then set aside.

Brown the ground meat in a skillet over medium heat and pour off the excess fat. Drain the sausages, cut into very thin slices and add to the meat, along with the onion, spaghetti sauce, cloves, sage and thyme. Simmer for 5 minutes.

To assemble, spread a thin layer of meat sauce over the bottom of a large, shallow ovenproof dish. Arrange a layer of noodles over the sauce, then top with some of the ricotta cheese mixture. Dot with small cubes of mozzarella cheese and cover with meat sauce. Continue to build successive layers of noodles, ricotta mixture, mozzarella and meat sauce, ending with a layer of noodles topped with meat sauce and bits of mozzarella.

Preheat oven to 350 degrees F.

Place the lasagne in the oven and immediately lower the heat to 325 degrees F. Bake for 25 to 30 minutes, or until the center is hot. Serve immediately.

MEATBALLS AND SPAGHETTI
YIELD: ENOUGH TO SERVE 6

1 Cup stale bread, coarsely crumbled
¼ Cup milk
2½ Pounds ground chuck
3 Tablespoons tomato catsup (or 1 tablespoon tomato paste)
2 Tablespoons prepared mustard
⅛ Teaspoon each thyme and sage
3 Tablespoons vegetable oil
5 Cups tomato purée
1 Cup water
½ Teaspoon fennel seeds
⅛ Teaspoon each ground cloves and oregano
1½ Tablespoons granulated sugar
¼ Cup red wine
1 Package (16 ounces) spaghetti
Parmesan cheese (optional)

Directions: Combine bread and milk, soak for 5 minutes, then drain off excess milk.

Mix meat, moistened bread, catsup, mustard, thyme and sage lightly with your fingers only long enough to incorporate ingredients. Shape into meatballs and fry in hot oil until brown on all sides.

Add tomato purée, water, fennel, cloves, oregano, sugar and wine and bring to a boil. Lower heat and simmer, covered, for 30 minutes, stirring occasionally.

Meanwhile, cook spaghetti according to package directions. Serve meatballs and sauce over hot, well-drained spaghetti, with a side dish of grated Parmesan cheese, if desired.

SPAGHETTI WITH BRANDIED SOUR CREAM SAUCE
YIELD: ENOUGH TO SERVE 6

4 Medium-size onions, peeled and
   finely chopped
2 Cloves garlic, peeled and minced
6 Tablespoons butter
3 Tablespoons olive oil
1½ Pounds ground round steak
   Salt and black pepper
2 Quarts Canned Tomatoes (see page 206)
4 Tablespoons tomato paste
1 Cup Basic Beef Stock (see page 191)
½ Teaspoon dried red pepper
3 Tablespoons minced fresh parsley
1½ Pounds thin spaghetti
¼ Cup brandy
1 Cup sour cream
1 Cup grated Parmesan cheese

Directions: Sauté onions and garlic in butter and oil until onions turn golden. Stir in meat. Season to taste with salt and pepper. Cook, breaking up any large pieces, until meat is lightly browned. Drain tomatoes, reserving 1 cup liquid. Add tomatoes, reserved tomato liquid, tomato paste, stock, red pepper flakes and parsley. Allow sauce to cook, stirring occasionally, for 1 hour or until thickened.

Meanwhile, cook spaghetti according to package directions. Stir brandy into spaghetti sauce and bring to a boil. Drain spaghetti thoroughly and heap onto serving plates. Pour sauce over and serve immediately, with sour cream and cheese on the side.

MEATBALLS, TOMATO AND SAUERKRAUT GOULASH
YIELD: ENOUGH TO SERVE 6

1½ Pounds each ground beef and ground pork
½ Teaspoon sage
¼ Teaspoon each salt, black pepper and
   caraway seeds
1 Cup soft bread crumbs
¼ Cup milk
1 Large can sauerkraut
4 Tablespoons vegetable oil
4 Medium-size onions, peeled and chopped
2 Green peppers, seeded and chopped
1 Tablespoon Hungarian sweet paprika
1 Tablespoon granulated sugar
4 Ripe tomatoes, peeled, seeded and chopped
½ Cup Basic Beef Stock (see page 191) or water
1 Bay leaf
1 Cup sour cream

Directions: Combine ground meats and spices. Soak bread crumbs in milk for 5 minutes. Drain ½ cup sauerkraut well and mince with a sharp knife. Squeeze bread crumbs dry and discard milk. Stir minced sauerkraut and bread crumbs quickly into meat mixture and shape into meatballs. Do not overwork the meat.

Sauté meatballs in oil until brown on all sides. Add onions, peppers, paprika and sugar and continue to cook until the onions are transparent.

Drain remaining sauerkraut and rinse under running water, then drain again and sprinkle over meatballs and vegetables, along with tomatoes, stock and bay leaf.

Cover and simmer goulash over low heat for 40 minutes. Adjust seasonings to taste. Stir in sour cream. Serve immediately over hot noodles.

MOROCCAN MEATBALLS
YIELD: ENOUGH TO SERVE 6

2 Slices bread
6 Tablespoons milk
3 Pounds ground chuck steak
2 Tablespoons raisins
½ Teaspoon each allspice, thyme and salt
3 Tablespoons vegetable oil
4 Large ripe tomatoes, peeled, seeded and cut into ½-inch cubes
18 Pitted prunes
18 Dried apricots
1¼ Cups tomato purée
1¼ Cups water
6 Tablespoons honey
2 Tablespoons soy sauce
1½ Teaspoons ground cinnamon
1 Teaspoon each meat concentrate and allspice
6 Cups hot, cooked rice

Directions: Crumble bread in a large bowl, sprinkle with milk and allow the mixture to stand for a minute or two, then mash to a paste. Drain off any excess liquid. Add meat, raisins and ½ teaspoon each allspice, thyme and salt. Mix thoroughly and form into 1-inch balls. Heat the oil and fry the meatballs until brown on all sides, but still rare within.

Place the meatballs in an ovenproof baking dish along with any pan scrapings. Arrange tomato cubes, prunes and apricots among them.

Preheat oven to 325 degrees F.

Combine tomato purée, water, honey, soy sauce, cinnamon, meat concentrate and remaining allspice and pour over meatballs. Cover and bake for 1 hour. Serve the meatballs hot on a bed of rice.

MEAT LOAF WITH TOMATO CATSUP
YIELD: ENOUGH TO SERVE 4 TO 6

2 Medium-size onions, peeled and minced
1 Large rib celery with leaves, very finely chopped
2 Tablespoons vegetable oil
2 Slices soft white bread, with crusts trimmed
⅓ Cup milk
2 Pounds lean ground steak
¾ Cup tomato catsup
3 Tablespoons Dijon mustard
⅓ Teaspoon each salt, powdered sage and dried thyme
⅛ Teaspoon black pepper
1 Large egg

Directions: Preheat oven to 350 degrees F.

Sauté the onions and celery in the oil until the onion is soft. Cut the bread into cubes, add the milk, allow to soak for 2 to 3 minutes, and then squeeze dry. Combine the meat with the onions, celery, bread, ½ cup catsup, mustard and seasonings. Mix the mixture gently with your fingers. Beat the egg lightly and stir into the meat mixture. Pack into loaf pan and smooth the top, and then spread the remaining catsup over meat. Bake for 1 hour. Serve hot.

BEEF STACK DINNER
YIELD: ENOUGH TO SERVE 6

2 Tablespoons butter
1½ Cups sliced mushrooms
2 Cups peeled and thinly sliced potatoes
1½ Pounds lean ground chuck
1½ Cups thinly sliced onions
1½ Cups diced green pepper
1 Pint canned tomatoes
1 Recipe Basic White Sauce (see page 187)
1 Teaspoon each salt and oregano

Directions: Heat butter in a large skillet and sauté mushrooms until golden. Place mushrooms over the bottom of a large casserole. Top with sliced potatoes. Spread the meat over the potatoes. Arrange onions and peppers on top. Drain and mash tomatoes, then add to the casserole. Top with white sauce. Sprinkle with salt and oregano before baking in a preheated 350 degree F. oven for 2 hours.

BEEF-STUFFED GREEN PEPPERS WITH TOMATO SAUCE
YIELD: ENOUGH TO SERVE 6

1 Tablespoon butter
1 Large onion, coarsely chopped
1½ Pounds ground beef
1½ Cups soft dry bread crumbs
¾ Cup cooked rice
½ Teaspoon salt
¼ Teaspoon dried thyme
½ Teaspoon ground sage
1 Cup tomato purée
1 Egg
6 Medium-size green peppers
1 Cup water

Directions: Heat butter and sauté onion until soft and transparent. Combine with beef, bread crumbs, rice, spices and ⅓ cup tomato purée. Beat egg lightly and blend into the meat mixture. Wash peppers, trim away the stems, seeds and inner white pith; place in a large saucepan and cover with boiling water. Allow the peppers to stand for 7 minutes, then drain thoroughly and stuff with the meat mixture.

Preheat the oven to 300 degrees F.

Stir 1 cup water into the remaining tomato purée and pour into the bottom of a square baking dish. Set the peppers upright in the dish and bake for 1 hour. Serve hot, topped with tomato sauce from the baking dish.

ITALIAN SAUSAGE CASSEROLE
YIELD: ENOUGH TO SERVE 6

6 Green peppers, seeded
   and cut in strips
6 Italian-style sausages, cut into 1-inch pieces
2 Tablespoons vegetable oil
¼ Pound Cheddar cheese, cut into cubes
3 Cups tomato sauce
4 Cups mashed potatoes
3 Tablespoons milk
½ Teaspoon oregano
1 Clove garlic, peeled and crushed
¾ Cup grated Parmesan (or other) cheese

Directions: Preheat oven to 350 degrees F.

Fry the peppers and sausage pieces in the oil, stirring frequently until the peppers are tender. Arrange sausage and peppers in the bottom of a rectangular glass baking dish. Place the Cheddar cheese cubes between the sausage pieces and pour the tomato sauce over all. Beat together the mashed potatoes, milk, oregano and garlic and use a pastry tube to make a decorative border. Sprinkle with Parmesan and bake for 40 minutes, or until top is golden brown. Serve immediately.

BAKED SHORT RIBS IN PORT WINE
YIELD: ENOUGH TO SERVE 6

10 Short ribs of beef
   Salt and black pepper
   Flour
¼ Cup vegetable oil
 1 Large onion, peeled and
     finely chopped
 3 Medium-size carrots, scraped
     and grated
 2 Ribs celery, finely chopped
 2 Cloves garlic, peeled and minced
 2 Teaspoons minced fresh thyme leaves
     or ½ teaspoon dried
 1 Bay leaf
   Salt and black pepper
 4 Tablespoons all-purpose flour
 5 Medium-size ripe tomatoes, peeled,
     seeded and chopped
 1 Cup port wine
 1 Cup Basic Beef Stock (see page 191)

Directions: Season ribs with salt and pepper and dredge in flour. Heat oil in a heavy Dutch oven and sauté ribs, turning occasionally, until brown on all sides.

Preheat oven to 375 degrees F.

Remove the ribs from Dutch oven, pour off fat, return ribs to pan and add onions, carrots, celery, garlic, thyme and bay leaf. Season to taste with salt and pepper, then sprinkle with 4 tablespoons flour. Bake uncovered 15 minutes, turn the ribs and bake 15 minutes longer. Add tomatoes and wine, cover and bake 1½ hours. Pour in stock, cover and continue to bake for 35 minutes, or until meat is very tender.

Set meat aside to keep warm. Skim off all fat from surface and strain sauce into a small saucepan. Simmer for 15 minutes, skimming any fat that rises. To serve, arrange ribs on a serving platter and cover with sauce.

CHILI CON CARNE
YIELD: ENOUGH TO SERVE 6

1½ Tablespoons vegetable oil
2 Pounds lean beef, cut into cubes
8 Medium-size ripe tomatoes, peeled, seeded
   and coarsely chopped
2 Medium-size onions, peeled and finely chopped
2 Large cloves garlic, peeled and finely chopped
3 Tablespoons chili powder
2 Teaspoons granulated sugar
1½ Teaspoons each salt, ground cumin and oregano
4 Cups canned red kidney beans
2 Cups cooked macaroni or rice

Directions: Heat oil in a heavy kettle or Dutch oven and brown meat well on all sides. Stir in tomatoes, onions, garlic, spices and the liquid from the can of beans. Bring to just under a boil, then lower heat and simmer the chili, covered, for 2 hours, stirring occasionally. If the chili becomes too thick, add a little water. Stir in kidney beans during the last 15 minutes of cooking. To serve, place 1 or 2 spoonfuls of cooked macaroni or rice in each bowl, then ladle hot chili over.

BAKED CHICKEN WITH SWEET-AND-SOUR TOMATO KRAUT
YIELD: ENOUGH TO SERVE 6

BASIC RECIPE
2 2½-Pound chickens, cut into pieces
  Flour
3 Tablespoons oil
4 Medium-size green tomatoes
3 Medium-size onions, peeled
5 Medium-size ripe tomatoes, peeled and coarsely chopped
2 Tablespoons granulated sugar
½ Teaspoon caraway seeds
1 Pound sauerkraut
½ Cup sour cream
3 Tablespoons minced fresh chives

Directions: Discard skin from chicken and dredge chicken pieces in flour. Shake off excess and brown chicken on all sides in oil, then cover pan and steam until slightly underdone. Set chicken pieces aside.

Cut green tomatoes and onions into ½-inch wedges and sauté in the same pan for about 8 minutes. Transfer these vegetables into a bowl and set aside. Simmer ripe tomatoes, covered, in the same pan for 10 minutes with the sugar and caraway seeds, then uncover and boil, stirring occasionally, until most of the liquid evaporates.

Meanwhile, drain sauerkraut, rinse, drain well again. Stir it into the tomatoes along with the reserved vegetables; simmer 10 minutes, then add sour cream. Taste and add more sugar if you like.

Preheat oven to 375 degrees F. Put chicken pieces in ovenproof serving dish, spoon sauce over, bake 20 minutes. Sprinkle with chives, serve hot.

BAKED CHICKEN WITH TOMATO KRAUT AND POTATOES
YIELD: ENOUGH TO SERVE 6

Ingredients for Basic Recipe Plus:
 6 Medium-size potatoes, peeled and cut in ¼-inch slices
½ Cup yogurt
½ Cup tomato juice
 2 Tablespoons Garlic Butter (see page 189)
   Paprika

Directions: Boil potato slices until slightly underdone. Drain well.

Follow directions for cooking chicken, tomatoes, onions and kraut, but stir in yogurt and tomato juice along with sour cream.

Preheat oven to 375 degrees F.

Arrange potato slices in bottom of a well-buttered ovenproof serving dish. Spoon the kraut mixture over the potatoes. Top the kraut with chicken pieces, then brush with garlic butter and sprinkle with paprika. Bake 20 to 25 minutes. Serve hot.

CORIANDER CHICKEN BAKED WITH TOMATOES
YIELD: ENOUGH TO SERVE 6
An exquisite chicken dish with Far Eastern flavor.

 1 Teaspoon ground coriander
½ Teaspoon black pepper
 2 2½-Pound chickens, cut into pieces
   Flour
⅓ Cup olive oil
   Salt
 2 Medium-size onions, peeled and finely chopped
16 Medium-size ripe tomatoes, peeled, seeded and chopped
 1 Teaspoon granulated sugar
 6 Tablespoons sherry
 2 Tablespoons minced fresh basil

Directions: Work coriander and pepper into chicken pieces. Dredge chicken lightly in flour, shake off excess and sauté in oil until golden brown on all sides. Transfer chicken to a large baking dish or casserole and season to taste with salt. Sauté onion in oil remaining in pan until soft and transparent. Spread onions over chicken pieces. Add tomatoes and sugar to pan and cook over high heat, stirring constantly, until the liquid evaporates and the mixture thickens to a paste. Remove from heat and stir in sherry. Season to taste with salt and pepper.

Preheat oven to 350 degrees F.

Pour tomato mixture over chicken, sprinkle with basil, cover and bake for 30 minutes. Remove cover and bake 30 minutes more, or until chicken is tender. Serve hot.

CHICKEN LIVERS AND CHERRY TOMATOES EN BROCHETTE
YIELD: ENOUGH TO SERVE 6

 2 Pounds chicken livers
24 Large cherry tomatoes (slightly underripe)
12 Pimiento-stuffed olives
   French Dressing I (see page 189)

Directions: Alternately thread chicken livers, cherry tomatoes and olives on skewers. Brush with dressing. Set on broiler rack 5 inches from flame and broil until livers are brown on the outside but pink on the inside, turning once. Serve immediately.

TOMATO AND GREEN BEAN STEW
YIELD: ENOUGH TO SERVE 6

¼ Pound country-cured slab bacon
   with rind removed
1 Tablespoon butter
3 Medium-size onions, peeled and
   finely chopped
3 Medium-size ripe tomatoes, peeled,
   seeded and chopped
3 Large potatoes, peeled and cut
   into ½-inch cubes
⅓ Teaspoon salt
   Black pepper
2¼ Cups Basic Clarified Beef Stock
   (see page 192)
¾ Pound green beans
¾ Teaspoon bottled beef concentrate
1¾ Tablespoons flour
⅓ Cup water

Directions: Cut bacon into ½-inch cubes and fry in butter in a heavy soup kettle until brown and crisp on all sides, then remove and set aside. Sauté onions until golden in the bacon fat. Stir in tomatoes, potatoes and salt and pepper to taste. Cook over low heat for 10 minutes, stirring occasionally. Add the stock and bring to a boil. Add the green beans and reserved bacon, lower the heat and allow the vegetables to simmer, covered, until all are tender but not mushy. Stir in beef concentrate. Blend flour and water and mix with ½ cup liquid from the kettle. Add this mixture to the stew and stir constantly until the gravy is thick and bubbling hot. Serve immediately.

PENNSYLVANIA DUTCH TOMATOES IN CREAM SAUCE
YIELD: ENOUGH TO SERVE 6

BASIC RECIPE
6 Medium-size ripe tomatoes
1 Cup flour
3 Tablespoons each butter and vegetable oil
⅓ Cup tightly packed light brown sugar
½ Teaspoon powdered marjoram
1 Cup heavy cream
   Salt and black pepper

Directions: Cut off and discard tops and bottoms and slice each tomato into 3 fairly thick slices. Dredge thoroughly in flour. Heat half the oil and butter in each of two large skillets. While the tomato slices are browning on the first side, sprinkle the other with sugar (about ¼ teaspoon on each).

Turn the slices carefully. Fry for 3 to 4 minutes, sprinkle with marjoram and pour ½ cup cream into each skillet. Lower the heat and cook several minutes longer. Arrange the slices on a heated platter and spoon the sauce over, then sprinkle with salt and pepper to taste and serve immediately.

CHICKEN BREASTS AND PENNSYLVANIA DUTCH TOMATOES IN CREAM SAUCE
YIELD: ENOUGH TO SERVE 6

Ingredients listed in Basic Recipe plus:
6 Good-size portions boned chicken
   breasts, skinned
6 Tablespoons lemon juice
2 Eggs

1 Teaspoon salt
⅔ Cup fine bread crumbs
6 Tablespoons vegetable oil

Directions: Slice through each piece of breast meat to make 12 thin, flat pieces. Marinate in lemon juice for 15 minutes. Blot dry with paper towels. Beat together eggs and salt. Dip chicken pieces in egg and bread crumbs and fry in hot oil until golden brown on both sides.

Meanwhile, prepare Pennsylvania Dutch Tomatoes in Cream Sauce as directed.

Arrange fried chicken on tomatoes and serve immediately with mashed potatoes, if desired.

PENNSYLVANIA DUTCH TOMATOES IN CREAM SAUCE WITH MASHED HERBED POTATOES
YIELD: ENOUGH TO SERVE 6

Ingredients listed in Basic Recipe plus:
8 Large potatoes, peeled
  Salt
2 Tablespoons each minced fresh sage
    and marjoram
3 Tablespoons butter
  Milk
12 Slices crisp country-cured bacon

Directions: Cook potatoes in salted water until tender. Mash with herbs, butter and enough milk to moisten slightly.

Meanwhile prepare Pennsylvania Dutch Tomatoes in Cream Sauce.

Serve hot mashed potatoes topped with hot tomatoes, sauce and bacon.

LEFTOVER MEATS WITH PENNSYLVANIA DUTCH TOMATOES IN CREAM SAUCE
YIELD: ENOUGH TO SERVE 6

Ingredients listed in Basic Recipe plus:
2 Pounds leftover turkey, ham, beef
    or other meat
3 Tablespoons butter
½ Cup chicken or beef stock or
    heavy cream
¼ Cup chopped fresh parsley

Directions: Arrange meat in a flat baking dish and dot with butter. Sprinkle with broth or cream and heat in a moderate oven.

Meanwhile, prepare Pennsylvania Dutch Tomatoes in Cream Sauce.

Spoon the tomatoes and sauce over the meat, sprinkle with parsley and serve immediately.

PENNSYLVANIA DUTCH TOMATOES IN CREAM SAUCE ON FRIED TOASTS
YIELD: ENOUGH TO SERVE 6

For lunch or light supper menus this is superb.

Ingredients listed in Basic Recipe Plus:
Ingredients for Fried Toasts
    (see page 185)

Directions: Prepare Fried Toasts according to directions.

Prepare Pennsylvania Dutch Tomatoes in Cream Sauce.

Spoon the tomatoes and sauce over hot fried toasts and serve immediately.

VEAL STEAKS WITH TOMATO-CREAM SAUCE
YIELD: ENOUGH TO SERVE 8

  Salt and black pepper
2 2½-Pound veal steaks, each ¾ inch thick
¼ Cup flour
3 Tablespoons butter
2 Cups Tomato-Cream Sauce (see page 128)

Directions: Work salt and pepper into the veal with your fingers, then dredge steaks with flour. Sauté in butter until lightly browned on both sides, turning once. Remove to a broiling pan. Using the same skillet, prepare the cream sauce as directed, scraping the browned bits around the edges of the pan into the mixture. Broil the steaks for 4 minutes on each side, turning once. Transfer steaks to a serving platter, cover with sauce and serve.

VEAL PROVENÇAL
YIELD: ENOUGH TO SERVE 6

4½ Pounds shoulder of veal, cut into 2-inch cubes
    Salt and black pepper
¼ Cup olive oil
3 Medium-size onions, peeled and coarsely chopped
1 Large clove garlic, peeled and finely chopped
1 Tablespoon fresh rosemary leaves or 1 teaspoon dried
1½ Cups dry white wine
1 Cup tomato juice
4 Medium-size ripe tomatoes, peeled and
    cut into 1-inch cubes
½ Cup stuffed green olives, blanched in 1 cup hot water
⅓ Cup water

Directions: Sprinkle meat with salt and pepper. Heat 3 tablespoons oil in a heavy soup kettle or Dutch oven and brown meat on all sides, stirring occasionally. Pour off fat from kettle and stir in onions and garlic. Cook for 5 minutes, then add rosemary, wine and tomato juice. Cover and cook over *very* low heat for 2 hours.

Remove meat from kettle and strain liquid. Carefully skim off all fat and return meat and liquid to kettle. Season tomato cubes with salt and pepper to taste. Heat remaining tablespoon oil in a skillet and sauté tomatoes for 10 minutes, stirring occasionally. Add tomatoes, olives and ⅓ cup water to kettle, then bring to a boil. Simmer for 10 minutes, skimming off any fat that rises to the surface. Serve hot over noodles or rice.

OSSO BUCO
YIELD: ENOUGH TO SERVE 6

---

1 Tablespoon butter
3 Tablespoons vegetable oil
6 3-inch pieces veal shank with surrounding meat
3 Medium-size carrots, scraped and grated
2 Large ribs celery, finely chopped
⅛ Teaspoon each rosemary and sage
1 Cup tomato purée
1 Cup Basic Chicken Stock (see page 192)
1 Cup dry white wine
2 Teaspoons cornstarch
½ Cup water
1 Teaspoon grated lemon zest (the thin outer skin of the fruit, with none of the bitter white underskin included)

¼ Cup minced fresh parsley
2 Cloves garlic, peeled and minced
　Salt and black pepper

Directions: Heat butter and oil in a large, heavy saucepan or Dutch oven and brown veal pieces on all sides (set shanks upright so marrow will not cook out). Add carrots, celery, rosemary and sage, then cover and simmer for 10 minutes.

Blend tomato pureé into stock and wine and add to meat and vegetables. Cover and simmer over *very* low heat for 2 hours, adding just enough stock or water from time to time to keep vegetables covered. Just before serving, transfer meat to a serving platter and keep warm. Mix cornstarch into ½ cup water and add to vegetables, stirring continually until sauce is thick and clear. Stir in lemon zest, parsley and garlic, season to taste with salt and pepper and serve at once over rice.

LAMB CHOPS IN GARLIC SAUCE
YIELD: ENOUGH TO SERVE 6

---

 3 Tablespoons olive oil
12 Rib lamb chops
    Salt and black pepper
 1 Clove garlic, peeled and crushed
⅓ Cup Basic Chicken Stock (see page 192)
⅓ Cup dry white wine
 1 Teaspoon tomato paste
 2 Teaspoons plus 1 tablespoon butter
36 Cherry tomatoes
 1 Tablespoon minced fresh parsley

Directions: Heat oil in large, heavy skillet. Season chops with salt and pepper, arrange in skillet and sauté over low heat until tender, turning once. Remove chops from skillet and set aside to keep warm. Blend crushed garlic clove with a little salt and add to skillet. Cook 1 minute, stirring constantly, then add stock, wine and tomato paste. Continue to stir as sauce comes to a boil, scraping up the brown bits clinging to the pan. As soon as the liquid is slightly reduced, stir in 2 teaspoons butter. In a separate saucepan, melt 1 tablespoon butter and sauté tomatoes until just heated through. To serve, arrange lamb chops in a circle on serving platter and pour sauce over. Heap tomatoes in center, garnish with parsley and serve at once.

FLOUNDER IN WINE SAUCE WITH CHERRY TOMATOES AND BRUSSELS SPROUTS
YIELD: ENOUGH TO SERVE 6

---

36 Brussels sprouts, trimmed
    and soaked in cold water for 15 minutes
36 Cherry tomatoes, peeled
 5 Tablespoons butter
½ Cup dry white wine
 6 Medium-size fillets of flounder
1½ Tablespoons flour
 2 Cups milk
 1 Tablespoon fresh thyme leaves
    Salt and white pepper

Directions: Bring Brussels sprouts to a boil in ½ inch of water. Lower heat, cover and cook until tender. Drain sprouts, cut each in half and keep warm.

Meanwhile, sauté cherry tomatoes for 2 minutes in 1 tablespoon butter, stirring gently all the while, then remove from pan with slotted spoon and set aside. Add 2 tablespoons butter and the wine to pan and poach fillets 2 to 3 minutes on each side. Carefully remove, set aside and keep warm. Melt remaining butter in pan and stir in flour, then add milk, thyme and salt and pepper to taste. Stir constantly over medium heat until sauce thickens.

Return fish to pan. (If fillets are underdone, complete their cooking at this point.) Return cherry tomatoes to pan and reheat 1 minute by carefully spooning sauce over. Arrange fish and tomatoes on hot plates. Stir the hot sprouts in remaining sauce and arrange on plates next to fish. Serve immediately.

JAMBALAYA WITH CORNBREAD DUMPLINGS
YIELD: ENOUGH TO SERVE 6

Here, feather-light cornbread dumplings enhance the hearty, Deep South flavor of Jambalaya.

9 Italian sausages
3 Strips country-cured bacon
2 Medium-size onions, peeled and chopped
2 Medium-size green peppers, seeded and chopped
2 ¾-inch slices fully cooked ham
6 Medium-size ripe tomatoes, peeled,
    seeded and cut in quarters
2 Cups tomato juice
3 Heaping tablespoons tomato paste
2 Small ribs celery, trimmed and cut in half
3 Tablespoons granulated sugar
1 Tablespoon meat concentrate
2 Small bay leaves
½ Teaspoon dried thyme
¼ Teaspoon each dried fennel seed
    and rosemary
½ Cup butter
3 Cups sifted all-purpose flour
1½ Cups yellow cornmeal
2 Tablespoons baking powder
1 Teaspoon salt
2½ Cups milk
¾ Pound fresh shrimp and/or oysters
    from your fish store

Directions: Prepare sausages according to directions given on page 195. Meanwhile, chop the bacon and sauté it in a deep, heavy kettle (one that can do double duty in your oven) over medium heat for 4 minutes. Drain and slice the sausages into ½-inch pieces, then add them, along with the onion, pepper and ham, to the kettle. Cook, stirring frequently, until onion is lightly browned. Stir in the tomatoes, tomato juice, tomato paste, celery, sugar, meat concentrate and spices. Cover the kettle and allow the mixture to simmer over low heat for 1 hour.

Preheat the oven to 425 degrees F.

Melt butter over hot water. Combine the sifted flour, cornmeal, baking powder and salt. Stir the butter into the milk and add to the dry ingredients, stirring only until lightly mixed. Raise the heat under the jambalaya until the mixture comes to a boil, then add the shrimp and/or oysters. Immediately lower the heat and drop the cornbread batter by spoonfuls onto the surface of the jambalaya. Remove the kettle from the heat and place in the preheated oven. Bake for 15 minutes. Serve immediately.

FISH FILLETS IN SAUCE PROVENÇAL
YIELD: ENOUGH TO SERVE 6

1 Recipe Tomato Sauce Provençal (see page 123)
3 Pounds fillets of flounder or sole
    Salt and black pepper
1½ Tablespoons fresh minced parsley
    Lemon wedges

Directions: Prepare sauce as directed and pour half into a shallow baking pan or dish, one that can do double duty on top of the stove. Preheat oven to 375 degrees F. Sprinkle fillets with salt and pepper to taste, then arrange in the dish. Cover with remaining sauce. Set dish over low flame and bring to a low boil. Remove from heat and cover with buttered wax paper, buttered side down. Bake for 8 to 12 minutes, or until the fish flakes when tested with a fork. Serve at once, topped with minced parsley and garnished with lemon wedges.

TOMATO TEMPURA
YIELD: ENOUGH TO SERVE 6

Yes, Virginia, there really is a tomato tempura— and it is delectable.

Tempura Batter
1 Egg
1 Cup water
1 Cup flour
4 Very firm, medium-size slightly
   underripe tomatoes
4 Green tomatoes
24 Butterflied shrimp or scallops
   (optional)
Vegetable oil for deep-frying

Directions: Beat the egg and water together lightly. Add the flour, 1 tablespoon at a time, stirring up and over with chopsticks (or a spoon). Do not overmix. The batter should be lumpy.

Cut tomatoes into eighths, discard all the seeds and drain pieces well on paper towels.

Dip tomato pieces in batter, drain off excess and fry one piece at a time in hot, deep oil (350 to 370 degrees F.), until golden brown. This will take about 2 minutes. Drain on paper towels and serve immediately.

Seafood may be prepared in the same fashion as tomatoes.

OMELETS
YIELD: ENOUGH TO MAKE 1 OMELET TO SERVE 2

The art of omelet making may seem a bit tricky at first, but the basic technique is easy to master if you start on a small scale and begin with omelets only large enough to serve two. When serving more than two, proceed in the same manner but make a succession of small omelets.

BASIC RECIPE
5 Eggs
2 Tablespoons water
  Salt and black pepper
1 Teaspoon butter

Directions: Beat eggs and water together and season to taste with salt and pepper. Heat butter to sizzling in an omelet pan or skillet over medium flame. Quickly pour in egg mixture and rapidly stir with a fork in a circular motion, lifting cooked part of omelet so that any uncooked egg runs underneath. As soon as eggs are set on the bottom but still soft and creamy on top, press the pan handle down and let omelet slide toward you and halfway up side of pan. Immediately flip omelet over toward the center of the pan, tilt pan in the opposite direction and let the omelet slip out of the pan on the side away from the handle, right onto a waiting plate.

TOMATO AND HAM OMELET
YIELD: ENOUGH FILLING FOR 3 SMALL OMELETS

Ingredients listed in Basic Recipe plus:
 1 Green pepper, seeded
½ Cup cooked ham, cut into shreds
 2 Tablespoons butter
 2 Medium-size ripe tomatoes, peeled, seeded and chopped
¼ Teaspoon granulated sugar

Directions: Parboil pepper for 4 minutes in boiling water, drain and cut into fine shreds. Sauté with the shredded ham in butter for minutes, then add tomatoes, sprinkle with sugar and cook until most of the moisture evaporates. Remove from heat and set aside. Prepare omelet mixture as directed. When eggs are firm but top is still creamy, spread tomato and ham filling over center, flip over, fold and slide onto waiting plate.

MUSHROOM OMELET WITH TOMATO SAUCE PROVENÇAL
YIELD: ENOUGH FILLING TO SERVE 6

Ingredients listed in Basic Recipe plus:
½ Pound fresh mushrooms, minced
 2 Tablespoons peeled and minced shallots
 2 Tablespoons butter
   Lemon juice
 3 Tablespoons sour cream
 2 Cups Tomato Sauce Provençal (see page 123)

Directions: Sauté mushrooms and shallots in butter until golden, then sprinkle with lemon juice. Cook over low heat until most of the moisture evaporates. Prepare and cook omelet mixture until eggs are set but still creamy on top. Spread with mushrooms and shallots along center and top with a dollop of sour cream, flip and fold over. Slip onto waiting plates and serve immediately topped with hot tomato sauce.

TOMATO OMELET WITH FRESH HERBS
YIELD: ENOUGH FILLING FOR 3 SMALL OMELETS

Ingredients listed in Basic Recipe plus:
 3 Medium-size ripe tomatoes, peeled, seeded
     and finely chopped
¼ Teaspoon granulated sugar
 1 Medium-size onion, peeled and finely chopped
 1 Tablespoon butter
 1 Tablespoon mixed minced fresh herbs

Directions: Sauté tomatoes, sugar and onions in butter until most of the liquid evaporates. Prepare and partially cook omelet. As soon as eggs are set on the bottom but still soft and creamy on top, spread some of the tomato filling across center and sprinkle with herbs. Flip, fold and remove omelet from pan according to directions.

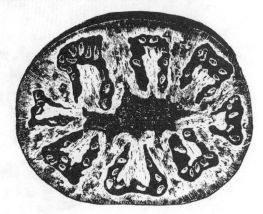

TOMATO AND SWISS CHEESE OMELET
YIELD: ENOUGH FILLING FOR 3 SMALL OMELETS

Ingredients listed in Basic Recipe plus:
1½ Tablespoons butter
2 Medium-size ripe tomatoes, peeled, seeded and chopped
¼ Teaspoon granulated sugar
1 Tablespoon minced fresh basil
½ Cup Swiss cheese cut into ¼-inch cubes

Directions: Heat butter and add tomatoes. Sprinkle with sugar and basil and cook until tomatoes give up their liquid. Keep mixture hot. Prepare omelet as directed to the point where eggs are set on the bottom but top is still soft and creamy. Spread tomato mixture over center and top with some cheese cubes. The cubes should be small enough to melt just a bit while the omelet finishes cooking. Flip, fold and slide omelet from pan as directed.

TOMATO-ZUCCHINI OMELET
YIELD: ENOUGH FILLING FOR 3 SMALL OMELETS

Ingredients listed in Basic Recipe plus:
1 Cup unpeeled, diced zucchini
½ Cup chopped cooked country-cured bacon
1 Tablespoon minced onion
2 Tablespoons butter
2 Medium-size ripe tomatoes, peeled,
   seeded and finely chopped
¼ Teaspoon granulated sugar

Directions: Sauté zucchini, bacon and onion in butter for 3 minutes. Lower heat, cover pan and cook for 4 minutes longer. With a slotted spoon, remove mixture from pan and set aside to keep warm. Add tomatoes to pan, sprinkle with sugar and cook over low heat, stirring, until most of moisture evaporates. Remove tomatoes from pan and stir into reserved bacon and vegetables.

Prepare omelet mixture and cook according to directions until eggs are set but still soft and creamy. Spoon some of the tomato-zucchini filling along center, then flip, fold and slide omelet from pan.

MADRAS TOMATO-EGG CURRY
YIELD: ENOUGH TO SERVE 6

1½ Cups uncooked rice
2 Onions, peeled and coarsely chopped
2 Small garlic cloves, peeled and crushed
3 Tablespoons butter
2½ Teaspoons curry powder
5 Large ripe tomatoes, peeled, seeded and chopped
2 Tablespoons tomato paste
2½ Cups Basic Chicken Stock (see page 192)
1½ Tablespoons granulated sugar
2½ Tablespoons flour
½ Cup water
6 to 8 Hard-cooked eggs

Directions: Cook rice according to package directions. Sauté the onions and garlic in the butter for 3 to 4 minutes. Stir in curry powder and cook for 3 minutes more. Add chopped tomatoes, tomato paste, chicken stock and sugar, then lower the heat and simmer mixture for 10 minutes. Mix flour and water together, and stir into curry mixture until slightly thickened. Slice one egg per portion and add to curry, cooking only long enough to heat. Serve at once over rice.

PEPPERY EGGS WITH TOMATOES
YIELD: ENOUGH TO SERVE 6

¼ Cup olive oil
8 Medium-size ripe tomatoes, peeled, seeded and chopped
½ Teaspoon granulated sugar
¼ Cup minced fresh parsley
½ Teaspoon black pepper
6 Eggs
   Buttered Toast Points (see page 185)

Directions: Heat oil in a large skillet and add toma-toes, sugar, parsley and pepper. Cook over medium heat, stirring frequently until the liquid evaporates and the mixture is smooth and thick. Lower the heat and carefully drop the eggs, one at a time, into the simmering sauce. Poach for 3 to 5 minutes, or until set, carefully spooning sauce over eggs as they cook. Serve eggs on toast points, with a bit of sauce spooned over each.

SPORTSMAN'S EGGS
YIELD: ENOUGH TO SERVE 6

3 Tablespoons butter
1½ Pounds chicken livers, halved
½ Cup minced onion
2 Tablespoons minced green pepper
1 Cup tomato sauce
1 Cup Basic Beef Consommé (see page 192)
¾ Cup dry white wine
6 Eggs
   Salt
   Buttered Toast Points (see page 185) or
      Fried Toasts (see page 185)

Directions: Heat butter in a large skillet and sauté chicken livers, onion and green pepper until lightly browned. Remove chicken livers and set aside. Add tomato sauce, consommé and white wine to the skillet and simmer for 8 minutes. Stir in chicken livers and continue to cook until livers reach the degree of doneness you prefer. In a separate pan, fry the eggs "as you like them."

Allow 1 egg and 4 chicken livers per serving and arrange on buttered toast points or fried toasts.

POACHED EGGS WITH ROSY TOMATO-CREAM SAUCE AND BACON
YIELD: ENOUGH TO SERVE 6

12 Eggs
    Buttered Toast Points (see page 185)
 2 Cups Rosy Tomato-Cream Sauce (see page 128)
12 Slices hot, fried country-cured bacon
12 Sprigs parsley

Directions: Prepare 2 poached eggs for each serving. Place on hot, buttered toast points and top with sauce and bacon strips, both hot. Garnish with parsley and serve immediately.

SPICED TOMATOES WITH PEAS AND POTATOES, PAKISTANI STYLE
YIELD: ENOUGH TO SERVE 6 TO 8

Exotic recipes like this one add interesting variety to meatless meals.

 5 Tablespoons each butter and vegetable oil
 2 Cloves garlic, peeled and crushed
 4 Large potatoes, peeled and cut
    in ½-inch cubes
1½ Cups fresh green peas
 1 Teaspoon chili powder
¾ Teaspoon each ground cumin, ground turmeric
    and ground ginger
 2 Teaspoons salt
 6 Medium-size ripe tomatoes, peeled,
    seeded and chopped
6 to 8 Eggs
 8 Scallions, with 3 inches green top, minced

Directions: Heat 3½ tablespoons each butter and oil, add the crushed garlic cloves and sauté the potato cubes, stirring frequently, until potatoes are fork-tender. Add peas and cook for 3 minutes more. Spoon these vegetables onto a large plate and set aside.

Add remaining butter and oil to skillet along with the spices and salt. Stir in tomatoes, potatoes, and peas, and cook over low heat until piping hot. Arrange vegetables on serving plates, top with fried eggs "as you like them," sprinkle with scallions and serve at once.

SCRAMBLED EGGS WITH TOMATO SAUCE
YIELD: ENOUGH TO SERVE 6

12 Eggs
 2 Tablespoons water or milk
    (optional)
    Salt and white pepper
 3 Tablespoons butter
 2 Cups hot tomato sauce
 3 Scallions, with 3 inches green top
 1 Cup grated cheese
    Buttered Toast Points (see page
    185)

Directions: Beat eggs (with water or milk, if desired) and season to taste with salt and pepper. Scramble in butter. Divide among hot serving plates.

Spoon tomato sauce over each portion, garnish with minced scallions and a sprinkling of grated cheese. Serve at once with hot, buttered toast points.

TOMATO SOUFFLÉ
YIELD: ENOUGH TO SERVE 6

2 Tablespoons butter
2 Tablespoons all-purpose flour
¾ Cup cold milk
¼ Teaspoon salt
1 Cup tomato purée
4 Egg yolks
5 Egg whites

Directions: Melt butter in a heavy pan. Blend in flour, then add cold milk and salt to taste. Cook, stirring constantly, until sauce thickens slightly.

Remove pan from heat and fold in purée. Beat in egg yolks, one at a time. When all ingredients are well blended, allow mixture to cool slightly.

Preheat oven to 350 degrees F.

Beat egg whites until they stand in stiff peaks and fold gently into tomato mixture. Turn at once into well-buttered soufflé dish or other deep baking dish. Bake for 30 minutes, or until soufflé is puffy and brown on top.

To make a less crusty soufflé, set dish in a pan of hot, not boiling, water while it bakes.

TOMATO SOUFFLÉ WITH HAM

When preparing the Basic Recipe, fold in ¾ cup minced cooked ham and 1 tablespoon minced chives along with the tomato purée. Continue as directed.

TOMATO-CHEESE SOUFFLÉ

Add ¾ cup grated Swiss cheese and 1 tablespoon minced fresh dill as you fold the tomato purée into the Basic Recipe. Proceed to beat in eggs and fold in egg whites.

TOMATO-ZUCCHINI SOUFFLÉ

Sauté 1 medium-size peeled and very thinly sliced zucchini in 1 tablespoon butter until vegetable is very soft. Combine with tomato purée when folding into Basic Recipe. Proceed as directed.

TOMATO-SEAFOOD SOUFFLÉ

Stir ¾ cup very finely chopped shrimp, lobster or crabmeat or the same amount of cooked, flaked fish into the tomato purée before adding to the Basic Recipe. Continue as directed.

MINIATURE CHEESE SOUFFLÉS IN TOMATO SHELLS
YIELD: ENOUGH TO SERVE 6

Perfect for a summer lunch, these individual cheese soufflés can also serve as a garnish to dress up a plain meat meal.

12 Large firm, ripe tomatoes
   Salt
 6 Tablespoons heavy cream
 2 Tablespoons flour
 6 Egg yolks
 2 Tablespoons melted butter
½ Teaspoon salt
   Pinch cayenne
 1 Cup grated Swiss cheese
 4 Egg whites

Directions: Cut ½ slice from the top of each tomato and scoop out seeds and pulp. Sprinkle tomato shells with salt to taste and drain, cut side down, for 30 minutes.

Meanwhile, mix together cream and flour in a saucepan. Add 3 of the egg yolks, melted butter and seasonings. Stir the mixture briskly over low heat until creamy and smooth. Remove from the heat and stir in 3 remaining egg yolks and cheese. Mix well and allow to cool.

Preheat oven to 375 degrees F.

Beat egg whites until stiff but not dry and fold into cheese mixture.

Spoon into tomato shells, filling them three-quarters full, and bake for 20 to 25 minutes, or until soufflés are nicely puffed and brown.

Serve immediately.

RATATOUILLE BAKED WITH EGGS
YIELD: ENOUGH TO SERVE 6

This is ratatouille with a difference—this version is baked with hard-cooked eggs. It is superb served hot and equally good served cold the following day.

2½ Pounds eggplant, peeled and cut
       into ½-inch dice
 1 Tablespoon salt
 2 Large green peppers, seeded
 2 Large sweet onions, peeled and coarsely chopped
 1 Cup vegetable oil
 6 Large ripe tomatoes, peeled, seeded
       and finely chopped
 3 Large cloves garlic, peeled and crushed
 1 Tablespoon fresh thyme leaves
1½ Teaspoons granulated sugar
¼ Teaspoon paprika
 4 Tablespoons wine vinegar
 6 Hard-cooked eggs, cut in quarters

Directions: Spread eggplant cubes on paper towels, sprinkle with salt, let stand 15 minutes, then turn, salt and let stand 15 minutes more. Rinse in cold water and pat dry with paper towels.

Boil the peppers for 5 minutes, then rinse under cold water. Dry and cut into ½-inch strips. Sauté with the onions in 2 tablespoons oil for 15 minutes, or until vegetables are tender but not brown.

In a large skillet, sauté eggplant cubes in ¾ cup hot oil until lightly browned on all sides.

Preheat oven to 375 degrees F.

Simmer the tomatoes with 2 tablespoons oil, garlic, thyme and sugar until most of the liquid has evaporated.

Stir the eggplant, onions, peppers, tomato mixture, paprika and vinegar together and spoon into an ovenproof baking dish. Arrange egg quarters on top, sprinkle each with a few drops of oil and bake for 15 minutes.

RATATOUILLE QUICHE
YIELD: 1 10-INCH QUICHE

1 Recipe Quiche Pastry (see page 184)
1 Pound eggplant, peeled and cut into ½-inch dice
1 Tablespoon salt
¾ Cup vegetable oil
1 Large sweet onion, peeled and coarsely chopped
1 Green pepper, seeded, parboiled for
    8 to 10 minutes, then seeded and chopped
1 Small zucchini, well washed but not peeled
1 Clove garlic, peeled
2 Teaspoons thyme leaves
½ Teaspoon granulated sugar
   Salt and black pepper
3 Eggs
1½ Cups Ripe Tomato Purée (see page 203)
   Dijon mustard
¾ Cup grated Swiss cheese

Directions: Prepare and refrigerate pastry.

Spread eggplant cubes on paper towels and sprinkle with salt. Let stand 15 minutes, then turn, salt and let stand 15 minutes more. Rinse in cold water and pat dry.

Sauté eggplant in hot oil until cubes are lightly browned on all sides. Remove from pan with a slotted spoon and drain on paper towels. Discard all but 3 tablespoons oil and in it sauté chopped onion and green pepper. Cut zucchini into small dice and add to pan, along with garlic, thyme and sugar, and cook until the vegetables are tender. Add salt and pepper to taste. Remove from heat and cool.

Beat the eggs and stir in tomato purée and cooled cooked vegetables.

Preheat oven to 375 degrees F.

Roll out, form and prebake pastry for 10 minutes.

Brush the bottom of the quiche shell with mustard and fill with the tomato-eggplant mixture. Sprinkle with cheese and bake for 20 to 25 minutes or until the top is set. Cool 5 minutes before serving warm.

RIPE TOMATO AND EGGPLANT QUICHE
YIELD: 1 10-INCH QUICHE

1 Recipe Cheese Quiche Pastry (see page 184)
1½ Pounds eggplant, peeled and cut
    into ½-inch dice
1 Tablespoon salt
¾ Cup vegetable oil
6 Strips lean country-cured bacon,
    coarsely chopped
3 Large ripe tomatoes, peeled, seeded and
    coarsely chopped
3 Eggs
1½ Cups Ripe Tomato Pureé (see page 203)
2 Tablespoons each chopped fresh thyme
    leaves and basil
    Salt and black pepper
    Dijon mustard
1 Cup grated Swiss cheese

Directions: Prepare and refrigerate pastry.

Spread eggplant cubes on paper towels and sprinkle with salt. Let stand 15 minutes, then turn, salt and let stand 15 minutes more. Rinse in cold water and pat dry.

Sauté eggplant in hot oil until cubes are lightly browned on all sides. Remove from pan with a slotted spoon and drain on paper towels. Discard oil and brown bacon pieces in the same pan. Remove with a slotted spoon. Sauté tomato in the same pan until liquid evaporates.

Beat eggs and stir in the eggplant, bacon, tomato, tomato purée, herbs and salt and pepper to taste.

Preheat oven to 375 degrees F.

Roll out, form and prebake pastry for 10 minutes.

Brush the bottom of the quiche shell with mustard, sprinkle with half the cheese and fill with the tomato-eggplant mixture. Sprinkle with remaining cheese and bake for 20 to 25 minutes, or until the top is set. Cool 5 to 10 minutes before unmolding. Serve warm.

WELSH RABBIT WITH GRILLED TOMATOES
YIELD: ENOUGH TO SERVE 6

1 Tablespoon butter
1¼ Pounds Cheddar cheese, grated
1 Cup flat beer, at room temperature
1 Tablespoon dry mustard
2 Teaspoons Worcestershire sauce
6 Medium-size ripe tomatoes
12 Strips country-cured bacon
    Bread crumbs
    Butter
24 Toast Points (see page 185)

Directions: Melt the butter in a heavy skillet and add cheese a handful at a time, stirring constantly with a wooden spoon. As the cheese melts, add ¾ cup of beer a bit at a time, and continue to stir until the mixture is free from lumps.

Mix the mustard and Worcestershire sauce with enough beer to make a smooth paste. Blend this into the cheese mixture. Keep the sauce warm.

Meanwhile, cut the stem ends from tomatoes, shake them to remove most of the seeds, then drain cut side down, for 5 minutes. Fry bacon until crisp and brown.

Top tomatoes with bread crumbs and bits of butter, then broil for 5 minutes about 5 inches from flame, or until the tops turn golden brown. To serve, arrange 4 toast points on each plate. Top with tomato and crisscross with bacon slices. Cover with cheese rabbit and serve hot.

TOMATO CURRY
YIELD: ENOUGH TO SERVE 6

This money-saving meatless meal is as flavorful as any you could prepare.

¼ Cup vegetable oil
 3 Large onions, peeled and thinly sliced
12 Medium-size ripe tomatoes, peeled,
      seeded and cut in quarters
 3 Cloves garlic, peeled and minced
 2 Teaspoons anchovy paste
 1 Teaspoon salt
½ Teaspoon each dried chili peppers
      and turmeric
 5 Tablespoons water
   Buttered Toast Points (see page 185)
      or rice

Directions: In a large, heavy skillet, heat the oil and sauté the onions for 3 to 4 minutes. Stir in the remaining ingredients. Cook over low heat, stirring frequently, for 20 minutes, or until vegetables are tender. Serve hot over toast points or rice.

BACON WAFFLES WITH GRILLED TOMATOES
YIELD: ENOUGH BATTER FOR 6 SERVINGS

Ingredients for 3 large Bacon Waffles:
 1 Cup sifted all-purpose flour
 1 Teaspoon baking powder
 1 Tablespoon granulated sugar
½ Teaspoon salt
 2 Eggs, at room temperature, separated
 1 Cup milk, at room temperature
 2 Tablespoons shortening, melted
 4 Strips crisply fried country-cured
      bacon, crumbled

Additional Ingredients:
 2 Cups Egg and Herb Sauce (see page 187)
 6 Grilled Tomatoes (see page 108)

Directions: Sift flour, baking powder, sugar and salt into large bowl. Beat egg yolks in a small bowl, then beat in milk and cooled shortening. Stir egg-yolk mixture into dry ingredients only enough to blend. Beat egg whites until stiff but not dry and fold them, along with the bacon bits, into the batter. Pour batter, about ⅓ cup at a time, onto a hot waffle iron and bake about 4 to 5 minutes.

Arrange half a waffle on each plate, spoon hot egg and herb sauce over and top each serving with a Grilled Tomato. Serve immediately.

SANDWICHES

A really delectable sandwich depends as much on appearance as it does on content. A sandwich that looks beautiful generally tastes fantastic no matter what the ingredients.

Here are a few tricks that canny sandwich makers can utilize to turn drab, everyday sandwiches into special treats.

- Trim crusts—crusts are the healthy but homey part of bread. Unless the sandwich is meant to be a hearty beer companion, get out the knife and trim. If your conscience hurts you, you may eat these later on or save them for another use. There is no way to get around it—you'll find that there is something very special about a sandwich that has doffed its tough, chewy outer edges.

- Don't overfill with too much of any one ingredient—a company sandwich should not be swamped with any one ingredient or combination of ingredients. Leave the belly-bursting to the local delicatessen.

- Don't forget the salt and pepper—any sandwich worth its salt, particularly one that includes tomato, is improved at least 50 percent by the simple addition of salt and pepper.

- The go-withs are important too—the tiny tomatoes, piles of relish, pickles, slices of avocado or egg are what make the difference between good and super. Never serve a sandwich on a tiny plate. Give it room to look spectacular and then surround it with extra goodies and perhaps a small dish of dressing or a wedge of lemon or lime. This is the time to use your ingenuity, your imagination . . . and those extra nibbles tucked away in the fridge.

- Always drain sliced, moist vegetables, like tomatoes or cucumbers, on paper towels before using.

OPEN-FACED SANDWICHES

These open-faced sandwiches, with their attractive, sunny sides up, offer an opportunity for you to show your creativity and imagination while treating your guests—superbly well. Trim the crusts to make them look special.

SMOKED SALMON, TOMATO AND ONION: Spread thinly sliced bread with Tomato–Cream Cheese Sandwich Filling (see page 105), cover with slices of smoked salmon and top with paper-thin slices of tomato and sweet onion sprinkled with chives and/or pepper.

SMOKED SALMON DELUXE: Spread thin slices of pumpernickel bread with Tomato–Cream Cheese Sandwich Filling (see page 105), cover with slices of smoked salmon and top with a bit of sieved, hard-cooked egg yolk.

TONGUE AND TOMATO WITH FRENCH DRESSING: Spread thin slices of rye bread with sweet butter, cover with overlapping slices of calf's tongue and top each with a peeled, seeded tomato slice and several slices of hard-cooked egg. Garnish with chopped sour pickle. Moisten with French Dressing II (see page 189). Serve cold.

BATTER-FRIED TOMATOES WITH HAM: Spread Toast Points (see page 185) with Dijon mustard, thin slices of ham sautéed in butter and Batter-Fried Tomatoes (see page 110). Serve hot.

CONFETTI COTTAGE CHEESE: Spread thin slices of pumpernickel with mayonnaise. Top with thin tomato slices and Confetti Cottage Cheese (see page 114). Garnish with avocado slices and serve cold with Tomato–Tabasco Salad Dressing (see page 130).

VEGEMATO: Spread white bread with Vegemato Sandwich Filling (see page 105). Top with thin tomato slices and minced fresh basil.

SALAMI AND CHERRY TOMATO: Spread thin slices of rye bread with Russian dressing. Top with paper-thin slices of salami and halved cherry tomatoes. Fill a pastry bag fitted with a fluted tube with cream cheese seasoned with horseradish and decorate the edges of the sandwich.

VEGEMATO SANDWICH FILLING
YIELD: ENOUGH TO FILL 8 SANDWICHES

2 Medium-size tomatoes, peeled and seeded
1 Large cucumber, peeled and seeded
5 Scallions, with 3 inches green top
1 Cup tightly-packed watercress leaves
5 Hard-cooked eggs
3 Tablespoons cream cheese,
   at room temperature
1¼ Cups Mayonnaise
   (see page 187)
2 Teaspoons prepared mild mustard
   Salt and black pepper

Directions: Coarsely chop tomatoes, cucumber, scallions, watercress and eggs. Blend together thoroughly cream cheese, mayonnaise and mustard. Combine all ingredients and season to taste with salt and pepper.

TOMATO–CREAM CHEESE SANDWICH FILLING
YIELD: ENOUGH TO FILL 8 SANDWICHES

5 Scallions, with 3 inches green top
2 Tablespoons sour cream
1½ Pounds cream cheese, at room temperature
4 Large tomatoes, peeled and
   finely chopped
   Salt and black pepper

Directions: Mince scallions and blend them, along with the sour cream, into the cream cheese. Drain tomatoes well, then blend into the cheese mixture along with salt and pepper to taste.

POOR BOY SANDWICHES
YIELD: ENOUGH TO SERVE 6

Slit in half lengthwise 1 or 2 loaves (depending on size) of French bread. Spread each half generously with soft butter. Slice the loaf (or loaves) in thirds or fourths, not quite through to the bottom crust. Use your imagination, or fill sandwiches in any of the following ways:

• Arrange fried oysters along one side of bread. Top each cut section with 1 fried egg, turned and cooked until white is firm and yolk still soft, then cover with thinly sliced tomatoes and crisp strips of country-cured bacon. Pour Salsa Piquante (see page 126) over all.
• Place a layer of fried oysters over one buttered side, then top with chicken salad, sliced tomatoes and crisp strips of country-cured bacon.
• Place fried oysters over one side of the loaf and top with cooked and sliced hot Italian sausage, tomatoes and hard-cooked egg slices.

REFRIED BEANS, AVOCADO, CHEESE AND TOMATO SANDWICHES
YIELD: 8 SANDWICHES

8 Pita
  Mayonnaise (see page 187)
3 Cups hot refried beans
¼ Pound Jack cheese, thinly shredded
1 Large sweet onion, peeled and thinly sliced
½ Head lettuce, thinly shredded
1 Avocado, peeled, seeded and thinly sliced
4 Ripe tomatoes, thinly sliced

Directions: Slice through the top layer of the Pita, taking care not to cut the bottom layer. Spread mayonnaise on the inside surfaces and fill the inside with layers of beans, cheese, onion, lettuce, avocado and tomatoes.

SAUSAGE SANDWICHES
YIELD: ENOUGH TO SERVE 6

12 Italian sausages
 3 Tablespoons vegetable oil
 3 Medium-size green peppers, seeded and cut
    into ½-inch strips
 3 Medium-size onions, peeled and sliced into thin rings
½ Pound mushrooms
 1 Cup tomato purée
½ Teaspoon granulated sugar
⅓ Teaspoon each black pepper and oregano
 2 Loaves Italian bread

Directions: Cook sausages according to directions on page 195. Meanwhile, heat oil in a separate skillet and sauté green pepper strips over medium flame for 5 minutes. Stir in the onion rings. Wipe the mushrooms with a damp cloth and cut into slices (fresh, tender mushrooms do not need to be peeled). Add to the peppers and onions and continue to sauté for 3 minutes, stirring occasionally.

Drain the sausages thoroughly and cut in half lengthwise. Push the vegetables to one side of the skillet. Raise the heat slightly and fry the sausages, cut side down, for 3 minutes. Turn the sausages over, cover with the vegetables, and fry for 3 minutes more. Stir in the tomato pureé, sugar, pepper and oregano and continue to cook for 1 minute, stirring constantly. Lower the heat. Cut the breads in half lengthwise. Pull out some of the soft insides, then warm the loaves under the broiler. Heap the sausage and vegetable mixture into the hollowed-out bread. Serve immediately.

CHEESE TOASTS WITH TOMATOES
YIELD: ENOUGH TO SERVE 6

12 Slices partially dry bread
2 Tablespoons butter
¼ Cup olive oil
2 Large cloves garlic, peeled
1 Pound Swiss cheese, cut into paper-thin slices
6 Medium-size ripe tomatoes, sliced

Directions: Trim crusts from the leftover bread. Heat 1 tablespoon butter and 2 tablespoons oil in each of 2 large skillets. Crush 1 clove garlic into each pan and fry the bread to golden brown on both sides, turning once.

Arrange bread on an ovenproof serving platter and top each slice with cheese and 2 slices tomato. Bake or broil until cheese melts and bubbles. Serve immediately.

TOMATO FONDUE
YIELD: ENOUGH TO SERVE 6

1 Clove garlic, peeled and cut in half
2 Tablespoons butter
2 Medium-size ripe tomatoes, peeled, seeded and chopped
1 Tablespoon minced fresh basil
3 Tablespoons dry white wine
   Pinch cayenne
2 Cups grated Cheddar cheese
1 Loaf slightly stale French bread cut into cubes

Directions: Rub the cut surfaces of garlic halves over the inside of a chafing dish or heavy saucepan. Discard garlic. Heat butter in pan until bubbly, then add tomatoes and basil. Cook over low heat, stirring frequently, for 8 to 10 minutes, then add wine and cayenne and cook only long enough to blend. Stir in the cheese, a handful at a time, and simmer until all cheese melts and the fondue is smooth. Serve hot with crusty cubes of French bread.

RATATOUILLE
YIELD: ENOUGH TO SERVE 6

1 Medium-size eggplant, peeled and cut
   into ½-inch cubes
   Salt
½ Cup olive oil
4 Medium-size onions, peeled and
   coarsely chopped
3 Green peppers, seeded and chopped
5 Ripe tomatoes, peeled, seeded and chopped
4 Small zucchini, cut in ½-inch cubes
1½ Cups chopped celery
1 Large clove garlic, peeled and crushed
1 Tablespoon each minced fresh basil
   and marjoram
   Salt and black pepper

Directions: Spread eggplant cubes on paper towels and sprinkle with salt. Let stand 15 minutes, then turn, salt and let stand 15 minutes more. Rinse in cold water and pat dry.

In a large skillet, heat the oil and sauté the onions until they are soft and transparent. Lower the heat, add the peppers and eggplant and cook for 5 minutes, stirring occasionally. Mix in the tomatoes, zucchini and celery, cover the skillet and allow to simmer over low heat for 50 minutes. Stir in the garlic and seasonings and cook 5 minutes longer. Serve hot or cold.

BROILED TOMATOES WITH EGG AND ANCHOVY TOPPING
YIELD: ENOUGH TO SERVE 6

6 Ripe, firm tomatoes
3 Tablespoons vegetable oil
8 Shallots, minced
1 Tablespoon each minced fresh parsley and
    minced fresh chives
2 Cloves garlic, peeled and crushed
2 Hard-cooked eggs
4 Anchovy fillets
¼ Teaspoon granulated sugar
1 Tablespoon softened butter
2 Tablespoons fine bread crumbs
  Butter

Directions: Turn oven to broil.

Cut the tomatoes in half crosswise and turn them upside down to drain for 10 minutes. Fry the cut sides of the tomatoes in hot oil for a minute or two, then arrange them in a well-buttered baking dish, cut sides up.

Mix the shallots, parsley, chives and garlic. Mince the eggs and anchovies and mix them, along with the sugar and softened butter, into the minced vegetable mixture. Spread the tomato halves with the topping, sprinkle with bread crumbs and dot with butter. Slide under the broiler until the tomatoes are heated through and the tops are lightly browned. Do not overcook. Serve immediately.

GRILLED TOMATOES
YIELD: ENOUGH TO SERVE 6

6 Large firm, ripe tomatoes
  Salt
1 Small clove garlic, peeled and minced
2 Teaspoons each softened butter and olive oil
¼ Cup bread crumbs
  Black pepper
6 Sprigs watercress

Directions: Remove ½-inch slice from stem end of each tomato. Shake each gently to seed, then sprinkle with salt. Allow to stand, cut side down, for 5 minutes. Mix together garlic, butter, oil and bread crumbs. Spread tomatoes with mixture. Season to taste with salt and pepper. Set tomatoes on broiling rack 4 to 5 inches below the flame.

Broil 4 to 5 minutes. Raise broiling pan closer to heat and broil only long enough to brown bread crumb mixture. Garnish each tomato with watercress before serving hot.

GRILLED TOMATOES WITH FRESH HERBS

Add 1½ tablespoons fresh minced basil, marjoram, thyme or sage to the bread crumbs.

GRILLED TOMATOES WITH CHEESE

Omit garlic from bread crumb mixture and substitute 3 tablespoons grated Parmesan cheese.

STEWED TOMATOES I

12 Good-size very ripe tomatoes, peeled and cut into eighths
1 Teaspoon cornstarch, mixed with a little cold water
  Salt and black pepper
1½ Teaspoons granulated sugar
  Minced fresh dill, thyme or marjoram
1½ Tablespoons butter

Directions: Place tomatoes in a glass, enamel or stainless steel saucepan and cook over medium-low heat for about 15 to 20 minutes, or until the juice has partially boiled away. Add cornstarch-water mixture to the stewed tomatoes and stir constantly until slightly thickened. Turn tomatoes into a serving dish, salt and pepper to taste, add sugar and dill. Dot with butter and serve immediately.

STEWED TOMATOES II

Follow recipe for Stewed Tomatoes I but omit the cornstarch and water and thicken with ¾ cup bread or cracker crumbs. Serve as directed.

STEWED TOMATOES WITH CHEESE

Follow recipe for Stewed Tomatoes I or II, but spoon tomatoes into an ovenproof dish and sprinkle with 1 cup grated Swiss, Parmesan or Monterey Jack cheese. Bake in a preheated hot oven until cheese melts. Serve immediately.

STEWED TOMATOES WITH HAM

Follow recipe for Stewed Tomatoes I or II, but add ½ cup minced ham immediately after tomatoes have been thickened. Serve as directed.

SWEET STEWED TOMATOES, QUEEN VICTORIA

YIELD: ENOUGH TO SERVE 6

These "stewed" tomatoes are actually baked. The texture and flavor are similar to the old-fashioned stewed variety but, in my opinion, are far superior. Delicious served as a side dish with steak.

12 Good-size very ripe tomatoes
8 Tablespoons granulated sugar
  Salt
  Butter
  Black pepper

Directions: Preheat oven to 500 degrees F.
  Dip tomatoes in scalding water and pull off the skins. Cut tomatoes into eighths, sprinkle with sugar and arrange in a well-buttered 9-by-13-inch glass baking dish. Bake for about 45 minutes or until the sugar and tomato juices have been reduced to a syrup. Salt to taste and serve immediately, dotted with butter and sprinkled generously with pepper.

FRIED TOMATOES WITH CHEESE
YIELD: ENOUGH TO SERVE 6

Perhaps because of my Pennsylvania Dutch heritage, fried tomatoes seem to me to be the best possible hot vegetable. If you have never fried a tomato—you really should.

4 Tablespoons butter
6 Large ripe tomatoes, cut
   in ½-inch slices
  Salt and black pepper
  Flour
  Buttered Toast Points (see page 185)
  Grated Cheddar cheese

Directions: Heat butter in a large skillet. Season the tomato slices to taste with salt and pepper, then dredge each slice in flour, shaking off any excess. Fry in the hot butter until light brown on both sides, turning once. Cut toast slices into rounds. Drain the tomatoes briefly on paper towels and arrange one slice on each toast round. Top each with grated cheese, slide under the broiler for 2 minutes and serve immediately.

FRIED TOMATOES WITH EGG-CREAM SAUCE
YIELD: ENOUGH TO SERVE 6

9 Medium-size ripe tomatoes
  Salt and black pepper
  Flour
6 Tablespoons butter
1 Cup heavy cream

1½ Teaspoons chopped fresh mint
    or ½ teaspoon dried
½ Teaspoon salt
⅛ Teaspoon granulated sugar
    Pinch grated nutmeg
2 Egg yolks

Directions: Slice the tops and bottoms from the tomatoes and cut in half, crosswise. Sprinkle each half with salt and pepper and dredge in flour, then sauté in 4 tablespoons butter to a golden brown, turning once.

Melt the remaining butter in a large saucepan over low heat. Blend in the cream, mint, salt, sugar and nutmeg. Allow the mixture to simmer for 8 to 10 minutes. Beat the egg yolks lightly and slowly add to the cream sauce, stirring constantly. Allow the mixture to heat briefly, but do not let it boil. To serve, arrange the fried tomatoes on serving plates and spoon the egg sauce over.

SAUTÉED CHERRY TOMATOES
YIELD: ENOUGH TO SERVE 6

Cherry tomatoes, when served as a vegetable, need not be peeled. However, when the tomatoes are to be included in any recipe with a subtle blend of flavors, they really should be.

2 Tablespoons butter
48 Cherry tomatoes

Directions: Heat butter in a wide skillet and sauté the tomatoes over low heat for 2 minutes, shaking the pan gently so tomatoes warm evenly. Serve as soon as they are heated through.

GARLIC CHERRY TOMATOES
YIELD: ENOUGH TO SERVE 6

2 Tablespoons butter
½ Clove garlic, peeled and crushed
24 Cherry tomatoes, peeled
    Salt and black pepper

Directions: Melt butter and sauté garlic over low heat for 2 minutes. Add tomatoes and sauté for 2 minutes more, shaking the pan gently until tomatoes are heated through.

Season to taste with salt and pepper.
Serve immediately.

BAKED TOMATOES
YIELD: ENOUGH TO SERVE 6

6 Ripe, firm tomatoes
4 Tablespoons bread crumbs
4 Tablespoons minced fresh chervil,
    parsley, thyme, dill or marjoram or
    a combination of these
  Salt and black pepper
  Granulated sugar
2 Tablespoons butter

Directions: Preheat oven to 450 degrees F.

Cut tomatoes in half crosswise and arrange them in a well-buttered baking dish. Sprinkle each half with 1 teaspoon each bread crumbs and herbs, salt, pepper and a pinch of sugar.

Dot with butter and bake until tops are lightly browned.

POTATO KEPHTIDES WITH CHEESE
YIELD: ENOUGH TO SERVE 6

These fried potato cakes have several secret ingredients—all delectable.

---

4 Cups cold mashed potatoes
3 Medium-size firm, ripe tomatoes, peeled, seeded and finely chopped
2 Scallions, with 3 inches green top, minced
2 Tablespoons butter, melted
8 Tablespoons flour
  Salt and black pepper
¼ Cup grated cheese
  Vegetable oil

Directions: Purée potatoes and thoroughly mix with tomatoes, scallions and butter. Add as much of the flour as needed to make a soft dough that is not too sticky. Season the mixture to taste with salt and pepper, then knead a bit with your fingers and roll out to ¾-inch thickness. Cut into 3-inch rounds, slit open one side and insert 1 teaspoon grated cheese in the center of each round. Fry to a golden brown on both sides in very hot oil, turning once. Drain briefly on paper towels. Serve steaming hot.

SAUERKRAUT IN TOMATO SAUCE WITH RAISINS
YIELD: ENOUGH TO SERVE 6

This combination may seem too mismatched to be tasty, but actually it is one of the most piquant side dishes to go with duck or pork.

---

3 Strips country-cured bacon, chopped
1 Large onion, peeled and chopped
2 Tablespoons flour
2 Cups tomato purée
¼ Cup light brown sugar
1 Quart sauerkraut, drained
2 Tablespoons dark raisins

Directions: Fry bacon for 2 minutes, stirring to separate pieces.

Add onion and sauté for 3 to 4 minutes, or until it is soft and transparent. Blend in flour until well incorporated with the fat. Mix tomato purée in well, then bring to a boil, stirring constantly. Add sugar, sauerkraut and raisins and simmer for 15 minutes.

What is a salad without tomatoes? Add beautiful red slices, wedges or bits of tomato to the most lifeless salad and suddenly it's a whole new salad bowl. From the traditional to the exotic, the tomato is definitely the salad bowl's best friend.

SALADE ESPAGNOLE
YIELD: ENOUGH TO SERVE 6

1 Small head Boston lettuce
6 Medium-size ripe tomatoes, thinly sliced
1 Large sweet onion, peeled and very thinly sliced
1 Medium-size cucumber, peeled and thinly sliced
2 Large green peppers, blanched in boiling
    water for 2 minutes, then seeded and sliced
1 Small can whole pimientos, drained and sliced
1½ Cups bread crumbs
¼ Cup olive oil
1 Clove garlic, peeled and minced
    Tomato–Tabasco Salad Dressing (see page 130)

Directions: Separate lettuce leaves, wash well and pat dry. In a large salad bowl, arrange lettuce and tomato, onion and cucumber slices in overlapping layers. Combine pepper and pimiento slices and mound in center of vegetables. Chill for 1 hour. Sauté bread crumbs in oil and garlic until crumbs are golden. Pour dressing over salad and sprinkle bread crumbs in a wide ring around mound of peppers and pimientos. Serve at once.

GREEK SALAD
YIELD: ENOUGH TO SERVE 6

1 Large head Bibb or Boston lettuce
½ Clove garlic, peeled
5 Medium-size ripe tomatoes, cut into eighths
2 Green peppers, seeded and cut into
    very thin rings
1 Medium-size cucumber, peeled and thinly sliced
6 Radishes, trimmed and thinly sliced
1 Cup Greek olives
6 Scallions, with 3 inches green tip, minced
½ Pound Feta cheese, crumbled
½ Cup olive oil
⅓ Cup lemon juice
½ Teaspoon salt
¼ Teaspoon each black pepper and oregano
2 Tablespoons each minced fresh basil
    and parsley

Directions: Wash lettuce well in ice water, dry thoroughly with paper towels and tear into bite-size pieces. Rub a large wooden salad bowl with cut side of garlic clove. Arrange tomatoes, peppers, cucumbers, radishes, olives, scallions and cheese attractively in bowl in the order listed. Chill.

Combine oil, lemon juice, salt, pepper and oregano in a jar, seal tightly and shake well. Pour dressing over salad, garnish with fresh herbs and serve at once.

BASIC STUFFED TOMATO RECIPE
YIELD: ENOUGH TO SERVE 6

6 Large firm, ripe tomatoes, peeled
3 Tablespoons each olive oil and tarragon vinegar
2 Cloves garlic, peeled and crushed

Directions: Cut ½ inch from tops of tomatoes. Carefully hollow out and save pulp for another use. Mix olive oil, vinegar and garlic, spoon this over the tomato shells and marinate for 20 minutes. Drain tomatoes and fill.

STUFFED TOMATOES WITH CHICKEN SALAD

Ingredients listed in Basic Recipe plus:
2 Cups diced cooked chicken
3 Hard-cooked eggs, coarsely chopped
1 Tablespoon chopped fresh chives
2 Teaspoons finely chopped capers
  Salt and black pepper
¾ Cup Mayonnaise (see page 187)

Directions: Prepare and marinate tomatoes following instructions given in Basic Recipe.

Combine chicken, eggs, chives and capers, season with salt and pepper to taste and mix with as much mayonnaise as necessary to bind the mixture. Spoon into tomato shells, chill and serve.

STUFFED TOMATOES WITH THREE-BEAN SALAD

Ingredients listed in Basic Recipe plus:
1 Cup cooked and drained red kidney beans
1 Cup cooked and drained chick peas
1 Cup cooked green beans
½ Sweet red onion, peeled and finely chopped
3 Hard-cooked eggs, coarsely chopped
  French Dressing II (see page 189)

Directions: Drain vegetables well and combine with onion and eggs. Mix with as much dressing as necessary to bind mixture. Refrigerate for at least 1 hour. Meanwhile, prepare and marinate tomatoes following instructions given in Basic Recipe. Spoon bean salad into tomato shells and serve.

CONFETTI COTTAGE CHEESE TOMATOES WITH AVOCADO SLICES
YIELD: ENOUGH TO SERVE 6

6 Large firm, ripe tomatoes
  Salt
3 Cups cottage cheese
3 Scallions, with 3 inches green top, minced
½ Cup Mayonnaise (see page 187)
1½ Tablespoons lemon juice
  Black pepper
2 Small avocados
1 Medium-size head Bibb lettuce
  French Dressing I or II (see page 189)

Directions: Cut ½-inch slice from stem ends of tomatoes, scoop out and reserve pulp, then sprinkle shells with salt to taste and drain in the refrigerator, cut side down, for 30 minutes. Remove seeds from pulp and drain pulp well. Combine cottage cheese with chopped, drained tomato pulp, scallions, mayonnaise, 1 tablespoon of the lemon juice and salt and pepper to taste. Mix well. Cover and chill for 30 minutes.

To serve, cut avocados in half lengthwise, peel, pit and cut into slices. Sprinkle with remaining lemon juice. Wash and dry lettuce well and arrange whole leaves on individual salad plates. Spoon cottage cheese mixture into hollow tomato shells and set on lettuce. Surround each filled tomato with a spiral of avocado slices. Serve immediately, with dressing in a side dish.

TOMATOES AND SWEET ONIONS WITH ROQUEFORT DRESSING
YIELD: ENOUGH TO SERVE 6

6 Medium-size firm, ripe tomatoes,
　　thinly sliced
1 Large sweet onion, peeled and very thinly sliced
⅓ Cup crumbled Roquefort cheese, at
　　room temperature
½ Cup French Dressing I (see page 189)
　　or Vinaigrette Dressing (see page 189)
3 Scallions, with 3 inches green
　　top, minced
1 Tablespoon minced fresh oregano

Directions: Arrange tomatoes on serving plates. Top each portion with onion slices, then refrigerate until thoroughly chilled. Mash cheese with a fork and combine with remaining ingredients. Pour over salad just before serving.

RIPE TOMATO AND SWEET ONION SALAD
YIELD: ENOUGH TO SERVE 8

8 to 10 Large, ripe tomatoes, peeled and sliced
2 Large sweet onions, peeled and sliced
1½ Cups your favorite dressing
　　(see pages 128 to 130)

Directions: Arrange tomatoes and onions in alternate layers on 8 salad plates. Serve with your favorite dressing.

TOMATO AND GREEN PEPPER SALAD WITH MUSTARD DRESSING
YIELD: ENOUGH TO SERVE 6

6 Medium-size firm, ripe tomatoes,
　　peeled and sliced
4 Medium-size green peppers, seeded
　　and sliced into thin rings
2 Tablespoons grated onion
4 Teaspoons Dijon mustard
¼ Teaspoon each salt, black pepper and ground thyme
¼ Cup cider vinegar
½ Cup olive oil
¼ Cup minced fresh parsley

Directions: Arrange tomatoes and peppers on a serving platter and refrigerate until well chilled. Stir onions, mustard and seasonings into the vinegar, then beat in the olive oil, 1 tablespoon at a time, until all is incorporated. Pour dressing over tomatoes and let stand 10 minutes before serving cold, sprinkled with parsley.

TOMATOES AND CUCUMBERS VINAIGRETTE
YIELD: ENOUGH TO SERVE 6

2 Medium-size cucumbers, peeled
Salt
6 to 8 Large ripe tomatoes
3 Scallions, with 3 inches green top, minced
Vinaigrette Dressing (see page 189)

Directions: Slice cucumbers *very* thinly and place in a shallow bowl. Sprinkle with salt, weight with a heavy plate and refrigerate for 1 hour. Drain. Slice tomatoes thinly and arrange attractively over the bottom of a large, shallow serving dish. Cover with a layer of cucumbers. Garnish with minced scallions. Sprinkle vegetables with dressing. Chill thoroughly before serving cold.

FRESH MUSHROOM AND TOMATO SALAD
YIELD: ENOUGH TO SERVE 6

6 to 8 Large ripe tomatoes, sliced
2 Tablespoons olive oil
1 Teaspoon each fresh sage and marjoram
1 Lemon
12 Large fresh mushrooms, thinly sliced
Black pepper

Directions: Arrange tomatoes attractively on a serving dish. Sprinkle with half the oil and herbs and about 1 tablespoon lemon juice. Arrange mushroom slices on tomatoes and sprinkle with remaining ingredients.

TOMATOES ANNA
YIELD: ENOUGH TO SERVE 6

5 Large, firm tomatoes, thinly sliced
9 Hard-cooked eggs, sliced
¾ Cup Mayonnaise (see page 187)
1 Tablespoon each minced fresh basil and chives

Directions: Arrange tomato slices attractively on a large serving platter. Chill well and pour off any accumulated juice. Top with a layer of sliced eggs. Spread with mayonnaise as you would ice a cake. Garnish with basil and chives. Serve cold.

SLICED TOMATOES WITH PEPPER AND OIL
YIELD: ENOUGH TO SERVE 6

6 Medium-size firm, ripe tomatoes, peeled
2 Large cloves garlic, peeled
¼ Cup olive oil
2 Teaspoons whole peppercorns

Directions: Cut tomatoes into thin slices and arrange in overlapping layers on a serving platter. Crush the garlic and add to the oil. Crush peppercorns with a mortar and pestle. Sprinkle tomatoes with oil and pepper, chill thoroughly and serve cold.

MARINATED TOMATO-ZUCCHINI SALAD
YIELD: ENOUGH TO SERVE 6

6 Small zucchini (about 1½ inches
    in diameter)
4 Medium-size ripe tomatoes
1 Green pepper, seeded
6 Scallions, with 3 inches green top
    French Dressing II (see page 189)

Directions: Wash zucchini well but do not peel. Cut into paper-thin slices. Cut tomatoes into ½-inch wedges and the green pepper into very thin rings. Chop scallions. Toss all ingredients in dressing and marinate in refrigerator for 1 hour.

MUSHROOM AND TOMATO SALAD
YIELD: ENOUGH TO SERVE 6

½ Pound mushrooms
6 Large leaves Romaine
4 to 6 Medium-size firm, ripe tomatoes,
    thinly sliced
2 Green peppers, seeded and cut into
    thin rings
4 Scallions, with 3 inches green top, minced
    French Dressing II (see page 189)

Directions: Wipe mushrooms with a damp cloth to remove any sand; fresh, white mushrooms do not need peeling. Slice mushrooms thinly. Wash and dry Romaine thoroughly, then tear into bite-size pieces and place in large salad bowl. Top with layers of tomatoes, mushrooms and peppers. Garnish with scallions. Chill well before serving lightly tossed with dressing.

MARINATED MIXED VEGETABLE SALAD
YIELD: ENOUGH TO SERVE 6

2 Medium-size green peppers, seeded
1 Tablespoon butter
1 Small head cauliflower, trimmed and
    cooked (or 2½ cups leftover)
1 Pound fresh beets, cooked, peeled
    and sliced
3 Medium-size firm, ripe tomatoes,
    thinly sliced
    French Dressing I or II (see page 189)
2 Tablespoons minced fresh tarragon

Directions: Boil green peppers in salted water for 3 minutes, then cut into 1-inch strips and sauté for 1 minute in 1 tablespoon butter. Remove from heat. Drain cauliflower.

In a large salad bowl, arrange layers of beets, tomatoes, cauliflower and peppers. Pour dressing over salad and garnish with tarragon. Marinate for 1 hour at room temperature. Serve without chilling.

SUMMER FESTIVAL SALAD
YIELD: ENOUGH TO SERVE 6

1 Head lettuce
2 Small zucchini, thinly sliced
2 Small cucumbers, peeled and thinly sliced
4 Small carrots, scraped and thinly sliced
8 Radishes, thinly sliced
6 Scallions, with 3 inches green top, chopped
8 Tomatoes, sliced and marinated in Vinaigrette Dressing
10 Sprigs fresh parsley
6 Hard-cooked eggs, quartered
    Vinaigrette Dressing (see page 189)

Directions: Wash and dry lettuce leaves and tear into pieces. Arrange leaves in salad bowl, then add zucchini, cucumbers, carrots, radishes and scallions. Arrange tomato slices, parsley and quartered eggs attractively on top and refrigerate until very cold. Toss salad with dressing at table.

SUMMER VEGETABLE MEDLEY
YIELD: ENOUGH TO SERVE 6

4 Medium-size ripe tomatoes, quartered
1 Green pepper, seeded and cut into ¼-inch strips
1 Sweet red pepper, seeded and cut into ¼-inch strips
12 Scallions, with 3 inches green top, split lengthwise
1 Small yellow summer squash, cut into ¼-inch slices
1 Small zucchini, cut into ¼-inch slices
2 Cups well-washed lettuce leaves
1 Medium-size cucumber, peeled and sliced
3 Small carrots, scraped and cut into thin strips
12 Radishes
    Niçoise Sauce (see page 129)

Directions: Arrange tomatoes, peppers, scallions, squash and zucchini attractively on lettuce leaves placed in bottom of a large salad bowl. Garnish with cucumber and carrots. Remove the root end from each radish and make thin, petal-shaped cuts around the radishes to create a rose effect. Set these around the edge of the salad. Chill well and serve with sauce in a dish on the side.

CHEF'S SALAD
YIELD: ENOUGH TO SERVE 6

6 Cups shredded salad greens
2 Cups cooked chicken, cut into thin strips
2 Cups smoked tongue, cut into ¼-inch-thick strips
2 Cups cooked ham, cut into ¼-inch-thick strips
2 Cups Swiss cheese, cut into ¼-inch- thick strips
3 Medium-size firm, ripe tomatoes, peeled
    and thinly shredded
2 Green peppers, seeded and shredded
12 Cherry tomatoes
½ Cup French Dressing I or II (see page 189)

Directions: Arrange greens over the bottom of a large salad bowl. Set meats and cheese in stacks like the spokes of a wheel over the greens, tucking shredded tomatoes and peppers in between. Garnish center of bowl with cherry tomatoes. Chill well. Serve with dressing on side.

SUPPER-IN-A-BOWL SALAD
YIELD: ENOUGH TO SERVE 6

3 Slices Italian bread, cut into ½-inch cubes
1½ Tablespoons butter, melted
1 Large garlic clove, peeled and crushed
6 Hard-cooked eggs
1½ Cups minced cold cooked chicken, ham or beef
1 Quart well-washed spinach leaves
4 Medium-size firm, ripe tomatoes, thinly sliced
½ Cup olive oil
¼ Cup wine vinegar
1 Teaspoon each salt and black pepper

Directions: Dry out bread cubes in a warm oven. Place in large salad bowl. Mix together butter and garlic, pour over bread cubes and toss well. Force eggs through a fine sieve, mix with bread cubes and meat and toss mixture well. Arrange spinach in a salad bowl, top with layers of sliced tomatoes and the bread-meat mixture. Combine oil, vinegar and seasonings in a screwtop jar, cover and shake well, then pour over salad. Toss and serve immediately.

COLESLAW IN TOMATO SHELLS
YIELD: ENOUGH TO SERVE 6

1 Small head cabbage
¾ Cup Mayonnaise (see page 187)
1 Teaspoon prepared mustard
3 Tablespoons milk or cream
2 Tablespoons lemon juice
2 Tablespoons granulated sugar
¾ Teaspoon poppy seeds
½ Teaspoon salt
6 Good-size ripe tomatoes

Directions: Strip the tough outer leaves from the cabbage and core it, then cut into quarters and rinse. Drain thoroughly and shred or chop into very fine pieces. Mix together the mayonnaise, mustard, milk, lemon juice, sugar, poppy seeds and salt. Pour the dressing over the cabbage and toss well. Refrigerate for at least 3 hours. To serve, hollow out and drain the tomatoes, reserving the pulp for another use. Pack coleslaw into the shells. Serve cold.

TOMATOES WITH CHICKEN SALAD SAUCE ROSY
YIELD: ENOUGH TO SERVE 6

6 Large firm, ripe tomatoes
 Salt and black pepper
3 Cups diced cooked chicken
2 Hard-cooked eggs, coarsely chopped
3 Scallions, with 3 inches top, minced
6 Flat anchovy fillets, chopped
1 Cup Rosy Tomato-Cream Sauce (see page 128)

Directions: Cut ½-inch slice from stem end of each tomato. Scoop out pulp and season tomato shells to taste with salt and pepper. Drain tomatoes on rack, cut side down, for 30 minutes. Combine chicken, hard-cooked eggs, scallions and anchovies with as much sauce as necessary to bind mixture. Spoon into tomato shells. Top each stuffed tomato with a dollop of sauce before serving cold.

FRESH HERB TOMATO SALAD WITH CHICKEN BREAST
YIELD: ENOUGH TO SERVE 6 TO 8

2 Heads Bibb lettuce
6 Tablespoons olive oil
2 Tablespoons tarragon vinegar
1 Teaspoon granulated sugar
½ Teaspoon salt
2 Cloves garlic, peeled and crushed
6 Large ripe tomatoes, peeled
1 Pound cooked breast of chicken, skinned,
    boned and cut into julienne strips
¼ Cup each minced fresh chives, dill,
    basil and parsley

Directions: Pull whole leaves from lettuce and crisp in ice water for a few minutes. Pat dry with paper towels and chill well.

Shake oil, vinegar, sugar, salt and garlic vigorously in a screwtop jar. Slice tomatoes into a shallow bowl, cover with dressing and refrigerate for ½ hour.

Just before serving, tear lettuce leaves into bite-size pieces and place in a large salad bowl. Carefully transfer tomato slices and arrange on lettuce pieces. Arrange chicken on tomatoes and sprinkle with herbs. Toss and serve immediately.

SALADE À LA RUSSE
YIELD: ENOUGH TO SERVE 6

6 Medium-size firm, ripe tomatoes
    Salt and black pepper
2 Medium-size potatoes, cooked, peeled and diced
1 Large McIntosh apple, peeled, cored and diced
½ Cup cooked, diced carrots
½ Cup cooked, diced beets
2 Tablespoons minced scallions
2 Small dill pickles, finely chopped
1 Cup Mayonnaise (see page 187)
    Dill sprigs

Directions: Cut ½-inch slice from stem end of each tomato. Scoop out pulp and season tomato shells to taste with salt and pepper, then drain tomatoes, cut side down, on a rack for 30 minutes. Combine ingredients with as much mayonnaise as necessary to bind mixture. Season to taste with salt and pepper and spoon into tomato shells. Chill well before serving cold garnished with dill sprigs.

ASPARAGUS SAUCE ROSY
YIELD: ENOUGH TO SERVE 6

2 Pounds asparagus, cooked and marinated overnight in
    Vinaigrette Dressing (see page 189)
5 Hard-cooked eggs, sliced
2 Cups Rosy Tomato-Cream Sauce (see page 128)
2 Tablespoons whole capers, drained

Directions: Drain asparagus spears and arrange on salad plates, with sliced eggs set attractively alongside. Top with sauce and garnish each serving with 1 teaspoon capers. Serve cold.

CUBED AVOCADO AND TOMATO SALAD
YIELD: ENOUGH TO SERVE 6

---

4 Medium-size firm, ripe tomatoes, peeled
    and cut into cubes
3 Ripe avocados, peeled, seeded and
    cut into cubes
10 Scallions, with 3 inches green top,
    minced
¼ Cup wine vinegar
1½ Tablespoons salad oil
    Salt and black pepper

Directions: Combine vegetables, add vinegar, oil, salt and pepper to taste and toss lightly until well mixed.

SOUTH-SHORE TOMATO ASPIC
YIELD: ENOUGH TO SERVE 8 TO 10

---

1 Quart tomato juice
½ Cup finely chopped celery leaves
2 Tablespoons finely chopped onion
1 Tablespoon granulated sugar
¾ Teaspoon salt
4 Whole cloves
6 Whole peppercorns
1 Small bay leaf
3 Tablespoons each gelatin, lemon juice
    and sour cream
1 Cup cooked flaked fish
3 Tablespoons minced fresh dill

Directions: In a large saucepan, mix together 3 cups tomato juice, celery leaves, onion, sugar and spices. Allow mixture to simmer, covered, for 15 minutes. Strain into large bowl. Combine gelatin with remaining cup tomato juice, let stand 5 minutes to soften, then dissolve in hot tomato mixture. Add lemon juice and sour cream and stir in thoroughly. Refrigerate until the aspic begins to set, then fold in fish and dill. Rinse 1½-quart mold with cold water and pour in aspic. Refrigerate until thoroughly set. Unmold on a chilled platter. Serve with crackers or toast points.

TOMATO ASPIC WITH CUCUMBER
YIELD: ENOUGH TO SERVE 6

---

2 Cups tomato juice
1 Cup white wine vinegar
4 Large cucumbers, peeled and
    thinly sliced
2 Envelopes unflavored gelatin
1 Tablespoon onion juice
    Salt, black pepper and cayenne

Directions: Place 1 cup tomato juice in a saucepan with vinegar, add cucumber slices and bring to a boil. Lower heat and simmer until cucumber is tender. Set a fine sieve over a bowl and purée cucumbers through with the back of a spoon. Dissolve gelatin in remaining cup of tomato juice, add to puréed cucumber and stir in onion juice, salt, pepper and cayenne to taste. Pour the mixture into a saucepan and stir over very low heat for 3 to 4 minutes. Oil a ring mold and fill with the aspic mixture. Chill until set. To serve, unmold on a serving plate and heap meat, vegetable or egg salad into the center. Decorate with peaks of mayonnaise forced through a pastry tube.

Here, perhaps more than anywhere else, is where the tomato proves its all-around usefulness. Tomato purée (see page 203)—and its products, the tomato sauces—has an entire cult of worshippers. Just fold a sauce around a pasta and before you know it your table will be surrounded by hungry guests crying "Mangia!"

Those other favorites, barbecue and hamburger sauces, are crowd-pleasers, too. Use small, slightly bruised or imperfect tomatoes in these and no one will be the wiser.

GOOD 'N EASY SPAGHETTI SAUCE
YIELD: ENOUGH TO SERVE 6

1½ Pounds ground round steak
 2 Medium-size onions, peeled and chopped
 1 Large clove garlic, peeled and minced
½ Cup grated carrot
 1 Tablespoon olive oil
 3 Cups tomato sauce
⅓ Pound mushrooms, thinly sliced
 1 Cup Basic Beef Stock (see page 191)
1½ Teaspoons fresh thyme leaves
 2 Teaspoons each fresh basil and oregano

Directions: Brown meat, onions, garlic and carrot in oil until meat is lightly browned. Add tomato sauce, mushrooms, stock and seasonings, then simmer, uncovered, over low heat for 20 to 30 minutes. Serve hot over well-drained spaghetti.

ITALIAN-STYLE TOMATO SAUCE
YIELD: ABOUT 5 CUPS

 1 Tablespoon butter
 3 Tablespoons olive oil
 1 Cup coarsely chopped onions
 1 Cup coarsely chopped carrots
 1 Cup coarsely chopped leeks
 3 Cloves garlic, peeled
½ Cup chopped celery
 4 Tablespoons chopped fresh parsley
 6 Tablespoons tomato paste
 3 Tablespoons flour
 4 Cups Basic Beef Stock (see page 191)
 2 Cups water
 1 Tablespoon each minced fresh oregano,
    tarragon and thyme leaves
½ Teaspoon whole peppercorns, crushed
 1 Teaspoon each salt and granulated sugar
 4 Medium-size ripe tomatoes

Directions: In a large, heavy kettle, melt the butter and add 2 tablespoons oil. As soon as the mixture bubbles, stir in the onions, carrots and leeks and sauté for 5 minutes. Crush the garlic cloves and add to the vegetables, along with the celery and parsley. Sauté for 2 minutes, then blend in tomato paste and flour. Add stock and bring to a boil, stirring occasionally. Stir in water, seasonings and sugar and bring to boil once again, then lower heat and allow to simmer gently, uncovered, for 45 minutes.

Meanwhile, heat remaining tablespoon oil in a separate skillet. Peel, core and seed tomatoes. Chop tomato pulp and sauté in oil until most of the liquid evaporates. Strain tomato sauce, add chopped tomato pulp and bring to a boil. Remove from heat and serve hot.

MEAT SAUCE FLORENTINE
YIELD: ENOUGH TO SERVE 6

1 Medium-size carrot, scraped and
    finely chopped
1 Medium-size onion, peeled and
    finely chopped
2 Teaspoons minced fresh parsley
3 Tablespoons olive oil
2 Pounds ground round steak
    Flour
1 Cup red wine
4 Medium-size ripe tomatoes, peeled,
    seeded and coarsely chopped
2 Cups Basic Beef Stock (see page 191)
    or water
1 Cup chopped fresh mushrooms
    Salt and black pepper

Directions: In a large, heavy saucepan, sauté carrots, onions and parsley in oil until lightly browned. Dust meat lightly with flour, add to pan and cook until lightly browned. Stir frequently and break up any large pieces of meat with a fork. Stir in wine, cook until most of liquid evaporates, then add remaining ingredients. Season to taste with salt and pepper and cook sauce over low heat for 1½ hours, or until quite thick. Serve with pasta (see page 186).

TOMATO SAUCE PROVENÇAL
YIELD: ABOUT 4 CUPS

Dry white wine and a generous addition of fennel seeds make this sauce especially delicious.

1 Large onion, peeled and minced
1 Cup chopped leeks
3 Tablespoons olive oil
16 Medium-size ripe tomatoes, chopped
3 Cloves garlic, peeled and chopped
2 Cups dry white wine
3 Cups Basic Chicken Stock (see page 192)
1 Teaspoon Tabasco sauce
1 Tablespoon fennel seeds
2 Teaspoons each minced fresh basil, oregano,
    thyme leaves and orange zest (the thin outer
    skin of the fruit with none of the bitter white
    underskin included)
    Generous pinch saffron
    Salt and black pepper

Directions: In a large, heavy skillet, sauté onion and leeks in olive oil until vegetables are softened but not browned. Add tomatoes and garlic, cover and simmer for 5 minutes. Remove the cover and boil, stirring occasionally, for 5 minutes more. Purée the vegetables and return them to the pan. Add wine, stock and seasonings and simmer, uncovered, for 45 minutes to 1 hour, or until sauce is nicely thickened.

TOMATO CATSUP

YIELD: 4 8-OUNCE JARS

This superb homemade catsup is darker in color (a deep, rich red) and more piquant than the commercial variety. It's much more like a steak sauce than everyday catsup.

10 Pounds (about 15 large) ripe tomatoes,
    peeled and seeded (you may include slightly
    imperfect specimens, but cut away all
    bad spots, please)
2 Sweet red peppers, seeded
2 Large onions, peeled
2 Cups granulated sugar (more if desired)
1 Teaspoon each paprika, salt and
    ground allspice
2 Teaspoons ground cinnamon
¼ Teaspoon ground cloves
½ Teaspoon each celery salt and dry mustard
½ Cup lemon juice

Directions: Remove stem ends from tomatoes, cut peppers and onions into quarters and put them through the fine blade of your grinder. Simmer the mixture in a large, heavy stainless steel kettle for 40 to 50 minutes, or until the bits of vegetable are quite soft.

Rub cooked vegetables through a strainer (whirling first in a blender or Cuisinart will make this easier). Do not give up too quickly on this process; every bit of strained pulp means more flavor and substance for your catsup. Ideally, only tomato seeds should be discarded.

Add all remaining ingredients except lemon juice. Mix well and cook over medium heat, stirring every 5 or 10 minutes, for 1½ hours. Stir in lemon juice and taste the catsup; add more sugar if you prefer a sweeter sauce.

Cook over medium-low heat, stirring every 5 minutes, until catsup is quite thick (about 1 hour longer). When the sauce begins to reach the consistency of the commercial variety, stir it more frequently. The catsup is ready to bottle when no liquid fills in the empty space if a spoon is drawn across the bottom of the pot.

Spoon the hot catsup into sterilized jars and top with commercial caps or paraffin. Use a funnel to avoid spilling. Seal and process in a boiling waterbath for 10 minutes according to directions on page 211.

BARBECUE SAUCE

YIELD: 2 CUPS

4 Tablespoons butter
2 Medium-size tomatoes, peeled, seeded and
    coarsely chopped
1 Medium-size onion, peeled and finely chopped
1 Medium-size green pepper, seeded and
    finely chopped
½ Cup tomato catsup
½ Cup brown sugar
2 Tablespoons Worcestershire sauce
2 Teaspoons lemon juice
¼ Cup mild yellow mustard
1 Teaspoon salt

Directions: Melt the butter in a saucepan. Add the remaining ingredients and cook over medium heat for 5 minutes, stirring frequently. Serve hot or cold over hamburgers.

TOMATO SAUCE POMIDORO
YIELD: 3 CUPS

4 Tablespoons each butter and olive oil
1 Medium-size onion, peeled and minced
1 Medium-size carrot, scraped and very
    finely chopped
1 Rib celery, minced
1 Clove garlic, peeled and minced
1 Tablespoon minced fresh basil
4 Pounds plum tomatoes, peeled, seeded
    and coarsely chopped
½ Teaspoon granulated sugar
    Salt and black pepper

Directions: Heat butter and oil together in a large, heavy kettle and sauté onions, carrots, celery, garlic and basil over low heat until soft. Add tomatoes and bring to a boil. Add sugar and salt and pepper to taste, then turn heat *very* low and simmer, covered, for 2 to 3 hours, stirring occasionally to keep sauce from sticking. The sauce should be fairly thick.

SALSA PIQUANTE
YIELD: ABOUT 3½ CUPS

6 Tomatoes, peeled and chopped
2 Medium-size sweet onions, peeled
    and chopped
2 Small chili peppers, finely chopped
¼ Teaspoon salt
¼ Cup vinegar

Directions: Place tomatoes, onions and chili peppers in a bowl. Sprinkle with salt and cover with vinegar.

FIRECRACKER SAUCE
YIELD: 4 PINTS

Only the courageous should tangle with this unusually fiery sauce.

12 Large ripe tomatoes, chopped
20 Long hot red peppers, seeded*
    and chopped
1 Quart vinegar
1½ Cups granulated sugar
1 Tablespoon salt
2 Tablespoons pickling spice, tied
    in cheesecloth

Directions: Boil tomatoes, peppers and vinegar in stainless steel saucepan until vegetables are soft. Strain and return to pan. Add remaining ingredients and boil until thick.

Discard spice bag. Pour immediately into hot, sterile jars and process in boiling waterbath for 5 minutes as directed on page 211.

*Wear rubber gloves to protect hands when seeding peppers.

QUICK AND EASY CHILI SAUCE
YIELD: ABOUT 4 PINTS

2 Quarts canned tomatoes
2 Large onions, peeled and chopped
1 Sweet red or green pepper, seeded
    and chopped
¾ Cup granulated sugar
1 Clove garlic, peeled and minced
½ Teaspoon salt
1 Teaspoon each mustard and celery seed
2 Teaspoons whole cloves, tied in cheesecloth
1 Cup vinegar

Directions: Boil tomatoes, onions, pepper and sugar in a large stainless steel pan until most of the liquid has evaporated. Add spices and vinegar and boil again until sauce is thick. Discard spice bag and pour the boiling hot sauce into hot, sterile jars. Seal immediately and process for 5 minutes in boiling waterbath as directed on page 211.

CHILI SAUCE
YIELD: 4 TO 5 PINTS

24 Large ripe tomatoes, peeled
 2 Large onions, peeled
 3 Large sweet red peppers, seeded
 2 Cloves garlic, peeled
 1 Hot red pepper
 2 Teaspoons each whole cloves and allspice
2½ Teaspoons ground cinnamon
 3 Cups vinegar
1½ Cups light brown sugar
 2 Tablespoons salt

Directions: Finely chop vegetables and boil with the spices in a large stainless steel pan until vegetable mixture is reduced by half. Stir constantly to keep from sticking. Add vinegar, sugar and salt and boil 5 to 10 minutes, or until fairly thick, stirring constantly. Seal in hot, sterile jars. Process 5 minutes in boiling waterbath according to directions given on page 211.

POWWOW SAUCE
YIELD: ABOUT 4 PINTS

Very zesty!

12 Large ripe tomatoes, peeled
12 Winesap apples, cored
 8 Large onions, peeled
 3 Green peppers, seeded
 1 Quart vinegar
3½ Cups light brown sugar
 2 Teaspoons salt
 1 Teaspoon each ginger and cinnamon

Directions: Put tomatoes, apples, onions and peppers through the coarse blade of your grinder. Combine all ingredients and simmer 1 hour. Ladle immediately into hot, sterile jars and process for 5 minutes in boiling waterbath as directed on page 211.

BEERY TOMATO GRAVY
YIELD: ENOUGH TO SERVE 6

Beer and tomatoes may not seem a perfect combination, but when they are combined with brown sugar, dry mustard and consommé the result is a gravy that is rich, piquant and unusually tasty.

8 Medium-size ripe tomatoes, peeled
¾ Cup all-purpose flour
2 Tablespoons each butter and vegetable oil
¼ Cup tightly packed dark brown sugar
½ Teaspoon dry mustard
½ Cup beer
½ Cup Basic Beef Consommé (see page 192)
  Salt and black pepper
  Mashed potatoes, Toast Points (see page 185)
    or Fried Toasts (see page 185)

Directions: Discard tops and slice tomatoes into thick slices. Dredge thoroughly in flour and fry in hot butter and oil until brown on one side. Sprinkle with sugar and dry mustard, then turn the slices and fry until brown on the other side. Pour in the beer and consommé and stir until the gravy thickens. Break up any large pieces of tomato, season with salt and pepper to taste and serve hot over mashed potatoes, toast points or fried toasts.

TOMATO FONDUE DIP
YIELD: 1½ CUPS

Use this sauce as an interesting change of pace when serving Fondue Bourguignonne.

8 Medium-size ripe tomatoes, peeled, seeded and chopped
½ Teaspoon granulated sugar

4 Tablespoons butter
  Salt and black pepper

Directions: In a stainless steel skillet, cook tomatoes and sugar in the butter, stirring frequently, until mixture is reduced to a smooth purée. Season to taste with salt and pepper before serving.

TOMATO-CREAM SAUCE
YIELD: ABOUT 2 CUPS

6 Medium-size ripe tomatoes, peeled, seeded and sliced
3 Tablespoons butter
  Pinch each ground nutmeg and thyme
1 Cup heavy cream

Directions: Sauté tomatoes in butter until soft. Sprinkle with nutmeg and thyme and stir in cream. Simmer over low heat until slightly thickened. Serve hot.

ROSY TOMATO-CREAM SAUCE
YIELD: ABOUT 2½ CUPS

It is rare to find a sauce as fresh-tasting and as adaptable as this one. Use it chilled to dress up almost any cold meat, fish or egg dish or hot to enhance the most simple entrée.

⅓ Cup chilled heavy cream
8 Ounces chilled cream cheese
2 Large cloves garlic, peeled and minced
¾ Cup tomato purée
2 Tablespoons minced fresh basil
8 Drops Tabasco (or more to taste)
  Salt

Directions: Use the back of a spoon or an electric beater to work heavy cream, 1 tablespoon at a time, into the cream cheese. Work in garlic and tomato purée in the same manner. Stir in remaining ingredients. Serve hot or cold as directed in your recipe.

NIÇOISE SAUCE
YIELD: ABOUT 2½ CUPS

4 Medium-size ripe tomatoes, peeled, seeded
    and chopped
2 Cups Mayonnaise (see page 187)
1 Sweet red pepper, seeded
    and minced
1 Tablespoon each minced fresh chives
    and tarragon

Directions: Cook tomatoes over medium heat, stirring frequently, until moisture evaporates and mixture is very thick. Remove from heat and chill. Combine mayonnaise, pepper and herbs. Stir in chilled tomato.

TOMATO MAYONNAISE
YIELD ABOUT 1½ CUPS

1 Cup Mayonnaise (see page 187)
2 Tablespoons tomato purée
2 Tablespoons heavy cream
  Dash Tabasco sauce
1 Medium-size ripe tomato, peeled, seeded and chopped

Directions: Mix together mayonnaise, purée, cream and Tabasco until well blended. Stir in tomato bits. Serve well chilled.

DWARF GIANT TOMATO

BURGERS WITH RED AND GREEN BARBECUE SAUCE
YIELD: ENOUGH TO SERVE 6

2 large onions, peeled and coarsely chopped
2 Tablespoons each vegetable oil and butter
4 Medium-size green tomatoes, peeled
4 Medium-size red tomatoes, peeled
2½ Tablespoons granulated sugar
1 Tablespoon wine vinegar
¼ Teaspoon salt
⅛ Teaspoon freshly ground black pepper
3 Pounds ground round steak
6 Hot buttered toast rounds or burger rolls

Directions: Fry onions in the oil and butter until lightly browned, then use a slotted spoon to transfer cooked onions to a small bowl.

Cut green tomatoes into ¼-inch vertical slices and the red tomatoes into ½-inch wedges, but keep each group separate. Sauté green tomato slices for 5 or 6 minutes, turning once. Add ripe tomato wedges. Sprinkle contents of the pan with sugar, vinegar, salt and pepper. Cook over high heat until the juice boils away.

Meanwhile fry the burgers in a separate pan "as you like them."

Stir onions into tomato topping and cook 1 minute more. Arrange meat patties on bread rounds and top with the vegetable mixture. Serve immediately.

TOMATO-TABASCO SALAD DRESSING
YIELD: 2 CUPS

⅔ Cup tomato purée
1 Heaping teaspoon granulated sugar
1 Teaspoon Tabasco sauce
¼ Cup minced onion
1 Clove garlic, peeled and crushed
1½ Teaspoons salt
½ Teaspoon black pepper
1 Teaspoon yellow mustard
½ Cup wine vinegar
1 Cup olive oil

Directions: Combine all ingredients except the vinegar and olive oil. Mix thoroughly, then alternately beat in the vinegar and oil, a little at a time, beginning with the vinegar. Cover tightly and chill thoroughly. Shake before using.

RED RELISH FOR HAMBURGERS
YIELD: 5 CUPS

3 Medium-size onions, peeled and
    finely chopped
2 Medium-size green peppers, seeded and
    finely chopped
2 Medium-size red peppers, seeded and
    finely chopped
6 Tablespoons butter
1¼ Cups Tomato Catsup
    (see page 124)
1¼ Cups light brown sugar
¼ Cup Worcestershire sauce
1½ Tablespoons lemon juice
3 Teaspoons dry mustard
1½ Teaspoons salt
½ Teaspoon Tabasco sauce
15 Whole cloves
1 Large stick cinnamon
⅓ Teaspoon ground cloves

Directions: In a medium-size saucepan, sauté onion and peppers in butter over medium heat for 1 minute, stirring constantly. Stir in remaining ingredients and continue to stir until mixture boils for 3 minutes. Serve hot or cold. Relish will keep one week stored, tightly covered, in your refrigerator or you may pack into hot, sterile jars, seal and process for 5 minutes in a boiling waterbath following directions on page 211.

TOMATO-PEAR RELISH
YIELD: ABOUT 4 PINTS

Here's a really special relish—cubes of sweet pear, tangy green tomato slices, red and green pepper in a tart tomato-y syrup.

16 Ripe plum tomatoes, peeled
 5 Large slightly underripe pears peeled and seeded
 4 Medium-size onions, peeled
 1 Large green pepper, seeded
 1 Large sweet red pepper, seeded
16 Green plum tomatoes
 2 Cups granulated sugar
¾ Cup cider vinegar
1½ Teaspoons salt
 1 Teaspoon each dry mustard and ground ginger
¼ Teaspoon cayenne pepper

Directions: Cut ripe tomatoes, pears, onions and green and red peppers into ½-inch dice and the green tomatoes into ¼-inch slices. Place sugar and vinegar over high heat and boil for 15 minutes. Combine diced fruits and vegetables, vinegar-sugar syrup and remaining ingredients in a large stainless steel pan, bring the mixture to a low boil and cook, stirring occasionally, for about 1 hour, or until the liquid is fairly thick and syrupy.

Spoon the hot relish into hot, sterile jars filled to within ¼ inch of the top, seal and process in boiling waterbath for 5 minutes following directions given on page 211.

TOMATO AND SWEET PEPPER RELISH
YIELD: 3 TO 4 PINTS

24 Ripe tomatoes, peeled
 2 Sweet red peppers, seeded
 2 Green peppers, seeded
 4 Onions, peeled
 4 Large ribs celery, trimmed
2¼ Cups granulated sugar
 2 Cups vinegar
25 Cloves
 1 Teaspoon ground ginger
 ¼ Teaspoon cayenne pepper
 2 Teaspoons curry powder
   Salt

Directions: Cut tomatoes, peppers, onions and celery into ½-inch dice.

Boil sugar and vinegar for 15 minutes in a large stainless steel pan. Add vegetables and spices, mix well and return mixture to a boil. Lower heat and simmer for 2 hours, stirring occasionally. Salt to taste.

Spoon into hot, sterile jars and process in boiling waterbath for 5 minutes following directions given on page 211.

RIPE TOMATO-CORN RELISH
YIELD: ABOUT 6 PINTS

12 Medium-size ripe tomatoes, peeled
     and seeded
 6 Medium-size green tomatoes
 2 Green peppers, seeded
 2 Sweet red peppers, seeded
 1 Large cucumber, unpeeled
 2 Large onions, peeled
 6 Ears fresh young corn
1⅔ Cups vinegar
1½ Cups granulated sugar
 1 Tablespoon plus 1 teaspoon salt
 2 Teaspoons mustard seed
 1 Teaspoon celery seed
 ½ Teaspoon ground allspice
 ¼ Teaspoon ground cloves

Directions: Coarsely chop tomatoes, peppers, cucumbers and onions. Cut corn from cob. Scrape cobs lightly to extract the milk from the base of each kernel.

Boil vinegar, sugar and spices for 5 minutes in a large stainless steel pan. Add the vegetables, bring to boil, then lower heat and simmer for 1½ hours. Pack in hot, sterile jars, seal and process in boiling waterbath for 5 minutes as directed on page 211.

PEACHY TOMATO CHUTNEY
YIELD: ABOUT 4 PINTS

Unbelievably delicious—juicy peach pieces, currants, red and green peppers and onion in a rich, spicy red-brown sauce.

5 Cups peeled and quartered ripe tomatoes
5 Cups firm peeled peaches, cut
    into ½-inch dice
1 Cup currants
2 Large seeded green peppers, cut
    into ½-inch dice
2 Large seeded sweet red peppers, cut
    into ½-inch dice
2 Large onions, peeled and cut
    into ½-inch dice
2 Cups granulated sugar
1 Cup honey
1 Cup white vinegar
1½ Teaspoons salt
½ Teaspoon ground cloves
1 Teaspoon each dry mustard, curry powder
    and ground ginger
¼ Teaspoon cayenne pepper

Directions: Bring all ingredients to a boil in a large stainless steel pan. Cook at a very low boil, stirring occasionally, until the syrup is fairly thick and just covers the fruits (about 1¼ hours or longer). Pack the chutney into sterile jars, filling to the top. Seal, refrigerate for short-term storage or, for extended storage, process in boiling waterbath for 5 minutes following directions given on page 211.

SWEET, HOT AND SALTY RELISH
YIELD: ABOUT 4 PINTS

15 Green tomatoes
7 Ripe tomatoes, peeled
1 Sweet red pepper, seeded
1 Sweet green pepper, seeded
1 Small hot red or green pepper
7 Ribs celery
8 Small green cucumbers
2 Large onions, peeled
6 Tablespoons salt
1 Cup vinegar
2 Cups tightly packed brown sugar
1½ Teaspoons dry mustard
2 Teaspoons powdered cinnamon
¼ Teaspoon ground cloves

Directions: Put all vegetables through a food chopper or mince finely. Place in a large glass or ceramic bowl and sprinkle with 4 tablespoons of the salt. Let stand overnight, then drain, rinse and drain well again.

Mix vegetables with remaining ingredients and boil 5 minutes in a large stainless steel pan.

Pack in hot, sterile jars. Cover the vegetables with liquid to within ¼ inch of the tops of the jars. Seal immediately and process in boiling waterbath for 15 minutes following directions given on page 211.

TOMATO CHUTNEY
YIELD: 1 CUP

8 Medium-size ripe tomatoes
½ Cup vinegar
4 Cloves garlic, peeled
2 Dried green chili peppers
2-Inch piece green ginger, peeled
2 Cups granulated sugar
½ Teaspoon salt

Directions: Peel, seed and slice tomatoes and place in a saucepan. Reserve ¼ cup vinegar and add the rest to the tomatoes. Cook until tomatoes are soft. Meanwhile, grind together the garlic, chili peppers and ginger. Mix with the reserved vinegar and add to the tomatoes along with the sugar and salt. Cook until the mixture thickens, then cool and chill.

EAST INDIAN TOMATO CHUTNEY
YIELD: ABOUT 4 PINTS

A spicy, sweet, exotic chutney—one of the most exciting condiments ever.

2 Pounds ripe plum tomatoes
1⅔ Cups vinegar
1 Ounce (about 10 to 12 cloves) garlic, peeled
1 Pound raisins
4 Cups granulated sugar
4 Ounces fresh ginger root, peeled
4 Teaspoons salt
4 to 5 Teaspoons cayenne pepper
25 Whole dates

Directions: Preheat oven to 450 degrees F. Arrange tomatoes on a baking sheet and bake for 15 minutes. Remove from oven, pull off skins and cut off stem ends. Boil whole tomatoes (and their accumulated juices) for 15 minutes with 1 cup vinegar. Meanwhile, mince garlic and half the raisins.

Boil sugar and remaining ⅔ cup vinegar for 5 minutes, stirring once or twice.

Mix all ingredients in a large stainless steel or unchipped enamel pan and cook until chutney is very thick, stirring frequently. Spoon into hot, sterile jars, seal and process for 5 minutes in boiling waterbath as directed on page 211.

"DOWN UNDER" TOMATO CHUTNEY
YIELD: ABOUT 1 CUP

3 Large tomatoes, peeled and seeded
1 Tart apple, peeled and cored
1 Large onion, peeled
2 Cloves garlic, peeled and sliced
  Vegetable oil (not olive)
1 Tablespoon paprika
1½ Tablespoons granulated sugar
2 Small bay leaves
  Salt

Directions: Coarsely chop tomatoes, apple and onion. Fry onions and garlic in deep, hot oil and drain well. Discard oil from pan and simmer tomatoes, apple, onion, garlic, paprika, sugar, bay leaves and salt to taste until apple is cooked and excess liquid has evaporated.

RED CABBAGE, BEET AND TOMATO CHUTNEY
YIELD: ABOUT 4 PINTS

8 Medium-size ripe tomatoes, peeled
6 Medium-size beets, peeled
3 Medium-size onions, peeled
½ Small head red cabbage, cored
10 Green plum tomatoes
10 Prunes, pitted
2 Tablespoons peppercorns
3 Cups granulated sugar
1½ Cups vinegar
2 Tablespoons salt
   (or more to taste)
2 Tablespoons mustard seed
1½ Teaspoons ground cinnamon
¼ Teaspoon ground cloves

Directions: Cut ripe tomatoes, beets, onions and red cabbage into ½-inch dice and green tomatoes into ¼-inch-thick slices.

Halve the prunes and set them aside to be used later.

Tie peppercorns in a cheesecloth bag.

Boil the sugar, vinegar, salt, mustard seed, cinnamon and cloves for 15 minutes in a large stainless steel pan, then add the tomatoes, beets, onions, cabbage and the bag of peppercorns. Cook at a low boil for 1 hour, stirring frequently. Add the prunes and continue cooking until the chutney is very thick.

Spoon into hot, sterile jars and process in boiling waterbath for 5 minutes following directions given on page 211.

TOMATO-APPLE-FIG CHUTNEY
YIELD: ABOUT 4 PINTS

5 Apples, peeled and cored
2 Medium-size onions, peeled
1 Large green pepper, seeded
2 Tablespoons whole mixed pickling spices
2 Pounds ripe plum tomatoes, peeled and quartered
3 Cups brown sugar
1½ Cups vinegar
2 Teaspoons salt
2 Teaspoons ground ginger
1 Cinnamon stick, broken into 1-inch pieces
1 Cup dried figlets (very small figs)
1 Sweet red pepper, seeded

Directions: Cut apples into ½-inch-thick slices and the onions and green pepper into ½-inch dice. Tie pickling spices loosely in a small cheesecloth bag. Bring all ingredients except figs and red pepper to a boil in a stainless steel pan. Boil gently for 45 minutes, stirring frequently. Add figs and red pepper and continue cooking for 45 minutes or until chutney is very thick. Again, stir frequently. Remove and discard spice bag, spoon the hot chutney into hot, sterile jars, then seal and process for 5 minutes in boiling waterbath as directed on page 211.

NOTE: ON PROCESSING PICKLES, CHUTNEYS, CATSUP, PICCALILLI, RELISHES AND OTHER PICKLED DISHES

Until recently, pickling recipes have not usually carried directions for processing in a boiling waterbath; however, the latest directive of the United States Department of Agriculture recommends such processing for all pickles, chutneys, piccalilli, relishes and other pickled dishes prepared by home canning.

While the large amounts of vinegar called for in these homemade specialties effectively prevent the growth of deadly botulism bacteria, unprocessed home-pickled foods do sometimes develop mold, the effects of which are unknown. To make food safer, USDA calls for processing as a precaution.

Unless otherwise indicated, fill all jars to within ⅛ inch of the top. Wrap jars of red sauces such as catsup and chili sauce in brown paper before storing. Wrapping preserves the condiment's quality and color.

USDA RECOMMENDED TIMETABLE FOR PROCESSING PICKLED DISHES*

	½ Pint	Pint	Quart
Chutneys, Relishes, Cross-cut Pickles, Piccalilli	5 mins.	5 mins.	10 to 15 mins.
Catsup		10 mins.	
Large Pickles			20 mins.

For fruits, tomatoes and pickled vegetables, use your boiling waterbath canner. You can process these acid foods safely in water. A steam-pressure canner is used when processing all common vegetables except tomatoes, since these low-acid foods require processing at a temperature higher than that of boiling water. You may, however, use your steam-pressure canner in any of the following recipes if you prefer.

*Start to count processing time as soon as water in canner comes to a second rolling boil.

RIPE TOMATO-STRAWBERRY PIE
YIELD: ENOUGH TO SERVE 6 TO 8

2 10-Ounce packages frozen sliced
    strawberries, with sugar added*
4 Medium-size firm, ripe tomatoes, peeled
1 Recipe Double-Crust Pie Pastry
    (see page 185)
6 Tablespoons flour
⅛ Teaspoon each ground nutmeg and ginger
    Generous pinch ground cloves
3 Tablespoons granulated sugar
3 Tablespoons butter
    Whipped cream

Directions: Defrost strawberries.

Preheat oven to 450 degrees F.

Cut tomatoes into ½-inch dice. Pour half the thawed berries, along with their syrup, into a pastry-lined 10-inch pie plate. Sprinkle with 3 tablespoons flour and half the spices. Top with half the tomatoes and 1½ tablespoons sugar, then dot with 1½ tablespoons butter. Repeat with an additional layer each of strawberries and tomatoes.

Cover with a latticework crust (see page 185) and bake for 15 minutes. Lower heat to 400 degrees F. and bake 25 to 30 minutes longer. The

*Frozen strawberries are recommended here, since strawberries and tomatoes are not in season at the same time. If fresh berries are used, purée some of them with sugar to produce a syrup.

pie should be thick and bubbling in the center as well as around the edges. Cool to room temperature and refrigerate. Serve cold with whipped cream.

RIPE TOMATO CANDIES
YIELD: ABOUT 4 DOZEN CANDIES

Candied fruit was highly prized by the ancient Greeks and Romans. This adaptation of an ancient recipe produces date-like candies with a mellow, fruity aftertaste.

4 Pounds ripe plum tomatoes, peeled
4 Cups light brown sugar
½ Teaspoon ground cloves
    Confectioners sugar
    Whole blanched almonds (about 4 dozen)

Directions: Cut a ¼-inch slice from the stem end of each tomato. Melt the sugar over low heat in two large, heavy skillets. Divide the tomatoes and cook half in each skillet, spooning the hot brown sugar syrup over them and turning each from time to time. When the tomatoes are candied and clear, use a slotted spoon to arrange them on lightly greased cookie sheets. Dry for 4 to 6 hours in a 200 degree F. oven. The candies are done when they have the appearance of dried dates. Pat each with a towel to remove any stickiness and sprinkle lightly with confectioners sugar. Place a blanched almond in the center of each. Refrigerate or freeze.

GRANDMOTHER'S TOMATO JUICE JAM CAKE
YIELD: ENOUGH TO SERVE 12 TO 16

Ingredients for Cake:
½ Cup butter (1 stick), at room temperature
1 Cup tightly packed light brown sugar
4 Eggs, separated
2 Cups all-purpose flour
1 Teaspoon baking soda
¾ Teaspoon each ground cinnamon and nutmeg
½ Teaspoon each ground cloves and allspice
1 Teaspoon lemon juice
3 Tablespoons milk
1 Cup Sweet–Tart Tomato Juice Jam
    (see page 141)
1¼ Cups chopped dates
Ingredients for Icing:
3½ Cups confectioners sugar
⅛ Teaspoon salt
4 Tablespoons butter, cut in thin slices,
    at room temperature
4 Tablespoons heavy cream
1 Teaspoon almond extract

Directions: Cream together the butter and sugar until the mixture is light and fluffy. Beat the egg yolks lightly with a fork, then stir thoroughly into the butter-sugar mixture.

Sift the flour, combine with the baking soda and spices and sift again. Stir the lemon juice into the milk, then mix with the jam. Add the dry ingredients to the creamed mixture alternately with the jam mixture, stirring well after each addition. Dust the dates with a little flour and add them to the batter.

Beat the egg whites until stiff but not dry and fold into the batter.

Preheat oven to 375 degrees F.

Butter two 8-inch cake pans and pour half the batter into each. Bake for 30 minutes or until layers begin to pull away from the sides of the pan. Cool on a wire rack after taking from the oven.

To prepare the icing, mix together the confectioners sugar and salt. Cream the butter with 1 cup sugar mixture until smooth. Alternately add the remaining sugar mixture and cream, a little of each at a time, beating well after each addition. Stir in the almond extract. Spread between the layers and over the top and sides of the cooled cake.

TANGY TOMATO-ORANGE ICE
YIELD: ABOUT 2 QUARTS

. . . An unusually subtle and refreshing summer dessert.

2½ Cups granulated sugar
3 Cups water
2¼ Cups tomato juice
1 Cup orange juice
1 Tablespoon lemon juice
2 Egg whites (optional)

Directions: Bring sugar and water to a boil over medium heat and boil for 5 minutes, then remove from heat and cool. Stir in tomato, orange and lemon juices, and pour through a strainer lined with cheesecloth into the metal freezer can of your ice cream freezer. Chill quickly, then churn and freeze. If a creamier product is desired, beat 2 egg whites until stiff and fold into the frozen sherbet.

SWEET-TART TOMATO JUICE JAM
YIELD: 2 PINTS

It's hard to believe that a jam made from tomato juice could complement hot, buttered toast in such a special way.

1¾ Cups tomato juice
⅓ Cup lemon juice, strained
4 Cups granulated sugar
½ Bottle liquid fruit pectin

Directions: In a large stainless steel saucepan, stir tomato juice, lemon juice and sugar until well mixed. Bring to a hard boil over high heat, stirring constantly. Immediately stir in pectin, bring to a full rolling boil and boil hard for 1 minute, stirring constantly. Remove from heat and skim off any light bits of froth with a metal spoon. Pour jam into hot, sterile jars or glasses. Cover with ⅛ inch hot paraffin.

TOMATO-HERB JAM
YIELD: 2 PINTS

Serve with hot or cold lamb.

¾ Cup boiling water
2 Tablespoons each sage and thyme
1 Cup tomato juice
1 Tablespoon tomato paste
½ Cup lemon juice, strained
4 Cups granulated sugar
½ Bottle liquid fruit pectin

Directions: Pour boiling water over herbs, cover and let stand 20 minutes. Strain. In a large, stainless steel saucepan, stir together the herb-water, tomato juice, tomato paste and lemon juice. Add sugar and stir until well mixed.

Bring to a hard boil over high heat, stirring constantly. Immediately stir in pectin, bring to a full rolling boil and boil hard for 1 minute, stirring constantly. Remove from heat and skim off any light bits of froth with a metal spoon. Pour into hot, sterile jars or glasses. Cover with ⅛ inch hot paraffin.

PEAR-TOMATO PRESERVES
YIELD: 1 PINT

16 Yellow pear tomatoes, peeled
4 Cups granulated sugar
Zest from 2 lemons and 1 orange (the thin outer skin of the fruit with none of the bitter white underskin included), cut in thin shreds
¼ Teaspoon ground ginger

Directions: Combine tomatoes with sugar, cover and allow to stand overnight. Drain syrup into saucepan until thick and cook, skimming any foam that rises to the surface. Stir in tomatoes, lemon zest, orange zest and ginger. Cook until tomatoes look clear and translucent. Pour into hot, sterile jars, seal and process in a boiling waterbath for 20 minutes according to directions on page 211.

Few juices are comparable to pure, rich tomato juice, and the recipe on page 203 adds extra freshness and nutrition simply because it's homemade.

If you have an abundance of ripe fruit, your own tomato juice is a must. If you'd like something a bit more exotic, any one of the following drinks should please you.

Remember, cold drinks are most inviting when they are served icy, in tall thin glasses with a wedge of lemon or lime. For someone special a frosted glass is a nice touch. Just put glasses in the freezer 10 minutes before using. Hot drinks should be served really hot in mugs if you have them.

TOMATO JUICE COCKTAIL
YIELD: ABOUT 1 QUART

2 Cups tomato juice
1 Rib celery, trimmed and cut in 1-inch pieces
1 ½-Inch strip green pepper
1 ½-Inch strip unpeeled cucumber
2 Sprigs parsley
1 Tablespoon each honey and lemon juice
½ Teaspoon salt
¼ Teaspoon Worcestershire sauce
1 Cup crushed ice

Directions: Whirl all ingredients except ice in your electric blender until liquified. Add ice and blend until ice is melted. Pour into glasses and serve immediately.

BEEF-TOMATO COCKTAIL
YIELD: 1 QUART

3 Cups tomato juice
1 Cup Basic Beef Consommé
   (see page 192)
1 Teaspoon onion juice
   Tabasco sauce
   (optional)

Directions: Combine juice, consommé and onion juice. Season with Tabasco to taste, if desired. Chill thoroughly. Serve cold.

BLOODY MARY
YIELD: ENOUGH TO SERVE 8

3 Cups tomato juice
12 Ounces vodka
2½ Tablespoons lemon juice
4 Teaspoons granulated sugar
2 Teaspoons Worcestershire sauce
1 Teaspoon Tabasco sauce
   Salt and black pepper

Directions: Combine tomato juice, vodka, lemon juice, sugar, Worcestershire sauce and Tabasco. Pour into a pitcher of ice cubes, then strain the beverage into 8 glasses. Season with salt and pepper to taste and serve immediately.

SEASIDE BLOODY MARY
YIELD: ENOUGH TO SERVE 8

Ingredients listed in Basic Recipe plus:
8 Clams or oysters, freshly opened

Directions: Prepare Bloody Marys as directed above. Slip one clam or oyster with its juices into each glass.

CLAM-TOMATO COCKTAIL
YIELD: 1 QUART

3 Cups tomato juice
1 Cup bottled clam juice
1 Tablespoon Worcestershire sauce
Tabasco sauce (optional)

Directions: Mix together tomato juice and clam juice. Stir in Worcestershire sauce and Tabasco to taste, if desired. Chill thoroughly before serving cold.

SWEET 'N' HOT TOMATO PUNCH
YIELD: ENOUGH TO SERVE 6

2 Cups water
¼ Cup granulated sugar
1 Cinnamon stick
5 Cloves
8 Cups tomato juice
6 Slices lemon

Directions: In a large stainless steel or enamel pan, simmer water, sugar and spices for 10 minutes. Add tomato juice and heat to just under a boil. Serve hot with a lemon slice in each cup.

MINTED TOMORANGE-ADE
YIELD: 1 QUART

2 Cups tomato juice
½ Cup granulated sugar
2 Cups mint leaves
2 Cups orange juice
½ Cup lime juice
Club soda

Directions: In a medium-size saucepan, bring tomato juice to a boil, then add sugar and mint leaves. Remove from heat and allow mixture to cool. Stir in orange and lime juices. Divide among ice-filled highball glasses and add soda to fill.

HOT, BUTTERED TOMATO JUICE
YIELD: ENOUGH TO SERVE 6

This is a great pick-me-up when you are coming down with a cold.

2 Tablespoons butter
¼ Cup rum
9 Cups Tomato Juice
1 Tablespoon sugar

Directions: Heat butter and rum in a saucepan. Set rum aflame and when it burns out, add remaining ingredients and heat to scalding. Serve hot.

Green Tomato Cookbook

Why cook with green tomatoes? One very good reason is because they are there in your garden in imminent peril of being done in by hornworms, grubs or sudden early frost. The second, and best, reason, of course, is that green tomatoes taste every bit as delicious as ripe ones once you realize that the former are a separate fruit and not just red tomatoes that are underachieving.

My search for green tomato recipes led me time after time to the pickle and relish files of friends, neighbors, relatives, professional cooks and old acquaintances. The more pickled recipes I found, the more I realized that, other than a few fried tomato concoctions, there just were not that many green tomato recipes to be found. But gradually as I tested, and received recipes from imaginative friends, I discovered that green tomatoes perform brilliantly in specialized recipes. They have a texture not unlike the sweet green pepper but are much more subtle in taste; they are more firm and less acidy when cooked than a ripe tomato; and in flavor, they are not too dissimilar to a tart apple.

I'm sure you are going to be amazed at the wide variety of dishes in which green tomatoes shine. Whatever you do, don't let the *idea* of cooking with green tomatoes put you off. Ripe tomatoes were once considered unpalatable, even dangerous to eat—a totally unjustified prejudice. The green tomato should be treated as a seasonal delicacy—a versatile and tasty vegetable in its own right. The more I tested, the greater was my respect for these friends of the garden.

Sometimes I wish my tomatoes would never get ripe.

GREEN TOMATO MULLIGATAWNY
YIELD: ENOUGH TO SERVE 8

Sweet-tart green tomatoes replace sweet-tart apples in this garden variety mulligatawny soup.

1 3½-Pound chicken, cut into pieces
3 Tablespoons butter
4 Medium-size green tomatoes
1 Medium-size green pepper, seeded
1 Large onion, peeled
2 Carrots, scraped
2½ Tablespoons flour
2 Teaspoons curry powder
3 Quarts Basic Chicken Stock (see page 192)
½ Cup shredded coconut
7 Whole cloves
2 Tablespoons granulated sugar
⅛ Teaspoon ground cinnamon
4 Medium-size ripe tomatoes, peeled and seeded

Directions: Brown chicken pieces in butter in a large, heavy soup kettle. Chop green tomatoes, green pepper, onion and carrots, add them to the pot and brown lightly, stirring from time to time. Blend in flour and curry powder, then stir in all remaining ingredients except ripe tomatoes. Simmer until chicken is tender.

Chop ripe tomatoes, add to soup and cook at a low boil for 15 minutes.

Set chicken pieces aside and strain the soup, using a spoon to force vegetables through a sieve back into the soup. Discard chicken skin and bones, cut meat into ½-inch cubes. Serve in hot soup.

GARDEN BOUILLABAISSE
YIELD: ENOUGH TO SERVE 4

1 Large onion, peeled and chopped
3 Cups green tomatoes, peeled, seeded
    and coarsely chopped
2 Tablespoons vegetable oil
2 Large potatoes, peeled and thickly sliced
3 Cups boiling water
1 Cup shelled peas
½ Teaspoon granulated sugar
2 Teaspoons fresh thyme leaves
    Generous pinch saffron
    Salt
2 1-inch strips orange zest (the thin outer skin of the fruit
    with none of the bitter white underskin included)
4 Eggs
    Fried Toasts (see page 185)

Directions: In a heavy, deep skillet, sauté onion and tomatoes in oil until the onion is soft and transparent. Add sliced potatoes and cook for 5 minutes, turning once. Add water, peas, spices and orange zest, then cover the skillet and cook over medium heat until potatoes are just fork-tender. Crack the eggs, one at a time, into the broth, pushing potatoes aside to make room for each egg. Spoon broth over the tops of the eggs as they cook. When the eggs are poached "as you like them," remove the soup from the heat. Place a slice of fried bread in each soup bowl and arrange a poached egg on each slice. Spoon the soup and vegetables over all and serve immediately.

THE CARDINAL.

COLD GREEN TOMATO-CREAM SOUP
YIELD: ENOUGH TO SERVE 6

3 Medium-size onions, peeled and
    finely chopped
2 Tablespoons butter
2 Cups Green Tomato Purée (see page 203)
1½ Tablespoons granulated sugar
2½ Cups Basic Chicken Stock (see page 192)
2 Cups heavy cream
  Pinch nutmeg
  Salt
  Unsweetened whipped cream (optional)
3 Tablespoons minced fresh chives or parsley

Directions: Sauté onions in butter until soft and transparent. Add purée, sugar and stock and simmer over low heat for 25 minutes. Remove and cool to room temperature. Stir in heavy cream, nutmeg and salt to taste. Chill thoroughly before serving cold with a dollop of whipped cream garnished with chives or parsley.

CREAMED TURKEY-MUSHROOM SOUP
YIELD: ENOUGH TO SERVE 6

2 Tablespoons butter
½ Pound fresh mushrooms, thinly sliced
4 Green tomatoes, seeded and coarsely chopped
3 Cups cooked diced turkey
4 Cups Basic White Sauce (see page 187)
3 Cups Basic Chicken Stock (see page 192)
1 Cup heavy cream
3 Tablespoons sherry
½ Cup grated Parmesan cheese

Directions: Melt 1 tablespoon butter in a large, heavy saucepan. Sauté mushrooms until golden. Remove with slotted spoon and set aside. Add remaining tablespoon butter to pan and sauté tomatoes for 5 minutes. Stir in turkey and sauté for 5 minutes, stirring occasionally. Add white sauce, stock and cream and cook over low heat until soup is hot, stirring frequently. Do not allow to boil. Stir in sherry and serve hot, garnished with cheese.

FRIED TOMATO-SLICE SOUP WITH CHICKEN SLICES
YIELD: ENOUGH TO SERVE 6 TO 8

This soup is unusual in two marvelous ways. First, the vegetable slices are fried in batter and added to the soup as a garnish and, secondly, it is served topped with salty, powdered nuts. It seems an unlikely combination but is, in fact, a delicious variation of a classic Far Eastern soup.

½ Cup dry-roasted peanuts
6 Tablespoons vegetable oil (not olive oil),
    more if necessary
4 Cloves garlic, peeled and minced
12 Scallions, with 3 inches green top
1½ Cups thin slices leftover cooked chicken (or turkey)
6 Medium-size green tomatoes
½ Cup all-purpose flour
4 Eggs, beaten
2 Quarts Basic Chicken Stock (see page 192)
½ Cup soy sauce

Directions: Using a mortar and pestle, pound the peanuts to a powder. Set aside. Heat 2 tablespoons oil and sauté the garlic, the scallions and the chicken. Remove from pan with slotted spoon and set aside.

Add remaining oil to pan. Cut ½-inch slice from stem ends of tomatoes and cut each tomato into 3 thick slices. Dip each slice first in flour and then in beaten egg, and fry to a golden brown on both sides, turning once. Add more oil if necessary to prevent slices from sticking.

Heat stock to steaming and add garlic-chicken mixture and soy sauce. Divide fried tomato slices among soup plates, ladle soup over and sprinkle with powdered peanuts.

Serve immediately.

CHILLED FRUIT AND TOMATO SOUP
YIELD: ENOUGH TO SERVE 6

Absolutely delicious!

5 Cups water
1 Cup dried apricots
4 Medium-size green tomatoes, seeded and chopped
  Zest grated from 1 lemon (the thin outer skin
    of the fruit with none of the bitter white
    underskin included)
2 Teaspoons cornstarch
3 Cups apricot nectar
  Lemon juice and granulated sugar
  Unsweetened whipped cream
⅛ Teaspoon nutmeg

Directions: Bring water to a boil, add apricots, tomatoes and grated lemon zest. Cook over low heat until fruits are soft. Purée the slightly cooled fruits in a blender or Cuisinart. Mix cornstarch to a paste with 2 tablespoons water and stir, along with the apricot nectar, into purée. Cook over low heat, stirring constantly, until clear and thickened. While soup is still hot, stir in sugar and lemon juice and nutmeg to taste; the soup should be tart but not too sour.

Chill thoroughly and serve with a dollop of unsweetened whipped cream sprinkled with nutmeg.

SWEET-AND-SOUR CABBAGE AND TOMATO SOUP
YIELD: ENOUGH TO SERVE 8

1 Small head cabbage, trimmed of wilted
    leaves and cored
7 Large green tomatoes, peeled and seeded
7 Ripe tomatoes, peeled and seeded
2 Carrots, scraped
2 Ribs celery, trimmed
10 Gingersnaps, crumbled
2 Teaspoons salt
½ Teaspoon each dill weed and celery salt
9 Cups water
  Black pepper to taste
¾ Cup granulated sugar
½ Cup light brown sugar
1 Teaspoon sour salt (citric acid)
  Salt

Directions: Shred cabbage and chop green and red tomatoes, carrots and celery. Bring all ingredients except the sugars, sour salt and salt to a boil. Lower heat, cover and simmer for 2½ hours. Add sugars and sour salt and cook over medium heat for 15 minutes more. Season with additional sugar, sour salt and salt to suit your taste. Serve hot.

HONIED DUCK BAKED WITH GREEN TOMATOES
YIELD: ENOUGH TO SERVE 6

No commonplace duck recipe this—but one so good you would have to sample to believe.

2 Ducks (about 4½ pounds)
8 Green tomatoes
¼ Cup thin strips of orange zest (the thin
    outer skin of the fruit without any of the
    bitter white underskin included)
6 Tablespoons honey
¼ Teaspoon salt
1 Cup orange juice
Buttered wild rice (optional)

Directions: Preheat the oven to 450 degrees F.

Prepare the ducks for roasting and set breast side down on a rack in roasting pan. Bake for 15 minutes. Lower heat to 350 degrees F., then turn the ducks breast side up and bake for 20 minutes more. Remove the pan from the oven and pour off and discard the duck fat. Take out the rack and return the ducks to the roaster breast side up.

Cut the tomatoes into eighths and scrape out the seeds. Arrange the wedges around the ducks, along with the orange zest. Mix honey, salt and orange juice. Return the ducks to the oven and bake for 45 minutes, basting with the honey mixture every 10 minutes. Raise the oven temperature to 450 degrees F., pour remaining basting mixture over ducks and bake 15 minutes longer, or until the skin is brown and the breast meat still slightly pink.

Remove the ducks to a serving platter, arrange tomato wedges around them and serve immediately with buttered wild rice.

DELICIOUS BAKED CHICKEN IN CREAM
YIELD: ENOUGH TO SERVE 6

Chicken in a delicate, creamy green tomato sauce with onion slices.

8 Whole chicken legs (thighs and
    drumsticks) with skin removed
  Flour
3 Medium-size onions, peeled and sliced
1½ Cups Green Tomato Purée
    (see page 203)
1½ Cups light cream
¼ Teaspoon salt
  Pinch nutmeg
  White pepper

Directions: Preheat oven to 375 degrees F.

Dredge chicken pieces in flour and place in oven-proof baking dish just large enough to hold them without crowding. Separate onion slices into rings and arrange over chicken. Mix purée, cream, salt, nutmeg and pepper. Pour this sauce over chicken and onions and bake 1 hour. Serve immediately.

CHICKEN WITH GREEN TOMATO CREAM
YIELD: ENOUGH TO SERVE 6

2 Small chickens, cut into pieces
Flour
2½ Tablespoons butter
1½ Cups Green Tomato Purée
   (see page 203)
1 Cup heavy cream
⅛ Teaspoon each nutmeg and salt
¼ Teaspoon granulated sugar
Hot noodles (optional)
2 Tablespoons chopped fresh chives

Directions: Discard skin from chicken and dredge chicken pieces in flour. Fry to a golden brown in the butter. Cover and steam chicken until done. Remove chicken pieces and set aside. Heat the purée in the same pan, stirring to incorporate any brown pieces stuck to the bottom. Stir in cream, salt and sugar (adding a bit more of the last, too, if necessary to suit your taste). Reposition chicken pieces in the pan and simmer over very low heat until sauce thickens slightly. Arrange noodles, if desired, and chicken on serving platter, cover with sauce and sprinkle with chives. Serve immediately.

CHICKEN AND TOMATO BISCUIT PIE
YIELD: ENOUGH TO SERVE 6

2 3-Pound chickens, cut in serving pieces
3 Cups water
4 Tablespoons butter
4 Large green tomatoes, seeded and chopped
1 Teaspoon granulated sugar
2 Tablespoons flour
2 Cups heavy cream
1 Tablespoon finely minced fresh chives
½ Teaspoon salt
⅛ Teaspoon black pepper
2 Cups all-purpose flour
3 Teaspoons baking powder

Directions: In a large soup kettle, bring chicken and water to a boil. Lower heat and simmer for 35 minutes, partially covered, turning once. Skim any scum that rises to the surface. Meanwhile, heat 2 tablespoons butter in a skillet and sauté tomatoes for 10 minutes, then sprinkle with sugar and set aside.

Remove chicken and broth from heat. Measure 1 cup of the broth and reserve. Pull the chicken meat from the bones in large pieces and arrange in an ovenproof baking dish. Melt the remaining 2 tablespoons butter in a saucepan and stir in 2 tablespoons flour until well blended. Remove saucepan from heat and mix in 1 cup heavy cream (be sure to mash out any lumps with a fork). Add reserved cup of chicken broth, return sauce to medium heat and cook, stirring constantly, until it bubbles and thickens. Combine sauce, tomato mixture and spices and pour this over the chicken pieces.

Whip remaining cup of cream until stiff. Combine and sift together 2 cups flour and baking powder, then fold in the whipped cream. Turn the dough out onto a lightly floured surface and knead for 1 minute. Roll the dough out to ½-inch thickness and cut into 2-inch rounds. Arrange rounds of dough over the chicken and tomato mixture. Bake in an oven preheated to 425 degrees F. for 25 minutes, or until biscuits are golden brown.

SWEET-AND-SOUR PINEAPPLE CHICKEN
YIELD: ENOUGH TO SERVE 6

2 Small chickens, cut in serving pieces
3 Tablespoons butter
8 Medium-size green tomatoes, cut
    into ½-inch wedges
1 Can pineapple chunks, drained
2 Cups Sweet-and-Sour Sauce (see page 188)

Directions: In a large stainless steel skillet, sauté chicken pieces in 2 tablespoons butter until golden brown on both sides, turning once. Lower heat, cover the skillet and allow chicken to cook until nearly done.

Preheat oven to 350 degrees F.

Set chicken aside. Add 1 tablespoon butter to pan and sauté tomatoes for 10 minutes, stirring occasionally.

Arrange tomato wedges and pineapple chunks over bottom of a large baking dish, set chicken on top and cover with sauce. Bake for 30 minutes, or until chicken is done and tomatoes are just tender.

CHICKEN LIVERS AMSTERDAM WITH GREEN TOMATOES
YIELD: ENOUGH TO SERVE 6

5 Medium-size green tomatoes, seeded and
    cut in ½-inch wedges
2 Medium-size onions, peeled and
    cut in ½-inch wedges
3 Tablespoons butter
2 Pounds chicken livers
½ Cup seedless raisins
2 Ounces brandy
2 Tablespoons Madeira
2 Cups sour cream
½ Teaspoon each salt and paprika
    Black pepper

Directions: In a large, heavy skillet, sauté tomato and onion wedges in 2 tablespoons butter until onion is golden, but vegetables still have a bit of crunch. Remove from pan with a slotted spoon and set vegetables aside.

Add remaining tablespoon butter to pan and sauté chicken livers until each is browned on the outside but still quite pink on the inside. Meanwhile, soak raisins in brandy for 10 minutes, then drain raisins, reserve brandy and add raisins to skillet. Warm brandy slightly and pour over livers and raisins, then ignite; when flames die away, add Madeira to skillet, along with tomatoes and onions. Stir in sour cream, scraping the sides of the pan to incorporate any browned bits. Add salt, paprika and pepper to taste. Cook over low heat, stirring constantly, for 1 minute. Cook only long enough to heat through. Serve immediately.

GREEN-TOMATO-CHICKEN CURRY
YIELD: ENOUGH TO SERVE 6

---

2 2½-Pound chickens, cut into pieces, or 6 chicken breasts
  Flour
3 Tablespoons vegetable oil
6 Medium-size green tomatoes, seeded
4 Medium-size onions, peeled
1 Apple, peeled, seeded and sliced
1 Tablespoon curry powder
2 Teaspoons granulated sugar
⅛ Teaspoon each nutmeg and salt
1 Cup heavy cream
  Buttered Toast Points (see page 185)

Directions: Discard skin from chicken and dredge chicken in flour. Shake off excess and brown chicken on all sides in oil, then cover pan and steam until slightly underdone. Cut meat into 1-inch cubes and set aside.

Slice tomatoes and onions into ¼-inch wedges and sauté them for 7 to 8 minutes in the pan in which the chicken was cooked. Stir in apple, curry powder, sugar, nutmeg, salt and chicken cubes and simmer, covered, for 5 minutes. Add cream and simmer over medium heat until slightly thickened. Serve immediately over hot toast points.

VEAL LOAF WITH GREEN TOMATO TOPPING
YIELD: ENOUGH TO SERVE 6

3½ Pounds ground lean veal
2 Cups minced onion
1 Cup fine dry bread crumbs
1 Egg, beaten
6 Tablespoons butter, softened
¼ Cup cider
¾ Teaspoon salt
⅛ Teaspoon each white pepper,
  celery salt and nutmeg
2 Cups seeded, chopped green tomatoes
½ Teaspoon granulated sugar
½ Cup Green Tomato Purée (see page 203)

Directions: Combine veal, 1 cup onion, bread crumbs, egg, 3 tablespoons butter, cider and spices in a large bowl and use your fingers to blend the mixture well. Heat the remaining butter in a skillet and sauté green tomato pieces together with the sugar and the rest of the onion for 3 minutes. Stir in tomato purée and cook at medium heat until all liquid boils away.

Preheat oven to 350 degrees F.

Pack the veal mixture into a loaf pan and spread the tomato sauce over the top. Bake for 1 hour.

VEAL STEAKS WITH GREEN TOMATO GRAVY
YIELD: ENOUGH TO SERVE 8

2 2½-Pound veal steaks, each ¾ inch thick
    Salt and black pepper
¼ Cup flour
3 Tablespoons butter
2 Cups Green Tomato Gravy
    (see page 181)

Directions: Work salt and pepper into the veal with your fingers, then dredge in flour. Sauté in the butter until lightly browned on both sides, turning once. Meanwhile, prepare the gravy as directed. Arrange steaks on a broiling pan and broil for 4 minutes on each side. Cover with gravy before serving hot.

KIDNEYS FLAMBÉ WITH GREEN TOMATOES
YIELD: ENOUGH TO SERVE 6

2 Tablespoons butter
5 Medium-size green tomatoes,
    coarsely chopped
2 Medium-size onions, peeled and chopped
¼ Teaspoon granulated sugar
6 Strips country-cured bacon, chopped
2½ Pounds veal kidneys, trimmed and thinly sliced
6 Scallions, with 3 inches green top, thinly sliced
6 Shallots, peeled and thinly sliced
2 Black truffles, thinly sliced (optional)
½ Teaspoon salt
⅛ Teaspoon black pepper
6 Tablespoons brandy
¾ Cup heavy cream
    Hot, cooked rice
18 to 20 Cherry tomatoes, peeled

Directions: Heat butter in a heavy skillet. Add green tomatoes and onions, sprinkle with sugar and sauté, stirring occasionally, until soft.

Meanwhile, in a separate skillet, fry bacon for 3 to 4 minutes. Sauté kidneys in bacon fat for 1 minute, then lower heat to medium, add scallions, shallots, truffles, salt and pepper, and cook for 2 minutes. Add brandy, heat slightly, then set aflame. When flame dies down, stir in heavy cream, mix well and cook over medium heat for 1 minute.

To serve, spoon hot rice onto heated serving platter, top with green tomatoes and onions, kidneys and cherry tomatoes heated for 1 or 2 minutes in pan in which kidneys were cooked.

GREEN TOMATOES STUFFED WITH HAM*
YIELD: ENOUGH TO SERVE 6

6 Large green tomatoes
10 Large mushrooms, sliced
3 Large onions, peeled and sliced
3 Tablespoons butter or oil
3 Slices white bread, with
    crusts removed
1 Cup cooked ham*
1 Medium-size ripe tomato, peeled
    and seeded
1 Tablespoon fresh thyme leaves
1 Large egg, lightly beaten
    Tomato sauce

Directions: Prepare tomatoes by cutting a ½-inch slice from stem tops to form lids. Carefully remove insides without damaging tomato shells. Sauté mushrooms and onions in butter or oil for 5 minutes, stirring occasionally. Put mushrooms, onions, bread, ham, ripe tomato and thyme leaves through coarse disk of your grinder (or coarsely chop). Add egg and stir until well mixed.

Preheat oven to 350 degrees F.

Stuff tomato shells, set lids on top and place upright in a shallow ovenproof dish. Pour ½ cup water into bottom of dish and cover with aluminum foil so steam does not escape. Bake for 20 minutes. Remove aluminum foil and baste tops and sides of tomatoes with tomato sauce. Raise heat to 375 degrees F. and bake 15 minutes more, or until tomato shells are tender. Serve immediately.

*Other leftover cooked meats may be substituted for ham.

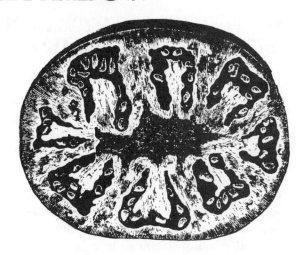

HAM SLICES BRASSERIE
YIELD: ENOUGH TO SERVE 6

4 Tablespoons butter
6 Medium-size green tomatoes, seeded
    and coarsely chopped
1 Large onion, peeled and cut
    into ½-inch dice
3 Slices fully cooked ham
    (each ½ inch thick)
6 Eggs, poached
    Mornay Sauce (see page 187)

Directions: Heat 2 tablespoons butter in a skillet and sauté tomatoes and onion until soft. In a separate pan, brown ham slices in remaining 2 tablespoons butter, turning once. To serve, arrange vegetables over ham slices, top each slice with a poached egg and cover with sauce. Place under broiler for 1 minute or until sauce is nicely glazed. Serve immediately.

ROAST PORK AND GREEN TOMATOES WITH SWEET-AND-SOUR SAUCE
YIELD: ENOUGH TO SERVE 6

4-Pound center-cut rib pork roast
  Salt and black pepper
2 Cups Sweet-and-Sour Sauce (see page 188)
10 Medium-size green tomatoes, cut into ½-inch wedges
1 Sweet red pepper, seeded and cut into ½-inch dice

Directions: Preheat oven to 450 degrees F.

Wipe pork roast with damp cloth and season to taste with salt and pepper. Set in roasting pan and roast for 30 minutes. Remove from oven, transfer to deep baking dish and cover with sauce. Lower oven temperature to 300 degrees F. and roast 1¾ hours, basting occasionally with sauce. Arrange green tomato wedges around pork, sprinkle red pepper over these and baste with sauce. Roast the meat, basting occasionally, for 45 minutes longer, or until pork is tender and cooked through. To serve, cut meat into slices, top with tomatoes and serve with sauce ladled over all.

PINEAPPLE PORK WITH RED AND GREEN TOMATOES
YIELD: ENOUGH TO SERVE 6

2 Pounds boneless pork shoulder,
  cut in 2-inch cubes
⅛ Teaspoon each salt and black pepper
3 Tablespoons vegetable oil
6 Green plum tomatoes, quartered and seeded
1 Large onion, peeled and chopped
1 Large green pepper, seeded and chopped
1 Large sweet red pepper, seeded and chopped
2 Cloves garlic, peeled and minced
3 Medium-size ripe tomatoes, peeled, seeded
  and chopped
1 Green chili pepper, seeded and chopped (optional)
1 Tablespoon chopped fresh coriander
  Basic Chicken Stock (see page 192) or water
1 20-Ounce can unsweetened pineapple chunks, drained

Directions: Sprinkle pork cubes with salt and pepper and fry in oil in a large, heavy saucepan until lightly browned on all sides. Remove meat with a slotted spoon and set aside. Sauté green tomato quarters for 10 minutes, stirring occasionally. Remove with a slotted spoon and set aside in a separate bowl. Add onion, green and red peppers and garlic to pan and sauté until onion is golden and transparent, stirring from time to time.

Add meat, ripe tomatoes, chili pepper, coriander and stock to cover. Simmer the stew, covered, for 1½ hours. Add reserved green tomatoes and pineapple chunks and continue to simmer, partially covered, until the meat is very tender (about 30 minutes).

POTTED BEEF WITH TOMATO GRAVY
YIELD: ENOUGH TO SERVE 6

2 Tablespoons vegetable oil
1 Slice salt pork, 2 by 3 inches
5 Green tomatoes, seeded and cut
    into segments ½ inch wide
2 Medium-size onions, peeled
    and sliced into rings
⅛ Teaspoon ground cloves
¼ Teaspoon ground ginger
1 5-Pound rump roast
1 Cup water
1¾ Cups tomato purée
1½ Tablespoons bottled beef concentrate
1 Tablespoon each granulated sugar
    and lemon juice
¼ Cup sour cream
    Hot cooked noodles

Directions: Heat oil in a heavy kettle and fry salt pork for 3 minutes, turning once. Add green tomatoes and onion rings and sauté until onions are soft and translucent, then set vegetables aside.

Combine cloves and ginger and work well into the surface of the roast with your fingers; then set meat in kettle, add water and allow the roast to simmer, tightly covered, for 4½ to 5 hours, or until meat is very tender.

Remove the roast from the kettle, wrap in aluminum foil and set aside. Discard the salt pork and pour the gravy into a large bowl. Cover the gravy and refrigerate 2 hours. Remove and discard fat. Strain gravy and measure 1 cup. Reserve and refrigerate any remaining gravy for other uses.

Combine the cup of gravy with the tomato purée, bottled beef concentrate, sugar and lemon juice; mix well and bring to a low boil. Reduce the heat and mix in the sour cream. Cut the meat into ½-inch slices and add to the kettle. Cover and simmer over very low heat for 1 hour. Stir in the reserved vegetables, heat and serve hot with noodles.

FRIED SCALLOPS DELMONICO
YIELD: ENOUGH TO SERVE 6

1 Quart bay scallops
3 Tablespoons lemon juice
2 Tablespoons olive oil
1 Cup bread crumbs
¼ Cup minced cooked ham
2 Tablespoons grated Parmesan cheese
1 Tablespoon minced fresh chives
2 Eggs, beaten
　Vegetable oil for deep-frying
8 Medium-size green tomatoes, cut into ¼-inch slices
3 Tablespoons butter
　Salt and black pepper
3 Hot, hard-cooked eggs
　Lemon wedges
　Tartar Sauce (see page 188)

Directions: Wash scallops, drain well and toss with lemon juice and olive oil. Let stand for 30 minutes, then drain well again. Combine half the bread crumbs with the ham, cheese and chives. Dip the scallops first in 1 beaten egg and then in the bread crumb mixture. Place in a wire basket and deep fry in hot oil until crisp and brown.

Beat 1 egg in a shallow bowl. Dip tomato slices first in egg and then in remaining bread crumbs. Fry in the butter and arrange on a hot platter. Season to taste with salt and pepper.

Pile the fried scallops on the fried green tomato slices, garnish with egg quarters and lemon wedges and serve with tartar sauce.

FROGS' LEGS WITH RED AND GREEN TOMATOES
YIELD: ENOUGH TO SERVE 6

 6 Tablespoons butter
18 Medium or 24 small frogs' legs
　Salt and black pepper
　Generous pinch cayenne
¾ Cup dry white wine
 3 Medium-size green tomatoes, seeded
　　and chopped
 3 Large ripe tomatoes, peeled, seeded
　　and chopped
 1 Medium-size onion, peeled and coarsely chopped
 1 Clove garlic, peeled and crushed
 4 Tablespoons minced fresh parsley
 3 Tablespoons vegetable oil
 1 Hard-cooked egg
 2 Tablespoons minced fresh chives

Directions: Heat butter in a large deep skillet and sauté frogs' legs over medium heat, on both sides, a few at a time. As soon as all the legs turn pearly white, sprinkle them with salt, pepper and cayenne, then add the wine and simmer for 5 minutes longer, turning the frogs' legs once.

Meanwhile, sauté tomatoes, onion, garlic and parsley in 3 tablespoons oil until the onion is transparent. Simmer for 10 minutes, then pour the mixture over the frogs' legs and simmer 5 minutes, or until frogs' legs are tender. Arrange on a heated platter. Force the hard-cooked egg through a fine sieve and use, along with the chives, to garnish the sauce. Serve at once.

LINGUINE WITH GREEN TOMATO CREAM SAUCE
YIELD: ENOUGH TO SERVE 4 TO 6

1 Pound linguine or thin spaghetti
  Salt
1 Large sweet onion, peeled and diced
2 Tablespoons butter
1½ Cups Green Tomato Purée (see page 203)
1 Cup heavy cream
1 Tablespoon whole black peppercorns

Directions: Prepare linguine in salted water according to directions on box.

Meanwhile, sauté onion in butter until golden and transparent. Add purée, then add heavy cream and simmer until sauce is nicely thickened. Meanwhile, coarsely crush peppercorns in a mortar with a pestle. Toss the drained linguine with the sauce, sprinkle with crushed peppercorns and serve.

RED AND GREEN TOMATO QUICHE
YIELD: 1 10-INCH QUICHE

1 Recipe Quiche Pastry (see page 184)
5 Strips country-cured bacon,
    coarsely chopped
2 Large sweet onions, peeled and chopped
4 Medium-size green tomatoes,
    seeded and chopped
4 Medium-size ripe tomatoes, peeled,
    seeded and chopped
½ Teaspoon granulated sugar
1 Tablespoon each minced fresh basil
    and thyme leaves
  Salt and black pepper
4 Eggs
  Pinch each cayenne and nutmeg
2 Cups hot milk
¾ Cup grated cheese

Directions: Prepare and refrigerate pastry.

Fry bacon until it is cooked through but not crumbly. Sauté onions for 3 minutes. Add tomatoes (green and red) and sauté until the liquid evaporates. Add sugar, herbs and salt and pepper to taste. Cool the vegetables. Roll out and form the quiche shell and spoon in the vegetables.

Preheat oven to 375 degrees F.

Beat eggs with salt, cayenne and nutmeg and add hot milk a little at a time, beating continually with a wire whisk. Continue to beat over low heat until the custard thickens slightly, then pour it over the vegetables in the pastry shell. Sprinkle the cheese overall. Bake for about 30 minutes or until the top is set. Serve hot.

GREEN TOMATO PIZZA
YIELD: ENOUGH FILLING FOR 6 6-INCH PIZZAS

This is pizza with a difference. The creamy puréed topping is much more delicate than the red tomato variety.

1 Recipe Pizza Dough (see page 184)
1 Tablespoon olive oil
1 Clove garlic, peeled and minced
2 Cups Green Tomato Purée (see page 203)
½ Cup heavy cream
　Pinch nutmeg
¾ Pound Fontina cheese, grated
　Basil

Directions: Prepare dough according to recipe directions. Allow to rise and double in bulk. Heat olive oil and sauté garlic for 2 minutes, then stir in the purée, cream and nutmeg. Cook, stirring frequently, until sauce thickens and most of the moisture has evaporated. Meanwhile, roll out pizza dough as directed. Spread cooled purée mixture over dough circles and sprinkle with cheese. Season to taste with basil. Bake as directed.

CARAMELIZED GREEN TOMATO SLICES
YIELD: ENOUGH TO SERVE 6

6 Large green tomatoes, cut
　　in ½-inch slices
　Flour
4 Tablespoons butter
⅔ Cup light brown sugar
　Heavy cream
　Salt

Directions: Dredge both sides of each tomato slice in flour, shaking off any excess. Sauté in the butter until the slices are brown on one side. Sprinkle each slice with sugar, then turn gently. Cook only long enough for the slices to caramelize and transfer to serving plates. Quickly mix a little cream into the pan drippings, season to taste with salt and stir briefly over medium heat. Pour over the tomatoes. Serve hot.

FRIED TOMATO SLICES
YIELD: ENOUGH TO SERVE 6

8 Large, firm green or ripe tomatoes
2 Eggs
1½ Teaspoons salt
1½ Tablespoons sugar
2½ Cups bread crumbs
　Vegetable oil or butter for frying

Directions: Cut tomatoes into thick slices. In a large, shallow bowl, beat together eggs, salt and sugar. Dip each tomato slice into the egg mixture and then in bread crumbs, and fry in hot oil or butter until brown on both sides. Serve immediately.

BATTER-FRIED TOMATOES
YIELD: ENOUGH TO SERVE 6

8 Large green tomatoes
1½ Cups all-purpose flour
⅛ Teaspoon salt
3 Eggs
1 Cup milk
   Vegetable oil for frying

Directions: Cut the tomatoes into thick slices. Combine the flour and salt and sift into a large bowl. Beat in the eggs, then add the milk and stir the mixture just long enough to moisten all ingredients. Heat 1 inch vegetable oil in a deep skillet. Dip the tomato slices into the batter and fry to a golden brown on both sides, turning once. Drain briefly on paper towels before serving hot.

SAUTÉED GREEN TOMATOES
YIELD: ENOUGH TO SERVE 6

6 Large green tomatoes
   Flour
12 Slices lean country-cured bacon
   Salt
   Toast Points (see page 185)

Directions: Cut each fruit into 4 thick slices. Dredge slices with flour. Fry bacon until crisp but not brown, then remove and drain on paper towels. Keep warm. Pour off all but 3 tablespoons bacon fat and sauté tomato slices until golden on both sides and just tender, turning once. Salt to taste. Serve on hot toast points, topped with pieces of bacon.

SCALLOPED SWEET POTATOES AND GREEN TOMATOES
YIELD: ENOUGH TO SERVE 6

Green tomatoes have the unique flavor and texture of candied fruit when they are baked, as these are, with dark brown sugar.

5 Medium-size sweet potatoes
4 Medium-size green tomatoes
6 Tablespoons dark brown sugar
½ Teaspoon salt
¼ Teaspoon grated nutmeg
3 Tablespoons butter

Directions: Cook the sweet potatoes in their jackets until tender, then drain and peel. Cut the potatoes and tomatoes into ¼-inch slices. Mix together the sugar, salt and nutmeg.

Preheat the oven to 375 degrees F.

Arrange the sliced potatoes over the bottom of a large, generously buttered baking dish that can go from oven to table. Top with a layer of tomatoes. Sprinkle with the sugar mixture, dot with bits of butter and bake for 50 minutes. Serve hot.

MEATLESS STUFFED GREEN TOMATOES
YIELD: ENOUGH TO SERVE 6

6 Large green tomatoes
6 Ribs celery
3 Large onions, peeled
3 Tablespoons butter or vegetable oil
4 Cups crushed stale bread
3 Tablespoons soy sauce
½ Cup catsup
1 Large egg, lightly beaten
  Tomato sauce

Directions: Prepare tomatoes by cutting a ½-inch slice from stem tops to form lids. Carefully remove insides without damaging tomato shells. Cut celery and onions into ¼-inch diagonal slices and sauté in oil until onion is transparent. Add stale bread, soy sauce, catsup and egg and stir until well mixed.

Preheat oven to 350 degrees F.

Stuff tomato shells, set lids on top and place upright in a shallow ovenproof dish. Pour ½ cup water into bottom of dish and cover with aluminum foil so steam does not escape. Bake for 20 minutes. Remove aluminum foil and baste tops and sides of tomatoes with tomato sauce. Raise heat to 375 degrees F. and bake 15 minutes more, or until tomato shells are tender. Serve immediately.

STEAMED GREEN TOMATO-DATE PUDDING
YIELD: ENOUGH TO SERVE 8 TO 10

This is one of the most delicious desserts ever.

1½ Cups pitted dates
½ Cup dark rum
1 Cup water
½ Cup vegetable shortening
6 Tablespoons butter
½ Cup each granulated sugar and
    light brown sugar
2 Eggs
½ Cup unsulfured molasses
1⅓ Teaspoons baking soda
2⅓ Cups all-purpose flour
1¼ Teaspoons baking powder
1 Teaspoon ground cinnamon
¾ Teaspoon ground nutmeg
½ Teaspoon salt
¼ Teaspoon each ground cloves
    and ginger
1 Cup seeded and chopped green
    tomatoes
1 Cup chopped walnuts

Directions: Place the dates in a small bowl. Boil together the rum and water for 1 minute, then pour over the dates and soak for 30 minutes. Meanwhile, cream shortening and 4 tablespoons butter together with the granulated sugar and ¼ cup light brown sugar. Beat the eggs with the molasses and fold into the creamed ingredients. Drain and chop the dates, reserving the liquid. Dissolve the baking soda in this reserved liquid and stir into the creamed mixture.

Combine flour, baking powder and spices, then sift together and blend with the creamed ingredients to make a batter.

Sauté green tomatoes in the remaining 2 tablespoons butter for 5 minutes, then add the remaining ¼ cup light brown sugar and cook 5 minutes more. Fold the green tomatoes, dates and nuts into the batter.

Butter a 2-quart pudding mold and pour in the batter. Arrange a cover of aluminum foil tightly over the mold. Set on a rack in a large kettle, ringed by crushed aluminum foil to keep it from touching the sides of the kettle. Add boiling water to a level three-quarters of the way up the sides of the mold. Top the kettle with tight sheet of aluminum foil and secure with a tight-fitting lid. Steam the mold over medium-low heat for 2 hours, adding more boiling water as necessary to keep the water level at its proper height. To test for doneness, remove the mold's foil cover and lightly press the center of the pudding. The pudding should be firm and springy. If not, recover as before and steam until the top tests done.

Serve hot with vanilla ice cream.

FARMHOUSE BREAD-SLICE PUDDING WITH CANDIED GREEN TOMATOES
YIELD: ENOUGH TO SERVE 4 TO 6

In the Early American tradition of "waste not, want not," this pudding turns ingredients on hand (plus a little cream) into a marvelous dessert.

---

6 Tablespoons butter
12 to 14 Slices white bread, trimmed
1 Cup seeded and chopped green tomatoes
¼ Cup light brown sugar
8 Tablespoons orange marmalade
4 Heaping tablespoons currants
¾ Cup granulated sugar
⅛ Teaspoon ground nutmeg
4 Eggs
½ Cup light cream
1½ Cups milk

Directions: Spread 5 tablespoons butter generously over one side of each bread slice. Line the sides and bottom of a buttered loaf pan with 6 slices, placing the buttered sides against the pan.

Sauté green tomatoes in 1 tablespoon butter 5 minutes, then add brown sugar and cook 5 minutes more. Spread 2 tablespoons marmalade over the unbuttered sides of the bread, then sprinkle with 2 tablespoons of the candied green tomatoes and 1 heaping tablespoon currants. Build 3 more layers with the remaining bread slices, buttered side down, covering each layer with 2 tablespoons marmalade, 2 tablespoons candied tomatoes and 1 heaping tablespoon currants. The final layer should be bread, but the pan should be no more than three-quarters full. Combine the granulated sugar and nutmeg with the eggs, milk and cream. Pour over the bread until the mixture just covers the top slices. Allow the pudding to stand for 1 hour.

Line the oven rack with aluminum foil and pre-heat the oven to 375 degrees F. Bake the pudding about 1½ hours, or until the top puffs and turns golden brown. Cool to room temperature after taking from the oven, then chill overnight. To un-mold, loosen by soaking the pan in 1 inch hot water for 30 minutes. Slide a sharp knife around the sides and turn out onto a plate. Chill before serving cold.

TOMATO BROWN BETTY
YIELD: ENOUGH TO SERVE 6

Anything tart apples can do, green tomatoes can do as well—if not better.

---

5 Large green tomatoes, seeded, chopped
    and well drained
1 Teaspoon each ground cinnamon and grated
    lemon zest (the thin outer skin of the fruit with
    none of the bitter white underskin included)
¼ Teaspoon each ground cloves and nutmeg
½ Cup melted butter
1 Cup light brown sugar
2 Cups fine bread crumbs
    Juice of one lemon
    Whipped cream

Directions: Simmer the tomatoes, cinnamon, lemon zest, cloves and nutmeg in 2 tablespoons butter for 5 minutes. Add the sugar and stir over low heat for 10 minutes more.

Preheat oven to 350 degrees F.

Combine bread crumbs and remaining butter, working together until well mixed. Press one-third of the bread crumb mixture into the bottom of a well-buttered baking dish. Layer half the tomato mixture over the crumbs. Sprinkle with half the lemon juice and top with another third of the crumbs. Spread with remaining tomato mixture, sprinkle with remaining lemon juice and top with remaining crumbs.

Cover the dish and bake for 40 minutes. Raise oven temperature to 400 degrees F. and continue to bake, uncovered, 10 minutes more, or until browned on top. Serve warm with whipped cream.

GREEN TOMATO–STRAWBERRY PIE
YIELD: ENOUGH TO SERVE 6 TO 8

---

2 10-ounce packages frozen sliced
    strawberries with sugar added*
4 Medium-size green tomatoes, peeled
1 Recipe Double-Crust Pie Pastry (see page 185)
5 Tablespoons all-purpose flour
    Cinnamon
4 Tablespoons light brown sugar
3 Tablespoons butter
    Whipped cream

Directions: Defrost strawberries. Preheat oven to 450 degrees F. Cut tomatoes into ½-inch dice. Pour half the defrosted berries and syrup into a pastry-lined 10-inch glass pie plate. Sprinkle with 2½ tablespoons flour and a bit of cinnamon. Top

*Frozen strawberries are recommended here, since strawberries and tomatoes are not in season at the same time. If fresh berries are used, purée some of them with sugar to produce a syrup.

with half the tomatoes and 2 tablespoons sugar and dot with 1½ tablespoons butter. Repeat with an additional layer each of remaining strawberries, flour and cinnamon, and tomatoes, sugar and butter. Cover with a latticework crust (see page 185) and bake for 15 minutes. Reduce the heat to 400 degrees F. and bake 25 to 30 minutes longer. The pie should be thick and bubbling in the center as well as around the edges. Cool on a rack to room temperature, then refrigerate. Serve with whipped cream.

Preheat oven to 450 degrees F.

Lightly beat 4 eggs together with sugar, vinegar, salt and nutmeg. Continue to stir while adding purée and hot milk, a little of each at a time, until mixture is well blended.

Pour into pie shell and bake for 5 minutes, then reduce heat to 350 degrees F. and continue to bake for 20 to 25 minutes, or until filling is set. Chill before serving cold, garnished with whipped cream flavored to taste with vanilla.

GREEN TOMATO–VINEGAR PIE
YIELD: ENOUGH TO SERVE 6 TO 8

If you are not familiar with old-fashioned vinegar pie this recipe will seem doubly strange, but do try it. It is superb.

½ Recipe Double-Crust Pie Pastry (see page 185)
4 Eggs
½ Cup granulated sugar
¼ Cup light brown sugar
2 Teaspoons vinegar
½ Teaspoon salt
¼ Teaspoon nutmeg
¾ Cup Green Tomato Purée (see page 203)
2¼ Cups hot milk
1 Cup heavy cream, whipped
Vanilla

Directions: Prepare, chill and roll out pastry and line a 10-inch pie plate.

GREEN TOMATO MARMALADE
YIELD: 6 PINTS

32 Green tomatoes, cored and very
    thinly sliced
8 Cups granulated sugar
1 Tablespoon salt
1½ Cups seedless raisins
    Zest (the thin outer skin of the fruit with none
    of the bitter white underskin included)
    from 1½ lemons, cut into thin shreds

Directions: In a large stainless steel pot, arrange alternate layers of sliced tomatoes and a mixture of sugar and salt. Allow to stand overnight, then bring to a boil over medium heat, reduce flame and simmer, uncovered, for 1½ hours, stirring occasionally to keep mixture from sticking. Stir in raisins and lemon zest and cook for 1½ hours longer. Stir more frequently to avoid burning as mixture boils away. Pour into hot, sterile jars, leaving ¼ inch of headspace. Process in a boiling waterbath for 10 minutes according to directions on page 211.

GREEN TOMATO LEATHER
YIELD: 1 LARGE SHEET. ABOUT 1½ POUNDS

---

3 Green tomatoes, seeded and cut in eighths
1 Box fruit pectin
¾ Cup water
½ Teaspoon baking soda
1 Cup sugar
1 Cup light corn syrup
1 Teaspoon lemon extract
  Granulated sugar

Directions: Run the fruit through the fine disk of a grinder.

Mix pectin, water and baking soda in a 2-quart saucepan. Mix sugar, corn syrup and tomato pulp in another saucepan. Cook both mixtures over high heat, stirring first one and then the other until the foam has thinned from pectin mixture and the tomato mixture is boiling rapidly . . . about 5 minutes.

Pour the pectin mixture in a slow steady stream into the tomato mixture, stirring constantly. Boil and stir one minute longer. Remove from the heat and stir in the lemon extract. Pour immediately into a buttered cookie sheet. Smooth the candy out with the back of a spoon. Let cool until firm . . . about 3 hours.

Sprinkle a flat surface (a wooden kitchen counter is best), with granulated sugar and turn the candy onto it. Turn the sheet to sugar the other side. Let stand overnight. Roll up the whole sheet in saran wrap or cut into pieces and store in a plastic box.

CANDIED GREEN TOMATOES
YIELD: ABOUT 4 DOZEN

Could it be that Jack Horner put in his thumb and pulled out a candied green tomato plum . . . ? These are as delicious as any candied fruit.

---

4 Pounds green plum tomatoes, peeled
4 Cups light brown sugar
½ Teaspoon ground cloves
  Confectioners sugar

Directions: Cut a ¼-inch slice from the stem end of each tomato. Place 2 cups sugar in each of 2 large, heavy skillets and melt over low heat. Divide tomatoes between the skillets and cook, covered, spooning the hot brown sugar syrup over and turning them from time to time. As soon as the tomatoes are clear and candied, use a slotted spoon to transfer them to lightly greased cookie sheets. Allow to dry for 4 to 6 hours in a 200 degree F. oven. The candies are done when they are dark and dry with the appearance of dried dates.

Pat each with a paper towel to remove any stickiness, then refrigerate or freeze.

Harvest time is pickling time and the real stars of your tomato garden are the greenies. Now, those firm, handsome fruits are seen in a new light . . . for long after their red counterparts are just a fond memory, they are still around, giving pleasure, livening up hamburgers and adding new spice to lamb and beef. The green tomato is the standard ingredient in many relish recipes. I've included here a few of the very best. Happy pickling!

GREEN TOMATO RELISH
YIELD: 2 TO 3 PINTS

20 Green tomatoes
12 Red or green sweet peppers, seeded
10 Large onions, peeled
⅓ Cup salt
6¾ Cups granulated sugar
2 Tablespoons each celery seed and mustard seed
4 Cups cider vinegar

Directions: Put green tomatoes, peppers and onions through the coarse blade of your grinder. Place in a large bowl and stir well, then cover with salt and let stand overnight. Rinse and drain the vegetables thoroughly.

Combine all ingredients in a large stainless steel or unchipped enamel saucepan, mix well and bring to a boil. Cook over medium heat for 20 minutes. Pack into hot, sterile jars and seal tightly. Store in the refrigerator.

Should you wish to store the relish without refrigeration, cook as directed above and pack into hot, sterile pint jars, allowing ½ inch of headspace, seal and process in a boiling waterbath for 5 minutes (see page 211).

INDIA RELISH
YIELD: 6 8-OUNCE JARS

3 Quarts green tomatoes, coarsely chopped
2½ Tablespoons salt
6 Cups finely chopped cabbage
4½ Cups cider vinegar
1 Cup finely chopped green pepper
1 Cup finely chopped sweet red pepper
1 Cup finely chopped onion
3 Cups granulated sugar
2¼ Teaspoons each celery seed and mustard seed
1 Teaspoon cardamom seed
½ Teaspoon dry mustard
½ Teaspoon whole peppercorns, coarsely crushed
1½ Teaspoons whole cloves
1 2-Inch stick cinnamon

Directions: Place chopped tomatoes in a large china or glass bowl. Mix in salt and toss thoroughly. Cover bowl loosely with a clean towel and let stand overnight.

Drain tomatoes well, place in a stainless steel saucepan and add cabbage and vinegar. Boil mixture 25 to 30 minutes, then remove from the heat and stir in peppers, onion, sugar, celery seed, mustard seed, cardamom seed, dry mustard, and peppercorns, cloves and cinnamon stick tied in a cheesecloth bag. Simmer over low heat, stirring frequently, until fairly thick, about 1½ hours.

Discard spice bag and pour relish into hot, sterile jars, leaving ½ inch of headspace. Seal and process in boiling waterbath for 5 minutes according to directions on page 211.

CARROT–GREEN TOMATO RELISH
YIELD: 3 PINTS

---

15 Green tomatoes, chopped
 4 Tablespoons salt
4½ Cups cider vinegar
16 Large carrots, scraped and chopped
¾ Cup chopped onion
¾ Cup chopped green pepper
½ Cup chopped sweet red pepper
 4 Cups granulated sugar
2¼ Teaspoons each celery seed and mustard seed
 1 Teaspoon cardamom seed
¼ Teaspoon dry mustard
 1 Teaspoon whole peppercorns, coarsely crushed
1½ Teaspoons whole cloves
 1 ¾-Inch stick cinnamon

Directions: Sprinkle the tomatoes with the salt, stir gently, then cover with cheesecloth and let stand overnight. Drain the tomatoes and transfer to a large stainless steel kettle. Add the vinegar and carrots and boil over medium heat for 25 to 30 minutes. Stir in the onion, peppers, sugar, celery seed, mustard seed, cardamom seed, dry mustard and

peppercorns. Tie the whole cloves and cinnamon stick in a cheesecloth bag and add it to the kettle. Return to low heat, stir once or twice and simmer about 1 hour, stirring occasionally, until the relish is fairly thick. Discard the spice bag and spoon into hot, sterile jars. Fill to within ¼ inch of the top. Seal and process in boiling waterbath for 5 minutes (see page 211).

HOT DOG RELISH
YIELD: ABOUT 4 PINTS

---

6 Medium-size green tomatoes
2 Large onions, peeled
½ Head cabbage, cored
6 Green peppers, seeded
¼ Cup salt
3 Cups vinegar
3 Cups granulated sugar
1 Cup water
1 Tablespoon each mustard seed and
   celery seed
1 Teaspoon turmeric
3 Sweet red peppers, seeded and
   finely chopped

Directions: Put tomatoes, onions, cabbage and green peppers through the coarse disk of your food grinder. Sprinkle with salt, let stand overnight, then rinse and drain well.

Boil the vinegar, sugar, water and spices for 5 minutes, add all vegetables and simmer for 10 minutes. Seal in hot, sterile jars and process in boiling waterbath for 5 minutes as directed on page 211.

GREEN TOMATO PICCALILLI
YIELD: 4 PINTS

16 Medium-size green tomatoes, chopped
5 Cups chopped cabbage (about 2 pounds)
1½ Cups chopped onion
1 Cup chopped green pepper
1 Cup chopped sweet red pepper
⅓ Cup uniodized salt
2 Cups firmly packed light brown sugar
3 Cups white vinegar
2 Tablespoons whole mixed pickling spices

Directions: Combine vegetables and salt, mixing thoroughly. Allow to stand overnight, then drain and press in a clean, thin white cloth to force out as much liquid as possible.

Mix the sugar and vinegar in a large stainless steel or unchipped enamel saucepan. Tie the spices in a cheesecloth bag; add to the pot and bring the sugar and vinegar to a boil. Add the well-drained vegetables and bring to a boil again, then lower the heat and simmer for 30 minutes, or until there is just enough liquid left in the saucepan to keep the vegetables moist.

Remove and discard the spice bag. Pour the hot relish into hot, sterile pint jars, leaving ½ inch of headspace. Process in a boiling waterbath for 5 minutes (see page 211).

AMBER RELISH
YIELD: 3 TO 4 PINTS

12 Green plum tomatoes
4 Large cucumbers, peeled
6 Medium-size onions, peeled
⅓ Cup salt
2 Quarts water
2 Cups vinegar
3½ Cups granulated sugar
½ Teaspoon cinnamon
¼ Teaspoon ground cloves
1 Teaspoon ground mustard
2 Teaspoons white mustard seed
1 Teaspoon turmeric

Directions: Cut tomatoes and half of the cucumbers into ¼-inch-thick slices. Chop remaining cucumbers and onions into ½-inch dice. Combine the vegetables, mix salt and water and pour over all. Soak in this brine 1 hour, then drain well.

In a large stainless steel pan, boil vinegar, sugar and spices for 20 minutes. Add drained vegetable mixture and cook at a low boil until onions are tender but still have a bit of crunch.

Spoon vegetables into hot, sterile jars and cover with the hot liquid, then seal and process in boiling waterbath for 5 minutes following directions given on page 211.

PENNSYLVANIA DUTCH CHOW-CHOW
YIELD: ABOUT 4 PINTS

5 Green tomatoes, any variety
2 Green peppers, seeded
1 Sweet red pepper, seeded
½ Small cabbage, cored
5 Green plum tomatoes
⅓ Cup salt
1½ Quarts water
4 Small onions, peeled
2 Large cucumbers
1 Cup lima beans
1 Cup green beans, cut in 1-inch pieces
3 Medium-size carrots, scraped and sliced
1¼ Cups vinegar
2 Cups granulated sugar
2 Tablespoons mustard seed
1 Tablespoon celery seed
2 Tablespoons turmeric

Directions: Coarsely chop 5 green tomatoes (*not* the plum tomatoes), the green and red peppers and cabbage. Cut green plum tomatoes, onions and unpeeled cucumbers into ¼-inch-thick slices. Place all the above in a large glass or ceramic bowl and cover with salt mixed with the water. Soak overnight, then drain, rinse and drain well again.

Parboil the lima beans, green beans and sliced carrots until they are barely tender, then drain them well.

Place the vinegar, sugar and spices in a large stainless steel pan and boil for 5 minutes. Add all ingredients and boil for 10 minutes more.

Pack in hot, sterile jars making sure the vegetables are covered with the syrup. Seal and process in boiling waterbath for 10 minutes following directions given on page 211.

SPANISH RELISH
YIELD: ABOUT 5 PINTS

24 Medium-size green tomatoes
3 Large green peppers, seeded
3 Large sweet red peppers, seeded
6 Large onions, peeled
¼ Cup salt
16 Medium-size ripe tomatoes, peeled, seeded and finely chopped
7 Ribs celery, minced
1 Quart cider vinegar
1½ Cups granulated sugar
1½ Teaspoons each whole cloves and ground cinnamon

Directions: Core green tomatoes. Put green tomatoes, peppers and onions through the fine disk of your grinder. Add salt, stir well and allow to stand overnight.

Drain and rinse the marinated vegetables, then drain well again. Place in large stainless steel kettle, add remaining ingredients, then boil until vegetables are tender. Spoon into hot, sterile jars, seal and process in a boiling waterbath for 5 minutes as directed on page 211.

TOMATO SLAW
YIELD: ENOUGH TO SERVE 6

½ Large head cabbage, cored
    and shredded
3 Medium-size green tomatoes,
    seeded and shredded
2 Sweet red peppers, seeded
    and shredded
3 Tablespoons butter
¼ Cup each milk and heavy cream
1 Tablespoon granulated sugar
1 Teaspoon each salt and dry mustard
½ Teaspoon black pepper
¼ Cup tarragon vinegar
2 Eggs
½ Teaspoon celery seed

Directions: Combine cabbage, tomatoes and peppers in a large bowl. Melt butter in the top of a double boiler set over hot water. Add milk, cream, sugar, salt, dry mustard and pepper. Cook, stirring constantly, until mixture is well blended and thoroughly heated through.

In a small saucepan, bring vinegar to a boil. Gradually add to milk mixture, a teaspoonful at a time, stirring well after each addition until the vinegar is well incorporated. Allow mixture to simmer for 5 minutes, then remove from heat.

Beat eggs, add 1 to 2 tablespoons of the hot dressing to eggs, then gradually add egg mixture, a little at a time, to dressing, beating constantly until thick. Stir in celery seed.

Pour warm dressing over vegetables and toss thoroughly. Refrigerate for 2 to 3 hours. Serve cold.

GREEN TOMATO, PEAR AND APRICOT CHUTNEY
YIELD: 4 PINTS

8 Green plum tomatoes, peeled and quartered
3 Large ripe pears, peeled and diced
2 Large onions, peeled and chopped
2 Large green peppers, peeled, seeded and chopped
1 Cup each seedless raisins and apricots
½ Cup white vinegar
1 Cup granulated sugar
1 Teaspoon salt
½ Teaspoon each ground ginger and dry mustard
⅛ Teaspoon cayenne

Directions: Bring all ingredients to a boil in a large stainless steel kettle. Lower the heat and simmer for 45 minutes, or until the chutney thickens.

Fill hot, sterile jars with the chutney to within ½ inch of the top. Seal and process in boiling water-bath for 5 minutes (see page 211).

GREEN TOMATO AND ONION PICKLES
YIELD: ABOUT 4 PINTS

24 Green tomatoes
 5 Small onions, peeled
 3 Tablespoons salt
 1 Cup granulated sugar
1½ Cups vinegar
 2 Teaspoons each mustard seed, celery seed,
    whole allspice and peppercorns

Directions: Cut tomatoes and onions into ¼-inch-thick slices. Place in a large glass or ceramic bowl and mix with salt. Let stand overnight, then drain, rinse and drain well again. Boil sugar, vinegar and spices for 5 minutes in a large stainless steel pan. Add the vegetables, simmer for 15 minutes, then bring to a boil. Pack immediately into hot, sterile jars, seal and process in boiling waterbath for 10 minutes as directed on page 211.

PICKLED GREEN TOMATOES
YIELD: ABOUT 2 QUARTS

 ½ Cup mixed pickling spices
6 to 8 Large branches of dill
 25 Medium-size green tomatoes
  1 Cup vinegar
 ¾ Cup salt
  1 Gallon water

Directions: Sprinkle ¼ cup pickling spices and several large branches of dill in the bottom of a 3-gallon crock. Fill jar with tomatoes to within 4 inches of the top. Mix vinegar, salt and water and pour over tomatoes. Cover with the remaining dill and pickling spices. Weight the tomatoes with a heavy plate to keep them submerged in the brine. Be sure to use only enough brine to cover the plate, since the tomatoes yield some of their juices as they pickle and the crock may overflow.

Keep the tomatoes at about 70 degrees F. and skim the scum from the top each day. The pickled tomatoes are ready to eat as soon as they are clean throughout with no white spots when they are cut (about 2 to 3 weeks).

OLIVE TOMATOES
YIELD: 2 PINTS

2 Pounds firm, green cherry tomatoes*
2 Cloves garlic, peeled
2 Sprays dill
1 Cup water
½ Cup vinegar
2 Tablespoons salt

Directions: Pack the tomatoes in hot, sterile jars. Put 1 clove garlic and 1 spray dill in each jar. Bring water, vinegar and salt to a boil, boil 1 minute, then pour over tomatoes. Seal immediately. The tomatoes will be ready to eat in 4 to 5 weeks.

*Pick only those that have a whitish cast at the bottom.

GRAPE-TOMATO CHUTNEY
YIELD: ABOUT 3 PINTS

---

4 Cups seeded and chopped
    green tomatoes
4 Cups full-size unripe grapes
4 Large cloves garlic, peeled
    and minced
¼ Cup chopped preserved ginger
1 Tablespoon each dry mustard and salt
1½ Cups cider vinegar
10 Whole cloves
2 Cups golden raisins
1½ Cups firmly packed light brown sugar
1 Cup currants

Directions: Using a large stainless steel saucepan, mix together tomatoes, grapes, garlic, ginger, mustard and salt. Add vinegar and cook over low heat until grapes are soft. Stir in remaining ingredients and simmer over low heat for about 1 hour, or until mixture is thick. Pour into hot, sterile jars, seal and process in a boiling waterbath for 5 minutes according to directions on page 211.

GREEN GODDESS CHUTNEY
YIELD: ABOUT 3 PINTS

---

4 Cups seeded and chopped green tomatoes
4 Cups peeled, cored and sliced tart apples
4 Large cloves garlic, peeled and minced
3 Tablespoons chopped preserved ginger
1 Tablespoon each dry mustard and salt
⅓ Teaspoon cayenne pepper
1½ Cups cider vinegar

2 Cups seedless raisins
1½ Cups firmly packed light brown sugar
¾ Cup finely chopped blanched almonds

Directions: Place tomatoes, apples, garlic, ginger, mustard, salt and cayenne in a large stainless steel saucepan. Add vinegar and mix well. Simmer over low heat for 10 minutes. Stir in remaining ingredients and continue to simmer for 1 hour, or until chutney is thick. Pour into hot, sterile jars, seal and process in boiling waterbath for 5 minutes according to directions on page 211.

FREEZER GARDEN RELISH
YIELD: ABOUT 6 PINTS

If canning is not your jar of relish, you might want to try this freezer-kept condiment.

---

4 Large green tomatoes
3 Sweet red peppers, seeded
4 Medium-size onions, peeled
4 Medium-size carrots, scraped
2 Medium-size cucumbers, peeled
2 Medium-size zucchini, peeled and seeded
1 Head cauliflower, trimmed and
    cut into florets
⅓ Cup salt mixed with 1½ quarts water
3 Cups cider vinegar
½ Cup all-purpose flour
¼ Cup each light brown and dark brown sugar
3 Tablespoons Dijon mustard
1 Teaspoon turmeric

Directions: Put all vegetables together through coarse disk of your food chopper. Place in glass or stainless steel bowl, cover with salted water to cover and let stand at least 6 hours. Drain, rinse and cover with water.

In a large stainless steel saucepan, bring vegetables and water to a boil. Remove and drain vegetables, discarding liquid. Set vegetables aside. Add remaining ingredients to saucepan and cook over medium heat, stirring constantly, until mixture is thickened. Lower heat, stir in reserved vegetables and cook over low heat until vegetables are tender and relish is very thick.

Cool quickly and pack into freezer containers, leaving ½ inch of headspace. Seal tightly and freeze at 0 degrees F. or below. To serve, partially defrost in refrigerator, then set in a saucepan over very low flame (or an asbestos pad) and heat slowly, stirring frequently. Cool before serving.

FREEZER MINT CHUTNEY
YIELD: ABOUT 5 PINTS

4 Medium-size white onions, peeled
4 Green apples, peeled and cored
2 Green tomatoes
2 Cups tightly packed mint leaves
2 Cups vinegar
2 Teaspoons each salt and
    prepared mustard
1½ Cups dried currants
1 Cup each granulated sugar and light
    brown sugar

Directions: Cut onions, apples and tomatoes into chunks and put through coarse disk of your food grinder together with mint leaves. Place in large stainless steel kettle. Add vinegar, salt and mustard, then simmer mixture slowly for 30 minutes, or until vegetables are tender. Stir in currants and sugar, raise heat and cook until liquid is reduced by half and turns syrupy. Remove from heat and and cool quickly. Pour into freezer containers, seal tightly and freeze at 0 degrees F. or below. Defrost in refrigerator before serving.

GREEN TOMATO STEAK SAUCE
YIELD: ABOUT 3 CUPS

12 Medium-size green tomatoes, sliced
6 Medium-size onions, peeled and sliced
2 Cups dark brown sugar
1 Tablespoon dry mustard
1 Teaspoon each salt and white pepper
2 Cups vinegar

Directions: Place tomatoes and onions in a large, stainless steel saucepan. Add the sugar and spices and, finally, the vinegar. Cover and simmer for 1½ hours, stirring occasionally, then remove the cover and simmer 1 hour longer. Strain the sauce, return to a boil and pour into hot, sterile jars. Seal and process in boiling waterbath for 5 minutes as directed on page 211.

GREEN TOMATO GRAVY
YIELD: ABOUT 2 CUPS

This is as good as any meat gravy.

8 Medium-size green tomatoes, peeled,
    seeded and sliced
3 Tablespoons butter
2 Teaspoons flour
½ Cup Clarified Beef or Chicken Stock
    (see page 191)
½ Cup light cream

Directions: Sauté tomatoes in butter until soft. Sprinkle with flour, then mash well with a fork. Add stock all at once and bring to a boil, stirring constantly. Lower the heat and stir in the cream, then simmer, stirring constantly, for 3 or 4 minutes or until the gravy thickens.

    Serve hot.

NOTE: ON PROCESSING PICKLES, CHUTNEYS, CATSUP, PICCALILLI, RELISHES AND OTHER PICKLED DISHES

Until recently, pickling recipes have not usually carried directions for processing in a boiling waterbath; however, the latest directive of the United States Department of Agriculture recommends such processing for all pickles, chutneys, piccalilli, relishes and other pickled dishes prepared by home canning.

While the large amounts of vinegar called for in these homemade specialties effectively prevent the growth of deadly botulism bacteria, unprocessed home-pickled foods do sometimes develop mold, the effects of which are unknown. To make food safer, USDA calls for processing as a precaution.

USDA RECOMMENDED TIMETABLE FOR PROCESSING PICKLED DISHES*

	½ Pint	Pint	Quart
Chutneys, Relishes, Cross-cut Pickles, Piccalilli	5 mins.	5 mins.	10 to 15 mins.
Catsup		10 mins.	
Large Pickles			20 mins.

Unless otherwise indicated, fill all jars to within ⅛-inch of the top. Wrap jars of red sauces such as catsup and chili sauce in brown paper before storing. Wrapping preserves the condiment's quality and color.

For fruits, tomatoes and pickled vegetables, use your boiling waterbath canner. You can process these acid foods safely in water. A steam-pressure canner is used when processing all common vegetables except tomatoes, since these low-acid foods require processing at a temperature higher than that of boiling water. You may, however, safely use your steam-pressure canner for all the following recipes.

*Start to count processing time as soon as water in canner comes to a second rolling boil.

Basic Recipes

QUICHE PASTRY (PÂTE BRISÉE)
YIELD: ENOUGH FOR 1 10-INCH QUICHE

¼ Pound cold butter (8 tablespoons)
1¾ Cups all-purpose flour
    Salt
1 Large egg yolk
1 Tablespoon plus 1 teaspoon oil
4 Tablespoons very cold water

Directions: Chop the chilled butter into small pieces with a large cold knife. Place the butter and flour in a large bowl. Cut the butter into the flour using two cold knives until the mixture resembles coarse meal.

Beat the egg yolk, oil and water together. Make a well in the center of the flour-butter mixture and pour in the egg mixture. Stir the liquid very slowly with a fork, incorporating the dry ingredients a little bit at a time, until about half the flour mixture has been moistened. Now use the fork to scrape the remaining dry ingredients down toward the center until a ball of rough dough has been made.

Flour your hands. Work the dough in the bowl, pushing it down and forward a few times with the heel of one hand until it is nicely blended. Form a ball, wrap in aluminum foil or waxed paper and refrigerate for at least 20 minutes. The dough will keep in the refrigerator for 4 days or in the freezer for 3 weeks.

CHEESE QUICHE PASTRY

All ingredients as listed in Quiche pastry, plus ¼ cup finely grated Cheddar or Parmesan cheese

Directions: Cut the cheese quickly into the flour-butter mixture just prior to adding the liquid. Proceed as directed but use a little extra flour when rolling pastry out.

PIZZA DOUGH
YIELD: 6 6-INCH PIZZAS OR 12 3-INCH PIZZAS

4 Cups all-purpose flour
1 Tablespoon granulated sugar
1 Teaspoon salt
½ Package (1½ Teaspoons) dry active yeast
¼ Cup lukewarm water
3 Tablespoons vegetable oil
½ Cup milk

Directions: Sift together flour, sugar and salt into large bowl. Stir yeast into lukewarm water, allow to dissolve, then mix into dry ingredients, along with oil. Add as much milk as necessary to make a fairly firm, manageable dough. Knead on a lightly floured surface for 10 minutes, or until dough is smooth and elastic. Divide dough into 6 equal pieces or, when making small pizzas, divide into 12 equal pieces.

Shape each piece of dough into a ball and set in a warm, draft-free place for 2 hours, or until each ball doubles in bulk. Roll each out to a thin, flat circle and top with your favorite filling. Preheat oven to 450 degrees F. and bake for 10 minutes. Serve hot.

DOUBLE-CRUST PIE PASTRY
YIELD: ENOUGH PASTRY FOR A DOUBLE-CRUST PIE

2 Cups all-purpose flour
1 Teaspoon salt
12 Tablespoons vegetable shortening
6 to 8 Tablespoons ice water

Directions: Combine flour and salt. Sift together into large bowl.

Cut in shortening with two knives or pastry blender until mixture resembles coarse meal. Sprinkle with 6 tablespoons ice water, stir with a fork, then press into a firm ball. (If pastry crumbles, work in remaining ice water.) Chill 15 minutes.

Divide dough in half. Roll out each half on a lightly floured pastry board. Do not overwork the dough.

TO MAKE A LATTICEWORK PIE CRUST

Roll top crust out as usual. Cut into strips ½ inch wide. Arrange half the strips in parallel rows. Crisscross the pie with remaining strips, weaving in and out if you prefer. Pinch off any excess and crimp strips to bottom of pastry shell.

TOAST POINTS
YIELD: ENOUGH TO SERVE 6

12 Slices white bread
Softened butter

Directions: Toast bread slices to desired degree of doneness. Trim crusts and cut slices diagonally into quarters.

Spread with soft butter before serving.

FRIED TOASTS
YIELD: 12 TOAST HALVES

6 Slices slightly stale bread
¼ Cup butter
¼ Teaspoon mixed herbs (optional)

Directions: Trim crusts from bread and cut each bread slice in half diagonally. Heat the butter in a heavy skillet, stir in the herbs and fry the bread to a golden brown on each side, turning once. Serve hot.

CROUTONS
YIELD: ABOUT 3 CUPS

12 Slices leftover bread, with crusts trimmed
3 Tablespoons each vegetable oil and butter

Directions: Cut the bread into small cubes and sauté in the oil and butter, stirring frequently, until golden brown on all sides. Cool before serving with soups and salads.

GARLIC CROUTONS

Prepare bread cubes as directed for croutons. Add 1 clove finely minced garlic to the hot oil and butter, then stir in the bread cubes and sauté to a golden brown.

GARLIC BREAD CRUMBS
YIELD: ABOUT 2 CUPS

2 Cups bread crumbs
2 Cloves garlic, peeled and minced
2 Tablespoons each butter and vegetable oil

Directions: Sauté garlic in butter and oil for 1 minute. Add bread crumbs and fry until crumbs are golden.

HOW TO MAKE PASTA
YIELD: ENOUGH PASTA TO SERVE 6

Here's a basic recipe for making those sublime Italian noodles that go so well with your favorite tomato sauces.

4 Cups flour
3 Eggs, lightly beaten
2 Teaspoons salt
½ Cup water

Directions: Sift flour into a wide, deep bowl. Use your fist to make a well in the center, then pour in the eggs. Add salt. Mix the dough by sprinkling the flour, a bit at a time, over the eggs and mixing it in with the fingers of one hand. When all the flour has been incorporated, add water, a few drops at a time, using only as much as necessary to make a soft, well-formed, but not sticky dough. Cover dough and set aside for 30 minutes.

On a lightly floured board, knead the dough for 10 to 12 minutes, or until it is smooth and elastic. Divide dough into 4 equal-size pieces and roll out, one piece at a time, into very thin, even sheets of pasta. Sprinkle each sheet lightly with flour and cut into desired pasta shape.

NOODLES

To make *fettucine* or *tagliatelle*, loosely roll up each sheet of dough, then cut rolled dough into ¼-inch strips. Set aside on dish towels so that noodles do not touch each other and allow to dry for 30 minutes. Cook for 5 minutes in a large amount of salted water.

To make *trenette*, roll out each sheet of dough to ¹⁄₁₆-inch thickness, then cut into long, very thin strips about ¹⁄₁₆-inch wide. Allow to dry for 30 minutes, then cook as directed.

If you happen to have your own pasta-making machine, the rolling-out and cutting process is considerably easier. Simply divide dough into 4 to 8 pieces, shape each piece into a long, narrow roll and flatten with rolling pin to a width slightly smaller than the width of your machine. Put each strip through the machine's rolling side three times, moving the rollers closer together with each subsequent rolling. Adjust your machine's cutting mechanism to desired width and cut dough into strips. Allow to dry, then cook as with hand-cut noodles.

To make *cannelloni*, roll out pasta dough to slightly less than ⅛-inch thickness, cut into 3-by-3½-inch rectangles, then spread on dish towels until dry, about 30 to 40 minutes. Cook 6 at a time in a large amount of boiling salted water, gently remove with a slotted spoon and slip immediately into cold water. Drain and spread on damp towels. Fill, roll up and bake (see page 78).

To prepare *lasagne* noodles, roll out dough to ⅛-inch thickness and cut into strips 2 inches wide and 8 to 12 inches long. Dry, boil and drain as with cannelloni noodles.

BASIC WHITE SAUCE
YIELD: 2 CUPS

4 Tablespoons butter
¼ Cup all-purpose flour
2 Cups cold milk
½ Teaspoon salt
   White pepper

Directions: Melt the butter over medium heat in a heavy saucepan. Stir in the flour. When the mixture is smooth, remove from the heat and add the cold milk all at once, stirring until the mixture is well blended and free from lumps. Return to medium heat and cook, stirring constantly, until sauce is creamy and thick. Season with the salt and white pepper to taste.

When a thinner sauce is desired, increase the amount of milk by ½ cup. To make a thicker sauce, reduce the quantity of milk to 1¼ cups.

MORNAY SAUCE

Add 1½ cup grated Swiss cheese and ⅓ cup grated Parmesan cheese to hot Basic White Sauce. Stir over low heat until cheeses melt.

BÉCHAMEL SAUCE

When preparing white sauce, sauté sliced onion in butter until soft, then discard onion and blend in flour. Substitute 1 cup cream for 1 cup of the milk and proceed as directed.

CURRY SAUCE

Melt butter as directed in Basic White Sauce. Add flour and 1 teaspoon curry powder. Proceed as directed.

EGG AND HERB SAUCE

Prepare Basic White Sauce as directed. Just before serving, stir 2 coarsely chopped hard-cooked eggs and 2 tablespoons mixed fresh or ½ teaspoon dried herbs (thyme, chervil, marjoram) into sauce. Season to taste with salt and black pepper.

MAYONNAISE
YIELD: ABOUT 2 CUPS

2 Egg yolks at room temperature
1 Tablespoon Dijon mustard
¾ Cup each olive oil and vegetable oil
1½ Tablespoons hot vinegar
      or lemon juice
   Salt and white pepper

Directions: Rinse a small bowl with hot water and wipe dry. Place egg yolks and mustard into the warmed bowl, mix well with a wire whisk, then set the bowl over boiling water for a few seconds, continuing to beat as mixture thickens slightly. Take care not to beat over the heat too long or mayonnaise will be too thick.

Remove egg mixture from heat. Mix oils together and gradually beat into eggs, ½ teaspoonful at a time, beating continuously and waiting until the previous addition has been thoroughly incorporated. The mixture should be creamy before beating in the next addition of oil.

When one-third to one-half of oil has been used, beat in the hot vinegar, then gradually add the remaining oil in small amounts as before, beating constantly after each addition. When all the oil has been absorbed, season to taste with salt and pepper.

TARTAR SAUCE
YIELD: 1½ CUPS

---

1 Teaspoon prepared mustard
1 Teaspoon salt
  Pinch cayenne
3 Egg yolks
1 Cup olive oil
1 Tablespoon white vinegar
1½ Teaspoons lemon juice
2 Tablespoons minced onion
1 Tablespoon minced capers
1 Tablespoon finely chopped pimiento-stuffed olives
1 Tablespoon finely chopped sweet pickle
1 Tablespoon minced fresh parsley or 1 teaspoon dried

Directions: Blend mustard, salt and cayenne into egg yolks. Gradually beat in the oil, 1 tablespoon at a time, until all is well incorporated. The sauce should be thick. Beat in the vinegar until completely absorbed, then beat in the lemon juice. Refrigerate until very cold. Mix in remaining ingredients just before serving.

SWEET-AND-SOUR SAUCE
YIELD: ABOUT 2 CUPS

---

2 Cups granulated sugar
1 Cup each vinegar and tomato juice
2 Tablespoons minced green pepper
1 Teaspoon salt
4 Teaspoons cornstarch
2 Tablespoons water
1 Tablespoon minced fresh parsley
2 Teaspoons paprika

Directions: Stir sugar, vinegar, tomato juice, green pepper and salt into saucepan. Cook over low heat for 5 minutes, stirring occasionally and skimming off any foam that may rise. Blend cornstarch into 2 tablespoons water to make a smooth paste; stir into vinegar mixture and continue to stir until mixture clears and thickens. Force sauce through a sieve with the back of a spoon and stir in parsley and paprika.

QUICK AÏOLI (GARLIC MAYONNAISE)
YIELD: ABOUT 1 CUP

Serve as a dip to accompany cherry tomatoes and crisp, fresh vegetable strips.

---

2 Tablespoons bread crumbs
3 Cloves garlic, peeled and coarsely chopped
1 Tablespoon lemon juice
2 Large egg yolks
⅛ Teaspoon each salt and black pepper
¾ Cup olive oil
  About 1 tablespoon boiling water

Directions: In an electric blender, whirl bread crumbs at high speed for about 5 seconds. Add garlic and lemon juice and blend at high speed until mixture is smooth. Beat in egg yolks and seasonings and continue to beat until mixture is quite stiff. Turn blender on high once more and gradually add oil, a few drops at a time at first, then slowly increase amount until oil runs in thin, steady stream. When half the oil has been incorporated, add 1 teaspoon boiling water to thin mixture a bit. Continue blending at high speed, stopping the action and adding another teaspoon or so of boiling water only if mixture becomes too thick for blender blades to turn easily.

When all the oil has been incorporated, sauce will be very thick. Scrape from blender jar with rubber spatula and turn into bowl. Chill before using.

FRENCH DRESSING I
YIELD: 2 CUPS

½ Cup wine vinegar
1 Teaspoon salt
   White pepper
1½ Cups olive oil (or other salad oil)

Directions: In a shallow bowl, beat vinegar together with salt and white pepper to taste and continue to beat while you slowly add oil. Pour into covered jar and chill. Shake well before using. This dressing will keep for several weeks in refrigerator. When a milder dressing is desired, substitute lemon juice for vinegar.

FRENCH DRESSING II
YIELD: ABOUT 1⅓ CUP

¼ Cup wine (or tarragon) vinegar
1 Teaspoon salt
½ Teaspoon each granulated sugar and dry mustard
¼ Teaspoon paprika
   Black pepper
1 Cup olive oil (or other salad oil)

Directions: Place all ingredients except oil in a screw-top jar. Cover and shake well. Add oil, cover and shake again.

Chill, then shake just before using.

This dressing can be varied in endless ways. Add fresh or dried herbs, minced onions or scallions, minced garlic, crumbled bits of cheese, catsup, anchovies, chutney, curry or anything your fancy dictates.

VINAIGRETTE DRESSING
YIELD: ABOUT 1 CUP

6 Tablespoons wine vinegar
½ Teaspoon salt
   Black pepper to taste
½ Teaspoon dry mustard (optional)
⅔ Cup olive oil (or other salad oil, or a combination)
¼ Cup finely minced fresh chervil, parsley or tarragon, singly or in combination

Directions: Beat the vinegar and seasonings together until well mixed. Add the oil and beat again. Add the herbs to the dressing just before serving or sprinkle them over the salad after tossing with the dressing.

GARLIC BUTTER
YIELD: ¼ POUND

¼ Pound butter (8 tablespoons) at room temperature
2 Cloves garlic, peeled and crushed
1½ Teaspoons minced fresh parsley
   Dash white pepper

Directions: Cream butter and blend in remaining ingredients. Pack into container, cover and refrigerate until needed.

BASIC BEEF STOCK
YIELD: 2 TO 3 QUARTS

---

3 to 4 Pounds beef bones, cut in small pieces
  by your butcher
2 Pounds veal bones
2 Large carrots, scraped
2 Large onions, peeled
4 Quarts water
 Leftover scraps of lean meat
1 Roast chicken carcass or chicken
  wings and necks
1½ Pounds lean beef
3 Large ribs celery with leaves
5 Sprigs parsley
8 Peppercorns
2 Teaspoons salt

Directions: Place the bones, 1 carrot and 1 onion, both sliced, in a roasting pan and roast for 30 minutes in a 450 degree F. oven. Transfer these to a soup kettle. Pour off the grease from the roasting pan, add 3 cups water and bring to a boil, deglazing by scraping brown bits stuck in pan. Add this to soup kettle along with the remainder of the water, meat scraps, chicken carcass and lean beef. Bring to a boil and skim off any scum that rises to the surface. When no more scum appears, add remaining vegetables, parsley, peppercorns and salt. Cover the kettle loosely—too tight a fit may cause your stock to cloud. Simmer over low heat for 4 to 5 hours. Cool and remove as much fat as possible with a spoon. Ladle as much stock as you can from the bones, then strain through a fine sieve or cheesecloth, chill and remove all fat. Discard the meat,

bones and vegetables—their flavor-packed nutrition has already passed into the stock. Divide the stock into pint or quart jars, cool further, then cover tightly and refrigerate, removing any fat that rises to the surface. Refrigerated stock keeps well, but bring it to a boil every 3 or 4 days to keep it fresh if not used immediately.

Frozen stock will remain at peak quality for several weeks when stored at 0 degrees F. or below. However, when preparing stock for the freezer, omit the peppercorns and salt. Spices can behave unpredictably when frozen. Pour the chilled and thoroughly skimmed stock into plastic pint or quart freezer containers, allowing 1 inch of headspace for expansion during freezing. Seal tightly and freeze. Thaw slightly in the refrigerator before reheating slowly over low heat. Season with salt and pepper to taste just before serving.

BASIC CHICKEN STOCK
YIELD: 2 TO 3 QUARTS

4 Chicken feet, cleaned and skinned
1 Roast chicken carcass
1 Veal knuckle
1 3-Pound chicken
8 Chicken necks
4 Quarts water
3 Medium-size carrots, peeled
2 Large ribs celery with leaves
1 Clove garlic, peeled
8 Peppercorns
⅛ Teaspoon ground thyme

Directions: Bring chicken feet, carcass and veal knuckle to boil in water to cover. Drain, return to pot.

Add whole chicken, chicken necks, water and vegetables and bring slowly to a boil over low heat. Skim off foam, add spices and simmer for 3 hours. Keep kettle covered loosely to prevent stock from clouding. Remove cooked chicken and reserve for other use. Strain stock through a fine sieve, cool quickly, then chill. Skim off any surface fat and reheat to use, or keep in refrigerator until needed. Refrigerated stock keeps well, but bring it to a boil every 3 or 4 days to maintain freshness.

Frozen stock will remain at peak quality for several weeks when stored at 0 degrees F. Omit the garlic and peppercorns, however, when preparing the stock for the freezer.

To freeze chicken stock, pour the cold and skimmed liquid into conveniently sized plastic freezer containers, allowing ½-inch headspace. Seal tightly and freeze. To use, thaw slightly in the refrigerator before reheating slowly over low heat. Season to taste with salt and pepper before serving.

BASIC CLARIFIED STOCK
YIELD: 2½ TO 3 QUARTS

Use this simple method to clarify a cloudy soup stock.

2½ to 3 Quarts well-skimmed Basic Beef Stock
    (see page 191) or Chicken Stock
  2 Egg whites
  2 Egg shells

Directions: In a large soup kettle, bring the stock to a boil. Beat the egg whites until they are foamy. Add whites and shells to the boiling stock, stirring constantly, then lower the heat and, still stirring, simmer at low boil for 10 minutes. Cool slightly. Allow the egg particles to settle. Arrange several layers of cheesecloth over a large bowl and strain the stock through. Refrigerate or freeze until needed for clear soup or sauces.

BASIC CONSOMMÉ

Prepare clear, delicious consommé by cooking Basic Beef or Chicken Stock further to reduce the quantity, and to concentrate and enrich the flavor. Easy-to-freeze consommé also takes less freezer space than basic stock, and all you need do to return it to stock condition is to add a little water. To freeze consommé, just pour into plastic containers, allowing 1 inch of headspace for expansion during freezing, then seal tightly and store at 0 degrees F. Thaw in the refrigerator before reheating slowly.

BEEF CONSOMMÉ
YIELD: ABOUT 2 QUARTS

1½ Pounds very lean chopped beef
  2 Egg whites
  2 Egg shells
  3 Quarts Basic Beef Stock (see page 191)

Directions: Place beef, egg whites and shells in a large soup kettle. Cover with cooled and skimmed stock and bring slowly to *just under* a boil, stirring constantly. Simmer over low heat for about 2 hours to reduce the stock and concentrate the flavor. Remove from the heat and allow the particles to settle, then strain through several layers of cheesecloth. Serve immediately, reheating over low flame if necessary. Otherwise, cool quickly and refrigerate or freeze.

CHICKEN CONSOMMÉ
YIELD: ABOUT 2 QUARTS

2½ to 3 Quarts Basic Chicken Stock
      (see page 192), cooked and skimmed
   2 Egg whites
   2 Egg shells

Directions: Place the stock in a kettle and bring to a boil. Cook over medium heat until the liquid is reduced by one-third. Stir in the egg whites and shells and continue to cook for 10 minutes while the soup clears. Remove from the heat and set aside for 10 minutes while the particles settle, then strain through several layers of cheesecloth. Return to low heat if serving immediately. Cool quickly and pour into refrigerator or freezer containers to store.

CHICKEN QUENELLES
YIELD: ENOUGH TO SERVE 6

½ Chicken breast, boned, skinned and cut
    into small dice
½ Egg white
 1 Tablespoon Chicken Velouté, chilled
    (see page 195)
   Pinch each salt, pepper and nutmeg
⅓ Cup heavy cream
   Basic Chicken Stock
    (see page 192)

Directions: Using an electric blender at high speed or a Cuisinart with the sharp metal blade, blend the chicken pieces until they are puréed, then force through a fine sieve. Chill mixture well in blender or Cuisinart container, then blend in the egg white a bit at a time along with the velouté, nutmeg, salt and pepper. Stop every few seconds to scrape down the container sides with a knife or spatula.

Blend in the cream gradually, mixing well after each addition. Shape the mixture into small ovals by molding between two teaspoons dipped in water. Butter a shallow enamel pan and arrange the quenelles in it so they do not touch and carefully pour in the lukewarm stock to almost cover the quenelles. Poach over very low heat until the quenelles are firm, about 5 to 7 minutes. Prepare the quenelles in two batches if your pan is not large enough to poach all of them at one time. To serve, stir 1 or 2 tablespoons chicken velouté into each of 6 bowls of hot stock or consommé and add several quenelles to each. These are also superb served as a garnish in other delicately flavored soups.

CHICKEN VELOUTÉ
YIELD: ABOUT 1 CUP

1¼ Cups Basic Chicken Stock (see page 192)
1 Sprig parsley
½ Cup chopped mushroom stems (optional)
2 Tablespoons butter
1 Tablespoon flour

Directions: Heat stock in a small saucepan. Add parsley and mushrooms, then simmer, partially covered, for 15 minutes.

In a separate saucepan, melt butter and blend in flour. Gradually add hot stock, stirring constantly, until mixture is smooth and thick. Continue to cook over low heat, stirring frequently and skimming the top occasionally, until velouté is reduced to ⅔ its original quantity. Strain sauce through a fine sieve before stirring into simmering beef or chicken consommé. To store velouté, stir from time to time as it cools to prevent a scum from forming on the surface, then cover and refrigerate until needed.

HOW TO PEEL TOMATOES

Tomato skins are easy to remove. Simply place 3 or 4 tomatoes at one time in a large strainer, then plunge into scalding hot water for 12 to 15 seconds, depending on the ripeness of the tomato. Cool under cold water for a few seconds, then pull off skins with your fingers or a sharp knife. To seed tomatoes, cut out the core and slice the fruit into eighths unless otherwise directed. Shake each piece until the seeds slip out or use your fingers to scoop seeds out.

Since skin and seeds are so full of nutrients, it is best to peel and/or seed tomatoes only when indicated in your recipe.

HOW TO COOK SAUSAGES

When cooking sausage links, arrange in a single layer in a skillet just large enough to hold them without crowding. Add enough water to reach halfway up the sides of the sausages, then cover and simmer for 5 minutes. Turn the sausages, recover the pan and simmer 5 minutes longer.

Pour off the water and blot excess moisture with paper towels. Add 2 to 3 tablespoons vegetable oil to the pan and cook over low heat until sausages are well browned on all sides. Pork should be eaten well done.

To cook sausage patties, heat a small amount of vegetable oil in a heavy skillet. Brown patties well on both sides until thoroughly cooked through.

PRESERVING

After all your attention (the digging, the raking, the composting), after weeks of waiting (the planting, the weeding, the mulching), nature has filled your garden with bright red fruit. Your gathering baskets overflow, your refrigerator swells with jewel-red tomatoes, your window ledges burst with harvest. Now, what to do with your bounty—purée and freeze them, home-can them, simmer them into jams and jellies? Any one of these procedures will preserve the abundance of your garden for your winter pleasure. Each of these methods is discussed in this last section, along with instructions for preserving early autumn, semiripened and green fruits in root cellars, pickle jars and brining crocks.

No matter which method you choose, you will have the comfort of knowing that the tomatoes you have grown and preserved are naturally delicious, uncontaminated by deadly sprays and nurtured by the sun instead of gas-ripened like those pink, plastic impostors that line your grocer's vegetable bins.

Freezing is an ideal method of preserving home-grown produce. It's easy, speedy and virtually fool-proof. Unfortunately, however, tomatoes are one of the few vegetables that behave disastrously when frozen in the raw and are absolutely useless unless you plan to use them in cooking after they thaw. Over the years I have experimented extensively with diverse methods of freezing tomatoes and have discovered that flavor is best and freshest when tomatoes are cooked up first and then frozen plain or stewed or in the form of juices, purées or pastes. Since strong flavorings—cloves, onions and garlic—may turn bitter during freezing, and milder flavorings—cinnamon, salt and so on—may disappear completely, it is best to add these *after* freezing and during the final cooking.

CONTAINERS

However you choose to prepare the tomatoes destined for your freezer, the kind of freezer protection you give them determines ultimate taste and quality. Suitable freezer packaging is any material or device that insulates food from the harmful effects of moisture loss and excess exposure to air.

Rigid plastic containers with tight-fitting, snap-on lids are ideal. Square or rectangular shapes take up less space than round ones and stack more compactly. Plastic-lined paper boxes are also practical, as are heavy-duty plastic bags if you're freezing tomatoes whole. To make the latter airtight, put in the tomatoes, twist the bag at the top, insert a straw and suck out as much air as possible. This draws the bag tightly against the sides of the tomatoes, preventing the formation of ice crystals.

You can also recycle some of the more common household containers you would otherwise throw away. Any container is actually suitable provided it is moistureproof, vaporproof, as airtight as possible, and you leave the proper amount of headspace between the food and the top of the container.

Waxed or plastic-coated milk or juice cartons make handy containers for cooked tomato dishes. Open the carton tops once the original contents have been consumed, wash, rinse thoroughly, dry well and store until needed. To use for freezer storage, pour in your sauce or purée, leaving ½ inch of headspace. Seal tightly with freezer tape before freezing.

Ice cream, some dairy products and other foods are frequently packed in reuseable plastic containers. Use them just as you do the store-bought kind, always allow ½ inch of headspace and seal with freezer tape. If any of these seem to be less than airtight, cover the outside with a layer of aluminum foil or plastic wrap to protect contents against freezer burn.

Even coffee cans, or any other metal cans with plastic lids, work well. Line these with plastic bags, leave ½ inch of headspace, then crisscross with freezer tape to insure airtight fit.

Ordinary wide-mouthed glass jars—peanut butter or mayonnaise jars, for example—or extra canning jars, if you have them, can also be used for freezing.

199

Glass jars with shoulders make removal of frozen foods a bit more difficult unless thawing is complete. They also have additional drawbacks. Glass is fragile and becomes more so when frozen, and careful handling is really a must! Then, too, if headspace is insufficient, the jars may burst, since liquids expand when frozen. If you do use glass (and I don't recommend it), leave a minimum of 1½ inches of headspace between jar top and contents.

Choose the container type according to what it will hold and the size on the basis of the size of the portions you prefer.

THE FREEZING PROCEDURE

Best results in freezing, as in canning, depend on getting your tomatoes from garden to freezer in short order. Check your supplies to make sure you have enough packaging materials before you begin. Have a large stainless steel or enamel kettle on hand if you plan to cook your tomatoes before freezing them, plus lots of ice for quick chilling afterwards. If you're following a recipe that calls for additional ingredients, assemble them beforehand, too.

Try, if possible, to prepare your freezer tomatoes and tomato dishes on the day they are picked. Just-harvested tomatoes may be stored in your refrigerator for up to 24 hours, but prolonged storage results in flavor and nutrition loss, a condition that freezing can only worsen.

Select young, tender, slightly immature tomatoes for freezing. Experiment with different varieties and see which ones suit your family's taste when defrosted and which types adapt best to freezing.

Package in containers appropriate to the method of preparation and seal carefully. Remember, excess air and dehydration are deleterious to the health of your frozen tomatoes.

FREEZING RAW TOMATOES

Tomatoes can be frozen successfully in an uncooked state if you freeze them whole and use them for cooking. Packaging tomatoes raw is the easiest method of freezing them, but because so much of their substance consists of water they tend to disintegrate and become grainy upon defrosting. Plum tomatoes are probably best for freezing raw because their water content is not as high as that of the slicing varieties.

To freeze raw tomatoes, merely wash whole, just ripe, unbruised specimens and assemble and package according to size. It is not necessary to peel or blanch them. Use plastic bags for storing—there's less chance that air will be trapped inside to form ice crystals (see directions for using plastic bags, page 199). For ease in peeling frozen whole tomatoes, run them under very hot tap water while still unthawed for a few seconds. The contact of hot against cold should crack the skins quickly, making peeling easy.

FREEZING RAW PEELED TOMATOES

If desired, you may peel your surplus crop before packaging and freezing. (For tips on how to peel, see page 195). Core and cut into quarters or small pieces, or core and leave whole. You should have enough juices left when you cut or chop to completely submerge the pieces when packed in rigid containers. If not, or if you prefer to freeze them whole, purée a few extra tomatoes and use to cover the fruit. The extra liquid will eliminate any air spaces. Take care to leave ½ inch headspace (1½ inches if glass jars are used), seal tightly and freeze. To use these tomatoes or tomato pieces, place the partially defrosted block in a saucepan, with or without a bit of extra water, then simmer gently over low heat.

FREEZING PRECOOKED TOMATOES

If you prefer to freeze stewed tomatoes, peel, core and prepare them as described above and cut into quarters or pieces. Simmer in a stainless steel or enamel pan over low heat, stirring frequently, until they soften. Cool quickly by plunging the cooking kettle into a bowl of ice water. When thoroughly chilled, divide the stewed tomatoes into rigid containers, leaving ½ inch of headspace (1½ inches if the containers are glass), seal tightly and freeze.

FREEZING TOMATO JUICE

Choose firm, well-ripened tomatoes. Loosen the skins by submerging a few tomatoes at a time in a kettle of boiling water until the skins burst. Peel, core and cut into quarters or eighths. Place in a large saucepan and simmer over low heat until soft, then use the back of a spoon to press the mixture through a very fine sieve into your freezer containers, leaving ½ inch of headspace in each (1½ inches when using glass jars). Seal tightly.

Chill the contents quickly, label each package with content, quantity and date and store at 0 degrees F. or below.

Leave an inch or two of space between packages when first putting them into the freezer to insure

the good air circulation necessary for rapid and even freezing. It's also a good idea to maintain a running inventory of quantities and varieties frozen. An accurate list will keep you advised of what's on hand and which varieties serve your purposes best.

Frozen tomatoes and tomato products can be safely stored up to one year, but for a maximum taste and nutrition, it's best to use them within 3 to 4 months. Always allow frozen tomatoes or tomato dishes to thaw in the refrigerator — partially (if used in cooking), or completely (if otherwise used), so that nutrient loss is kept to a minimum.

STRANGE ARE THE WAYS OF FROZEN SAUCES

Although tomato sauces, purées, pastes and juices may be prepared with onions, garlic and so on and subsequently frozen, these added ingredients are frequently distorted in your freezer to produce bitter and unpleasant off-flavors. On the other hand, salt, herbs and spices when frozen often fold their flavors and silently steal away. Since unflavored tomato products generally remain constant and fresh-tasting, it seems wisest to add flavorings during final, postfreezer cooking. Here follow my favorite recipes for Freezer Tomato Purée, Freezer Tomato Paste and Freezer Tomato Juice with directions for transforming these into a bouquet of predictably delicious sauces, drinks and so on.

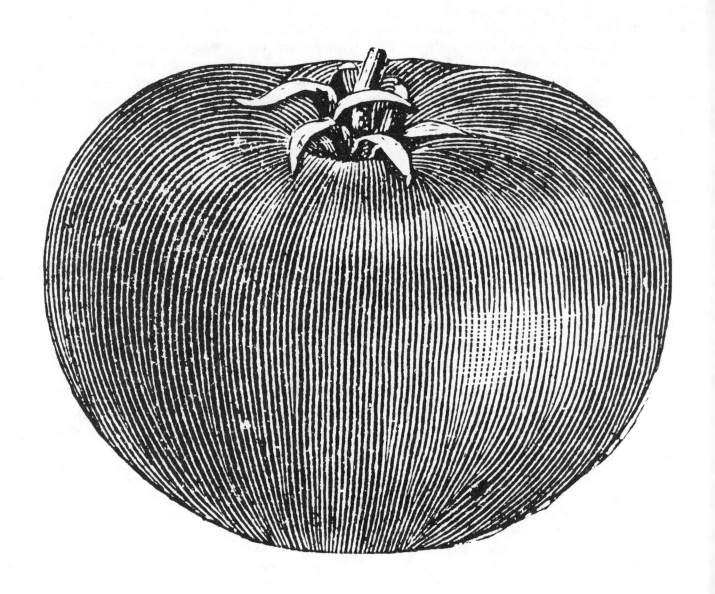

EASY TOMATO JUICE
YIELD: 1 QUART

---

12 Medium-size ripe tomatoes, cored
½ Teaspoon granulated sugar
  Lemon juice
  Salt

Directions: Squeeze tomatoes, or put through a juicer. Add sugar, lemon juice and salt to taste. Refrigerate until serving time.

RIPE TOMATO PURÉE
YIELD: ABOUT 2 CUPS

---

16 to 20 Fully ripe tomatoes
  1 Tablespoon butter or olive oil
  ½ Teaspoon granulated sugar

Directions: Wash the tomatoes and cut them into eighths. Heat the butter or oil in a heavy stainless steel pan. Add the tomatoes and sugar and cook, uncovered, over medium heat until the juices have evaporated. Run the cooked tomatoes through a food mill or rub through a strainer. If the purée is at all watery, return it to the pan and simmer until most of the juices have evaporated and the purée has a nice thick consistency. Cool quickly and freeze at 0 degrees F. or use immediately.

QUICK AND EASY RIPE TOMATO PURÉE
YIELD: ABOUT 2 CUPS

---

16 to 20 Fully ripe tomatoes
  1 Tablespoon butter or oil
  ½ Teaspoon granulated sugar

Directions: Wash the tomatoes, cut into quarters and whirl in a Cuisinart using the sharp steel blade. When the tomatoes are liquified, pour them through a strainer into the hot butter or oil in a heavy stainless steel pan. Add sugar and cook over medium heat until most of the juices have evaporated and the purée has a nice thick consistency. Cool quickly and freeze at 0 degrees F. or use immediately.

TOMATO PASTE

Turn tomato purée into paste by simmering it until it is thick enough to stick to a spoon. Place the pan containing the purée on an asbestos pad; stir almost constantly to prevent scorching. Cool quickly and freeze at 0 degrees F. or use immediately.

GREEN TOMATO PURÉE
YIELD: ABOUT 1 QUART

I puréed green tomatoes this year and found to my surprise that they impart a unique, sweet mellow flavor to dishes. As versatile as the ripe variety, it is a "should try" for every tomato gardener.

---

5 Pounds green plum tomatoes
¾ Cup water
2½ Tablespoons granulated sugar

Directions: Finely chop tomatoes and place in a large stainless steel saucepan along with the water and sugar. Bring to a boil over medium heat, then lower heat and simmer, covered, for 2 hours, or until tomato bits are very soft. Smooth the purée by putting it through a food mill or whirling it in a Cuisinart or blender. Freeze at 0 degrees F. following directions given on page 201.

Summer, that indolent season, has come and gone (though its memory remains like candy tucked into the cheek for savoring), and with it have gone those delicate leafy vegetables and the fleshy fruits of summer. Your garden is still bushy with broccoli and Brussels sprouts, cauliflower and parsnips, those frost-fearless favorites, and, of course, tomatoes hang heavy with fruits at varying stages of ripeness.

Now that nights have a nip to them and frost is just around the corner, what will you do with your late-blooming fruits and vegetables? Soak them in pickle brine, simmer them into relishes and preserves? Layer them in the dormant depths of the root cellar? Any one of these can transform your foods and preserve them for winter eating, but only root cellar storage can extend the season on fresh produce in the form that nature made them.

The root cellar, once the only practical way to store fruits and vegetables, is still a functional extension of gardening. In the old days a cool, moist lean-to shed, or an excavated cellar with stone walls and earthen floors, was a traditional feature of most country homes. Nowadays, poured concrete basements, central heating, ping-pong tables and workshops have preempted the root cellar, but although commercial cold-storage techniques, freezing and the like have turned the root cellar from a necessity to something of a luxury, it is still surprisingly convenient, practical and economical to boot.

You can improvise a more than adequate root cellar in any excavated area where cool temperatures, good ventilation and proper humidity can be uniformly maintained. Ideally your root cellar should consist of a dirt floor, two windows for cross-ventilation and a series of wooden shelves. You can approximate these conditions by partitioning off a northern (preferably northeast) corner of your basement, provided it has at least one window. A slatted wooden floor set several inches above your concrete floor makes a perfectly adequate substitute for the classic packed-earth floor, but you can also construct a floor of sorts with planks set on bricks or concrete blocks, and use these same materials to improvise shelves. The precise methods or materials you use aren't terribly important, so long as you keep the air circulating around your stored vegetables (produce will mildew if it's set on concrete floors or placed against concrete walls).

Isolate your root cellar from the rest of the basement with two interior walls (ideally 2-by-4 studding and insulation board—perhaps Celotex), which will shield your root cellar from the drying effects of furnace heat. To complete the job, hang a door of the same materials and edge it with felt weather stripping for a tight fit. If there are any overhead heating ducts, be sure to insulate these as well. Next, set up your storage shelves, hang up a thermometer, open the window and you're in business.

The tomatoes you select for root cellar storage should be sound green specimens just this side of ripening. Small, dark green fruits will, in all probability, never ripen, so discard these or use them for relishes. Choose instead good-size tomatoes that are whitish-green on the bottom. Tomatoes that have begun to turn pink should be ripened in the kitchen. Harvest fruit late in the season but before the first frost. Make sure those destined for storage have no bruises, cuts or defects of any kind (use any that are slightly less than perfect in green tomato recipes, pages 145 to 181) and handle them carefully to prevent accidental damage.

Some expert gardeners suggest that you wash and dry the tomatoes gently before storage, but I prefer to gently wipe . . . not wash. Separate those fruits that are beginning to ripen from those that are very green. In either event, pack them in single layers according to degree of ripeness in long, clean, shallow cardboard or wooden boxes. Shred clean paper or use enough salt hay or straw to surround each individual tomato and keep it from touching its neighbor.

Ideal storage temperatures for green tomatoes range between 50 and 60 degrees F. It's a good idea to check daily and to keep the temperature uniform by opening (or shutting) the windows. In a very cold snap, set the tomato boxes on the highest and therefore warmest of your shelves. Use your windows to regulate air circulation and moisture, too, and, if necessary, supply extra humidity by setting pans of water or moist sand on the floor. A humidity gauge is probably a worthwhile investment if you're storing different kinds of vegetables.

Ripening tomatoes in a root cellar should assure you of a continuing fresh supply for up to two months after harvest. Check on progress at least once a week, separate the red tomatoes from their slower ripening neighbors and allow them to finish ripening in your kitchen away from direct sunlight or in your refrigerator.

Canning is the time-honored, and heretofore the most popular, method of preserving surplus produce. Nowadays, many gardeners feel uneasy about canning and prefer to home-freeze instead, but there is nothing mysterious, complex or dangerous about the canning procedure, when properly performed. Canning is simply the process of destroying food-spoiling yeasts, molds, bacteria, spores and other microorganisms present in air, water and soil. When you properly process your tomatoes in standard canning jars you kill off these organisms, and when you seal the jar lids tightly enough, you prevent others from entering.

Canning requires meticulous preparation, which makes it time-consuming and fairly arduous but it remains the most economical and practical way to preserve foods, particularly if these are not to be used for some time. It is true, however, that improperly canned produce, tomatoes or any other food, can cause sickness or even death. Botulism, most notorious and deadly among the types of food poisoning, is caused by a microorganism which grows in low-acid food where careless processing creates conditions favorable to its growth. When using any home-canned food, be sure to check for signs of spoilage. Puffed or bulging jar lids, leaks, jars that spurt when the lid is lifted, mold or unpleasant odors may all indicate that something is wrong. If any of these signs are present—don't take chances—discard the food! In addition, follow the basic rule of cooking any home-canned product at a rapid boil, covered, for 15 minutes, before you so much as taste it.

Time was when home-canners could count on the relatively high acid content of tomatoes to prevent the growth of spoilage microorganisms inside their sealed jars. Changes in plant varieties, however, have resulted in some new types of tomatoes which, unlike former varieties, are pleasantly less acid. Just to be on the safe side, it's a good idea to add 2 teaspoons vinegar (or lemon juice, if you prefer) to each quart of tomatoes you can. This insures a proper level of acidity and an extra margin of safety while it improves canned fruit flavor. This is particularly important when processing your crop as whole or cut-up tomatoes or as sauce, paste, purée or juice. Most recipes for canned tomato delicacies like relishes, catsups and pickled tomatoes call for vinegar and need no extra acid, nor do tomatoes processed in the steam-pressure canner, since temperatures are high enough to destroy bacteria.

SELECTING TOMATOES FOR CANNING

Since your canned product is only as good as your original produce, be sure that the tomatoes you choose for canning are high-quality specimens at

🍅206

their peak of perfection. It is better to turn slightly imperfect tomatoes into tasty tomato sauce or all-purpose purée and consign them to your freezer than to take a chance on canning them.

Varieties especially good for canning include Rutgers, Marglobe, Beefsteak, Ponderosa, Campbell 1327, Heinz 1350, Spring Giant Hybrid, Spring Boy, Jubilee, Long Red, Crimson Giant, Doublerich, Springset and Roma. Roma, a very versatile red, plum-shaped tomato, is excellent for tomato purée and paste, as are Red Top and the later-maturing San Marzano. Red Top is also popular for canning or puréeing.

For preserves, try Yellow Plum, Red Pear or Yellow Pear. Tomato juice aficionados will find Rutgers, Roma, Earlibell and Springset to their taste, and pickle lovers will particularly relish Maritimer.

Canning yields the best results when your tomatoes are prepared for processing straight from the garden. Wash them carefully and thoroughly in several changes of water to remove all dirt and dirt-borne bacteria, removing the tomatoes and rinsing the pan well between washings. Drain well and sort according to size and ripeness. Be sure to handle gently to avoid bruising.

The number of quarts of canned food you will get from any quantity of tomatoes depends mainly on their quality, variety, maturity and size. Whether the tomatoes are canned whole or cut into halves, quarters or slices also makes a difference; so does whether you pack them raw or hot. A rough estimate is that 2½ to 3½ *pounds of fresh tomatoes* will yield 1 quart of canned. You may figure 4 medium-size tomatoes make 1 pound.

CANNING EQUIPMENT
CANNERS

There are two types of canners used in home canning. The *Boiling Waterbath Canner* (see directions for use on page 211) will process your whole, quartered or chopped tomatoes or such tomato and pickled vegetable combinations as chutneys, catsups and conserves. Standard waterbath canners are available, but any large metal cooking pot will do nicely if:

- it is deep enough to permit water to boil briskly at a level 3 to 4 inches above the tops of the sealed jars
- it comes equipped with a tight-fitting cover
- it has room for a rack to keep the jars from touching each other or falling against the canner's sides during processing

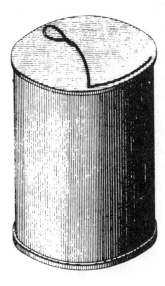

A steam-pressure canner (see below) is also eminently serviceable for waterbath canning provided it's deep enough. Simply arrange the jars in the rack and cover them with water to a level 3 to 4 inches above the sealed lids, then place the canner cover on top without fastening it. Leave the petcock or weighted gauge wide open to allow steam to escape.

The *Steam-Pressure Canner* (see directions for use on page 212) is essential for processing tomatoes prepared with other vegetables or with meats. These combinations need to be canned at higher temperatures than boiling water can supply, since they are low in acid and therefore more susceptible to those microorganisms hardy enough to survive a temperature of 212 degrees F.

The standard steam-pressure canner comes equipped with a rack and tight-fitting cover which is centered by a petcock or weighted gauge. Manufacturers usually include specific instructions for using new canners, but if you have lost or misplaced yours, here are some general rules for any steam-pressure canner.

1. Pour several inches of boiling water into the bottom of the canner.
2. Arrange your filled and sealed jars in the canner rack. Be sure that steam can circulate freely. If your canner allows room for 2 jar layers, stagger the second so that jars do not touch.
3. Fasten the cover securely so that steam escapes only through the petcock or weighted-gauge opening.
4. Set the canner over medium-high heat until steam pours steadily from the vent for 10 minutes and drives all air out of the canner. Then close the petcock or put on the weighted gauge.
5. Thorough processing demands that pressure rise to 10 pounds. As soon as pressure reaches that figure (or the figure given in the Pressure Compensation Chart, page 213), start counting processing time and maintain the pressure at 10 pounds for the entire time specified. Keep the pressure from rising and falling by regulating the heat under the canner. *Never open the petcock to lower the pressure,* and be sure that there are no drafts blowing on the canner.
6. As soon as processing time is up, carefully remove the canner from the heat.
7. Let the canner cool slowly. Never try to hurry cooling along by dousing the canner with water or refrigerating it. When the inside pressure registers zero, wait 10 minutes, then slowly open the petcock or take off the weighted gauge. Unfasten the far side of the cover first, tilting it up so that the steam escapes away from you. As you lift each jar from the canner, set it upright several inches from its neighbor on a rack or folded towel to cool. Never place any hot jars on a cold surface or in a draft.

JARS

The safest jars are those especially made for canning. Unlike jars designed for other commercial uses, only standard canning containers can effectively withstand the high temperatures required by steam-pressure and/or waterbath canning. Make sure that yours are clean and in perfect condition before using them.

LIDS

There are two main types of lids manufactured for standard canning jars. One is the porcelain-lined zinc cap with shoulder rubber ring. The other is a two-piece cap consisting of a metal screwband and flat metal lid. Whatever type you use, be sure to follow manufacturer's directions to assure a secure seal.

THE CANNING PROCEDURE

The key to successful preservation of flavor in canning lies in getting your tomatoes from garden to jars to canner as quickly as possible. For this reason it is important to ready all your equipment before canning day.

Begin by checking your supply of standard canning jars and lids. Make sure they are clean and in perfect condition. Discard any jars with chips or any lids that are dented or rusted. Purchase new jars and lids if necessary—some two-piece lids need brand new seals each time you can. In any case, carefully read and follow manufacturer's directions for handling and sealing your jars. Each jar *must* have the proper vacuum seal to prevent spoilage.

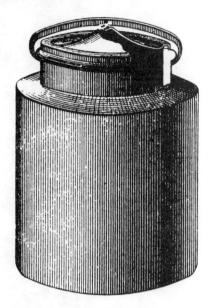

The pressure gauge on your steam-pressure canner must be accurate so that correct processing temperatures can be reached. If your canner has a weighted gauge, clean it thoroughly. If it features a dial gauge, ask your county home-demonstration agent, dealer or canner manufacturer to check it. The safety of your canned food depends on your canner's reaching 10 pounds of steam pressure. Any gauge that is off by more than 5 pounds should be replaced. If your gauge is inaccurate by less than 5 pounds, follow the Pressure Compensation Chart on page 213. Finish your preliminary preparations by drawing a string through the petcock and safety-valve openings to clean them.

On canning day, wash your jars, lids and bands in hot, soapy water, then rinse and dry them well. Wash and rinse both canner and cover thoroughly. (If you're using the steam-pressure canner, don't

submerge the cover.) Dry both pieces well.

Prepare the firm, ripe tomatoes you have selected for canning. (For tips on peeling see page 195.)

USING THE BOILING WATERBATH CANNER

Tomatoes canned in a boiling waterbath are processed by either the *cold* (or *raw*) *pack* method or the *hot pack* method.

In the *raw pack* method, peeled, uncooked tomatoes are packed whole, halved or quartered into canning jars to a level ½ inch from the top. Only salt and vinegar (or lemon juice) are added: ½ teaspoon salt and 1 teaspoon vinegar or lemon juice to each pint, and 1 teaspoon salt and 2 teaspoons vinegar or lemon juice to each quart (see page 206).

In the *hot pack* method, the tomatoes are precooked. Bring whole, halved or quartered peeled tomatoes to a boil in a glass, stainless steel or unchipped enamel saucepan (no cast-iron or copper pans, please). Stir frequently to keep the tomatoes from sticking. Pack into canning jars, leaving ½ inch of headspace at the top. Add ½ teaspoon salt and 1 teaspoon vinegar or lemon juice to each pint, 1 teaspoon salt and 2 teaspoons vinegar or lemon juice to each quart.

Whatever method you use, be sure that the tomatoes are covered by their juices. Run a knife or spatula around the inside of each jar so that all air bubbles are forced out. Wipe the necks and tops of each jar and fix the lids according to manufacturer's directions.

Fill the canner about two-thirds full of hot water, then arrange the jars upright on the rack. The water should reach a level of at least 3 to 4 inches higher than the tops of the jars. Add more hot water if necessary, but avoid pouring it directly on top of the jars. Cover the canner and bring the water to a boil.

As soon as the water boils, start the timing and process for the *entire recommended time*. Cutting corners at this point may prove disastrous—bacteria can be killed only by applying high temperatures for a specific time period. Process pint jars of raw-packed tomatoes for 40 minutes, quart jars for 50 minutes. Process pint jars of hot-packed tomatoes in boiling water for 35 minutes, quart jars for 45 minutes. If you live in a high-altitude area, increase processing time by 1 minute for each 1,000 feet above sea level.

When processing time is up, immediately remove the jars from their boiling waterbath and set them several inches apart on a rack or folded towel, away from any draft, so that they can cool evenly. Follow the manufacturer's directions if your seals are the type that need further adjustment.

USING THE STEAM-PRESSURE CANNER

Steam-pressure canners are designed to process foods that are especially vulnerable to the pathogenic bacteria which are even resistant to a temperature of 212 degrees F. Tomatoes combined with meats and certain vegetables must be processed at temperatures that exceed the boiling point.

After readying your canning equipment (see above), prepare your tomatoes and other ingredients according to the recipe you have selected (see pages 131 to 137). Divide the mixture among the jars, leaving the amount of headspace specified in the recipe. Eliminate any air bubbles by carefully running a knife or spatula around the inside of each jar, then wipe the necks and tops. Arrange the lids according to manufacturer's directions.

Pour several inches of boiling water into the bottom of the canner and set the jars into the canner rack. Follow the directions that came with your canner or the general procedure described on page 208. Thorough processing is imperative. Pressure must rise to 10 pounds *before* you start to count processing time and must be maintained at 10 pounds for the entire time specified in the recipe. If you live in a high-altitude area, increase the pressure by 1 pound for each 2,000 feet above sea level. (High altitudes may affect the accuracy of a weighted gauge. Make sure yours is correct.)

When processing time is up, slide the canner from the heat. Allow it to cool until interior pressure descends to zero. Wait an additional 10 minutes before slowly opening the petcock or removing the weighted gauge. To avoid steam burns, lift the cover on the side opposite you first. Follow manufacturer's directions for adjusting the seals after taking the jars out of the canner. Allow the jars to cool in a draft-free place as directed in water-bath canning.

CHECKING AND STORING YOUR CANNED TOMATOES

The final step in the canning process is to check the seals on your cooled jars. Test each seal by pressing down on the center of the jar lid. If the lid is rigid and resists the pressure of your finger, the jar is properly sealed. If you suspect a faulty seal or find a leaky jar, eat the tomatoes immediately or treat them as if they were fresh and repack and process all over again.

The screwband that comes with the special two-piece seal may be removed if you wish and the jars stored without it, but wait until jar and contents have cooled completely. The lid alone will provide a tight seal, and you eliminate the possibility that the band may rust with time and prove troublesome when you're ready to open the jar.

Wipe the jars and label them, listing contents and date. If you've canned more than one batch in one day, add the lot number, too.

Pick a dry, dark storage place for your canned tomatoes. They will keep better where the temperature remains cool and constant. Use the oldest ones first, and always check for signs of spoilage before opening. Carefully dispose of any jar that displays one or more of the danger signals listed on page 206.

CANNING TOMATOES:
PRESSURE COMPENSATION CHART

If the gauge reads high:
1 pound high, process at 11 pounds
2 pounds high, process at 12 pounds
3 pounds high, process at 13 pounds
4 pounds high, process at 14 pounds

If the gauge reads low:
1 pound low, process at 9 pounds
2 pounds low, process at 8 pounds
3 pounds low, process at 7 pounds
4 pounds low, process at 6 pounds

NOTES

- All tomatoes are washed, peeled and seeded unless otherwise stated.
- Herbs fresh from your garden add an extra dimension, a more subtle flavor to your tomato cookery than their dried counterparts. But if fresh herbs are not available, substitute ¾ teaspoon dried for each tablespoon garden-picked.

  Drying concentrates the natural oils of herbs, making small amounts much more flavorful. Crush or chop fresh herbs to extract maximum flavor. Dried herbs yield their concentrated fragrance more easily when soaked in oil or vinegar shortly before using.
- All pepper is freshly ground unless otherwise stated.
- All vegetables and fruits are well washed.

INDEX OF GARDENING

INDEX OF RECIPES

ABOUT THE AUTHOR

YVONNE YOUNG TARR is a veteran cookbook writer. Her books include *Super-Easy Step-by-Step Cheesemaking, Super-Easy Step-by-Step Winemaking, Super-Easy Step-by-Step Sausagemaking, Super-Easy Step-by-Step Book of Special Breads, The Up-with-Wholesome, Down-with-Store-Bought Book of Recipes and Household Formulas, The Ten Minute Gourmet Cookbook, The Ten Minute Gourmet Diet Cookbook, 101 Desserts to Make You Famous, Love Portions, The New York Times Natural Foods Dieting Book, The Complete Outdoor Cookbook, The New York Times Bread and Soup Cookbook* and *The Farmhouse Cookbook.* She is married to sculptor William Tarr. They have two children, Jonathon and Nicolas.

GRAPHIC CREDITS

The text of this book was set in Cheltenham, a typeface designed by Bertram Grosvenor Goodhue specifically for Ingalls Kimball, Cheltenham Press of New York. The Cheltenham face appeared in 1902; it owes little or nothing to historical inspiration, and in that sense it is truly a twentieth-century type design.

The text type was photo-composed by Superior Printing, Champaign, Illinois. The book was printed and bound by Colonial Press, Clinton, Massachusetts.

Production and manufacturing were directed by David Rivchin.

The cover illustration and design, and the hand-lettered type on the part-title pages, are by William Murphy.

Book design and graphics are by Elissa Ichiyasu. Design and graphics were directed by R. D. Scudellari.